50th Cotton Bowl Classic COOKBOOK

50th ANNIVERSARY

Russell M. Gardner
Chris Farkas

LIBRARY OF CONGRESS CATALOG NUMBER 86-091249
INTERNATIONAL STANDARD BOOK NUMBER 0-9613874-1-6

ADDITIONAL COPIES MAY BE OBTAINED BY ADDRESSING

COTTON BOWL CLASSIC COOKBOOK: 50th ANNIVERSARY
Gardner-Farkas Press, Inc.
P.O. Box 33229
Fort Worth, Texas 76162

COTTON BOWL CLASSIC COOKBOOK may be obtained
for fundraising projects or retail outlets at wholesale
rates. Write above address for more information.

FIRST EDITION, NOVEMBER 1986, 10,000

PRINTED BY WIMMER BROTHERS, INC.
5930 LBJ FREEWAY
DALLAS, TEXAS 75240

FOREWORD

Those who enjoy sports seem to have a greater zest for life. The sportsman's joy for living is obvious in this wonderful collection of more than 400 recipes commissioned to celebrate 50 years of the Cotton Bowl Classic and 150 years of Texas history.

Along with being a fine reference for hearty appetites, this volume reflects the history of the Cotton Bowl in a special pictorial section, and the extensive Game recipes are illustrated by an internationally renowned wildlife artist. These two features alone make for entertaining reading and add value as a collector's item.

But the real meat and potatoes of this cookbook are the recipes. You'll be surprised and delighted at the fare many of your favorite celebrities chose to share. And you'll get an interesting insight into their personalities if indeed it is true that "we are what we eat."

The Cotton Bowl is privileged to be a part of this project. Our thanks to all who shared their prized recipes.

We invite our readers to savor the results of these recipes with a sportsman's gusto. Enjoy with vigor. Soon and often.

THE COTTON BOWL ATHLETIC ASSOCIATION

Dan S. Petty
President

Jim L. Brock
Executive Vice President

Dedication

Member institutions of the Southwest Athletic Conference

Officers, Directors, Committeepersons, and Staff of the Cotton Bowl Athletic Association

Dr. and Mrs. William R. Gardner

Mrs. Frank Farkas

Mr. and Mrs. Theodore Pibil

Mr. and Mrs. Stearns H. Gardner

In Memory of:

J. Curtis Sanford — father and founder of the Cotton Bowl Classic

Col. Frank Farkas

Mr. Frank W. Maddox

Mr. and Mrs. E.P. Maddox, Jr.

Mrs. Oscar Lynch

THE COTTON BOWL CLASSIC

Not too many folks have first-hand memories of the first Cotton Bowl, partly because it's been 50 years since January 1, 1937 and partly because only 15,000 attended the matchup between TCU and Marquette in Fair Park Stadium. But, it was a perfect beginning for what has become an age-old classic, featuring the nation's top two passers, Sammy Baugh of TCU and Buzz Buivid of Marquette. The Frogs won that one, 16-6.

The idea for a post-season football classic that might someday rival California's Rose Bowl belonged to the late J. Curtis Sanford, a Dallas oil man, who promoted that first game as a private enterprise and covered expenses with $6,000 out of his own pocket. With an economic depression still gripping the country, and tremors of global unrest becoming more apparent, Sanford's dream of a Texas sports spectacle was deemed unrealistic by many observers.

Time has vindicated Sanford's vision. It took a few years to gain momentum, and it took a tie-in with the Southwest Conference to assure future success. The 1941 game, an outstanding contest between Texas A&M and Fordham, was the first sponsored Classic by the SWC, and the first in a long line of sellouts. A then capacity crowd of 45,000 watched the Aggies squeeze out a 13-12 victory.

The following year, the Southwest Conference made the alliance permanent by voting to send its championship team to the Cotton Bowl each year to serve as the host school. The Cotton Bowl Athletic Association became an agency of the conference. The CBAA is a non-stock, non-profit organization incorporated under the laws of the State of Texas. All funds remaining after the schools' shares of the receipts are awarded, and after actual operating costs are paid, accrue to the SWC. No other bowl association or bowl game is tied so closely with a college athletic conference. No other conference has been so enriched from a post-season game. Last year, each conference school received $240,000 from the Cotton Bowl. Texas A&M, the Classic's host team, earned over $700,000 with its New Year's Day appearance against Auburn. The Cotton Bowl has contributed more than 55 million dollars to intercollegiate athletics with the Southwest Conference receiving almost 31 million dollars.

The honor role of gridiron greats who have appeared in the Cotton Bowl through the last half century includes such standouts as: Bo Jackson, Doug Flutie, Earl Campbell, Bart Starr, Joe Theismann, Joe Montana, Eric Dickerson, Roger Staubach, Doak Walker, Jim Brown, Kenny Stabler, John Cappelletti, Dan Marino, Dicky Maegle, Sammy Baugh, Bryon "Whizzer" White, James Street, Jim Swink, Lance Alworth, Bob Lilly, Martin Ruby, Norm Van Brocklin, Bobby Layne, Joe Routt, Ki Aldrich, John Kimbrough, Banks McFadden, Holt Rast, Tommy Nobis, Joe Labruzzo, Duke Carlisle, Ernie Davis, and Charlie "Choo Choo" Justice. It's a list that reads like a who's who of football, and those are just a few of the many Hall of Famers who have stepped onto the Cotton Bowl turf in the first 50 years of the Classic.

The 1987 Cotton Bowl will be played before more than 72,000 fans, plus a CBS television and radio audience of millions across the nation. And for providing the teams and 60 minutes of action and excitement, the two institutions will receive checks in excess of $2,000,000.

The Cotton Bowl – it's a Classic!

ACKNOWLEDGMENTS

Board of Directors and Staff of the Cotton Bowl Athletic Association

Mrs. Caroline Hunt Schoellkopf

Mrs. Jane Justin
Compiler and publisher of "Mother Jane's Prescription for Hunger"

Mrs. Fran Chiles
Author of "Parties, Parties"

Nell B. Robinson, Ph.D., R.D.
Chairman, Department of Nutrition and Dietetics, Texas Christian University, Fort Worth, Texas

Mr. Philip Tate
Director of Sports Publications-Southwest, Host Communications, Dallas

Front cover artwork
Donald F. Mitchell, S.W.S., Turtle Creek Gallery, Dallas, Texas

Cover design and graphics
Louis Daniel, Louis Daniel & Company, Fort Worth, Texas

Foreword
Dan S. Petty, Jim Brock

Introduction
Jim Brock

Game Section
Mary Penner, Mary Penner Studios, Fort Worth, Texas

Wine and Food
Ray Raney, wine consultant and vice president, Kings Liquors, Fort Worth, Texas. Member American Institute of Wine and Food and German Wine Society
Willis C. McIntosh, Bailla, Confrerie de la Chaine des Rotisseurs, Fort Worth Chapter

Diners' Dictionary
Jim Bradford, President, Dining Publications, D/FW Airport, Texas

President Reagan and Vice President Bush paintings (color section)
Sherry Beadle, Sherry Beadle Productions, Dallas, Texas

Willie Nelson Painting
Debbie Crites, portrait artist

Lee Trevino Sketch
Gene O'Rourke, Gene O'Rourke and Company,
Fort Worth, Texas

"Salute to the Champion," Texas A&M Print
Delton Gerdes, Gerdes Design, Houston, Texas

Photography
Bradley Photographers, Dallas, Texas
Lee Angle Photographers, Fort Worth, Texas

Recipe Editor
Teresa Cage, Teresa Cage Communication, Austin,
Texas

Back Cover Artwork
Ted Watts, Sports Artist from Oswego, Kansas
commemorating the 50th Anniversary of the Cotton
Bowl Classic. The painting, which originally
appeared on the cover of the 50th Cotton Bowl
Classic program, salutes Cotton Bowl greats from
Sammy Baugh to Doug Flutie. Copies of the official
game program for the 50th Cotton Bowl Classic are
available by sending check or money order for $7.00
to: 50th Cotton Bowl Program, P.O. Box 47420, Dallas,
Texas 75247.

Thanks to: Noble Leslie DeVotie, Vito Ciraci, C. Harold
Brown, Richard E. Miles, Craig Claiborne, Charles
Ringler, Dotty Griffith, Bill Johnson, Karen Haram, Lynn
Hohertz, Peter A. Schwartz, Kim Dawson, Linda Cason,
Lael Byers, Debbie Wilson, Ann Shira, Mike Justice,
Laura Bellomy, Pam Seal, Le Anne Rains, Buckshot
Price, Bob Richards, Gene F. Jankowski, Martin
Clayton, Reagan Murray, Bob Lilly, Jr., Duke Chairez,
Edmund W. Schenecker, II, Eddie Gaylord, Gerry
Goodman, Roger Latham, Richard P. Dale, Mark Hill,
Kathryn Nelms, Vivian Rowan, Katie Henderson,
Nelson Ryan, Lon Lowenthal, Harlan Streater, Dinah K.
Duncan, Merlin Priddy, Jean Galvin, Ken Tracey,
Lyndall Kirkley, Molly Henderson, Jack Rattikin, Jr.,
Sonja Conway, Col. "Rocky" Rosacker, Jill Davis, Ann
McCulloch, Barbie Nichols, Jim Hudson, H E. Dickey,
Jr., Jan Wiethorn, Lori Harris, Jane Keel, Charlie Turner,
Morgan Ross Patterson, Steve Martin, Lori Milam,
Emory Nash, Mary Gonzales, Mary Ann Van Horn,
Dana Lattin, Susan Westbrook, Karen Bayless, Brent
Morford, Jr., Sheila Morford, Ruth Barfield, Mylar
Productions, Sheila Simmons, Autumn Durham, Nancy
Glass West, Linda Henson, Darla Thornton Lyon,
Phyllis Watson, Ruth Allen-Ollison

CONTENTS

RECIPE FOR LIFE

Take a full cup of sifted humanity
And add an overflowing cup of love.
Pour in slowly the ingredients
God sends down from Above:

A cup of trust
And one of integrity.
A cup of ambition
Strengthened with humility.
A cup of joy
And one of woe;
A cup of laughter
Blended with sorrow.
A cup of loyalty
And of commonsense;
A dash of courage
And a pinch of intelligence.

Mix well for the years of your life on Earth
And bake in humanity's large oven.
This recipe will reach maximum maturity,
And be delicious for breakfast in Heaven!

Joydelle Garrett Wolfram

Appetizers
Beverages

COTTON BOWL OFFICERS 1986-87

JIM RAY SMITH
Chairman

DAN S. PETTY
President

JIM WILLIAMS, JR.
1st Vice President

JOHN STUART
2nd Vice President

JIM BROCK
Executive Vice President

CBAA BOARD OF DIRECTORS
1986-87

Donny Anderson
Jim Aston
Sam J. Beard, Jr.
C.T. Sparkey Beckham
Archie Bennett, Jr.
Jim Brock
Bill Burford
John W. Carpenter, III
Guy Carter
Alan J. Chapman
Richard Chapman
Ronald Clinkscale
Walt Coughlin
J.W. Davis
Joe Dealey, Sr.
Jane Ray Dietrich
Buddy Dike
Ken Dowell
Otto Eisenlohr
Jim Erwin
Wilbur Evans
Finley Ewing, Jr.
Bob Frymire
Wayne Gallagher
Fred Gentile
Leonard Green
Walker G. Harman
Harry C. Hoover, Jr.

J.L. Huffines, Jr.
Fred Jacoby
Michael T. Johnson
Erik Jonsson
Phil Lineberger
Malcolm Louden
Bill McKenzie
Felix McKnight
Rodger Meier
Jack Miller
Mike A. Myers
Tom O'Dwyer
J.R. Parten
Dan S. Petty
Dewey Presley
Louis Ramsay, Jr.
Field Scovell
John Field Scovell
Burt Shryock
Harry Shuford
Jim Ray Smith
John Stuart
A. Starke Taylor, Jr.
Jere Thompson
John Thompson
Dan Williams
Jim Williams, Jr.
Charles Wooldridge

Brent Musburger

Buffalo Chicken Wings

30 chicken wings, about 5 pounds
1/4 cup all purpose flour
1 teaspoon salt
1/2 teaspoon black pepper
vegetable oil
6 tablespoons butter
6 tablespoons Louisiana Red Hot
    Sauce (not Tabasco)
blue cheese dressing
celery and carrot sticks

1. Cut off small tip from each wing and discard. Cut each
wing into 2 pieces. Wash and pat dry. Combine flour, salt
and pepper and place in paper bag. Dredge chicken wings, a
few at a time, in the flour mixture.

2. Place oil in a heavy skillet to the depth of 1 inch.
Heat oil to 350 degrees and fry wings, about one third at
a time, until they are golden brown and crisp. Drain well.

3. In a small saucepan melt butter and stir in hot sauce.
Pour mixture over chicken wings, cover, and shake until wings
are evenly coated. Place on a serving platter along with
celery and carrot sticks. Serve blue cheese dressing along-
side. Makes 6 servings.

Enjoy

Brent Musburger

Don Meredith Productions, Inc.

DON'S FAVORITE STUFFED MUSHROOMS

(appetizer or to accompany entree)

Serving size: Approximately 2 each

Ingredients:

20 Large mushrooms, scrubbed, with stems removed and drained on a paper towel
1   Package Jimmy Dean Sausage (large)
1   Package Philadelphia Cream Cheese (large)
1/3 Onion, minced
1   Clove of garlic, minced
1   Pinch of cinnamon (optional)

In a large skillet, crumble the sausage and add the onion, garlic and cinnamon. Cook until brown, but not crisp.

Drain all grease carefully. Add to drained meat, cream cheese and blend well.

Stuff mushroom caps with mixture. Bake in a large Pyrex dish for 30 minutes at 350º. Serve hot.

CRABMEAT MOLD

1 can (10 3/4 oz) Cream of Shrimp soup

2 3-oz. pkgs. cream cheese

1/4 cup finely chopped onion

1 cup mayonnaise

2 envelopes unflavored gelatin

1 cup cold water

2 7-oz. cans crab meat, or 1 lb fresh

1 cup finely chopped celery

In medium saucepan, combine soup, cream cheese and onion. Heat until cheese is melted, stirring. Blend in mayonnaise, remove from heat.

In another saucepan, sprinkle gelatin over water. Over low heat, stir until gelatin dissolves. Stir into soup mixture. Add crab meat and celery.

Pour mixture into 6-cup mold. Refrigerate 6 hours or until firm.

Unmold. Serve with crackers.

Confrérie de la Chaîne des Rôtisseurs
Fort Worth Chapter

WILLIS C. McINTOSH

BAILLI

SHRIMP TOAST

1 pound raw shrimp
1 (8-ounce) can water chestnuts, minced
2 scallions, minced
1 teaspoon minced fresh ginger root
1 teaspoon salt
1/2 teaspoon sugar
1 tablespoon cornstarch
1 egg, lightly beaten
1 tablespoon sherry
6 slices 2-day-old bread
2 cups vegetable oil

Shell, devein, wash and drain shrimp; mince very finely. Combine
thoroughly with water chestnuts, scallions, ginger root, salt, sugar,
cornstarch, egg and sherry. Cut the crusts from the bread, then cut
into 4 triangles. Spread one heaping teaspoon of the shrimp mixture
onto each bread triangle. Heat oil to 375 degrees. Gently lower the
triangles, shrimp side down, into the hot oil and cook for 30 seconds;
turn and fry a few more seconds. Shrimp toast should be golden brown
when perfectly cooked. Drain on paper towels. Serve immediately, or
keep warm in a low oven.

Willis "Mac" McIntosh
Carriage House Restaurant

ESCARGOTS

1 Cup Butter
4 Cloves Fresh Garlic
1 Tablespoon Chicken Stock
2 Tablespoons Chicken Baby Food
2 Teaspoons Dijon Mustard
1½ Tablespoons Chopped Shallots
2 Teaspoons Chopped Parsley
½ Teaspoon Nutmeg
1 Oz. White Wine (Chablis preferred)
¼ Cup Breadcrumbs
1 Can Consomme Soup

Shells: Deep fry shells in peanut oil; drain and sprinkle insides with garlic salt

Snails: Drop snails in 1 can undiluted/boiling consomme soup. Cover and let stand for 10 minutes. Pass snails through hot peanut oil for a few seconds and drain.

Sauce: Saute the pressed/mashed garlic and shallots in butter until soft. Add the remaining ingredients and simmer for 30 minutes. Do not allow mixture to boil. Add snails and 1/2 of breadcrumbs to mixture last 10 minutes.

Serving: Stuff shells with snails. Pour remaining sauce over shells and sprinkle with remaining breadcrumbs.Top with slices of sweet onion.

Place snails/serving plates in 350° oven. Heat until mixture is bubbly. Be careful not to allow edges of onions to burn.

Serves Four.

Best wishes,

Larson

C. R. LARSON
Rear Admiral, U.S. Navy
Superintendent

TEXAS A&M UNIVERSITY

Department of Intercollegiate Athletics — Aggieland, Texas 77843-1228

Jackie Sherrill
Athletic Director and
Head Football Coach

PECANS PIQUANT

1 thick pat butter   2 cups pecans, unsalted
1/3 cup Worcestershire   Salt
2 dashes Tabasco

Melt butter, add Worcestershire and Tabasco, mix well.
Remove from heat. Add pecans, mix well for 4 or 5
minutes. Line cookie sheet with paper towels and spread
nuts evenly. Place in 300° oven, crisp for 15 to 20
minutes. Watch carefully or they will burn. Pour them
on clean towels, salt. Cool and store in airtight
cannister.

YELL LEADER ARTICHOKE DIP

1 can artichoke hearts, drained
1 cup mayonnaise
1 cup grated Parmesan cheese

1 (4-ounce) can chopped green chilies
(optional, for wimps)

Mix ingredients, transfer to baking dish and bake at 350° for 1 hour. Serve with crackers.

Laura Bellomy

SEVEN LAYER DIP PILE UP

3 avocados, mashed
Lime juice
3 tablespoons sour cream
3 tablespoons mayonnaise
½ package taco sauce mix

1 to 2 large cans jalapeño bean dip
½ package Longhorn cheese, grated
Firm tomatoes, peeled and chopped
1 small can chopped, black olives
Green onions with tops, chopped

Mash avocados with lime juice; set aside. Blend sour cream, mayonnaise and taco sauce mix. In serving bowl, layer bean dip, mashed avocados, sour cream mixture, grated cheese, tomatoes, olives and green onions. Serve with chips or crackers.

Mr. and Mrs. Walter Coughlin (Ann)
Cotton Bowl Director

BLACK EYED PEA FIRST DOWN DIP

1 can jalapeño black eyed peas
½ onion, finely chopped
1 small can green chilies, drained and
  chopped or mashed

1 stick margarine or butter
1 (8-ounce) jar sharp Cheddar cheese
  spread
Garlic clove or salt, to taste

Drain and mash peas. In a saucepan, mix peas with onion and chili peppers. Add margarine and cheese spread. Cook over low heat until margarine and cheese have melted.

Mrs. Glynn Gregory (Virginia)
Cotton Bowl Committee

BLACK EYED PEA DIP

4 cups black eyed peas, cooked and drained, or canned peas
4 canned jalapeños
1 tablespoon juice of jalapeños
½ medium onion, chopped

1 (4-ounce) can chopped green chilies
Dash garlic powder
10 ounces sharp cheese, grated
1 stick margarine

Combine peas, jalapeños, pepper juice, onion, green chilies and garlic powder in a blender; process until smooth. Set aside. In a double boiler, heat pea mixture with grated cheese and margarine; stir and heat until bubbly. (May heat the mixture in a covered pan in a 300° oven, removing from heat and stirring occasionally.) Serve with tortilla chips.

Pam Horton
Texas Christian University

SUPER BLUE DEVIL DIP
Men love this dip.

1 cup mayonnaise
1 cup sour cream
1 tablespoon Beau Monde seasoning

1 tablespoon dill weed
1 tablespoon shredded parsley

Blend ingredients. Serve with carrot and celery sticks or avocado chunks on toothpicks.

Mrs. Richard E. Miles (Karen)

HOT MUSTARD DIP

1 cup dry mustard
1 cup vinegar
1 cup sugar

½ teaspoon salt
2 eggs

Soak mustard and vinegar overnight in top of double boiler. Add sugar, salt and beaten eggs. Cook over hot water until thick. This is delicious for turkey, ham, meats, sandwiches or most anything.

Mrs. George W. Bailey (Novella)

CLASSIC MILESTONE

1935 - J. Curtis Sanford, a Dallas oil man, conceived the idea for a Texas sports spectacular to rival California's Rose Bowl.

SCORE KEEPERS' SPINACH DIP

1 cup mayonnaise
1 cup sour cream
1 green pepper, chopped
3 green onions, chopped

1 can water chestnuts, chopped
1 package Knorr's Swiss vegetable soup
  mix
Dash garlic powder
1 package frozen spinach, uncooked,
  drained

Mix ingredients well; chill. Serve with corn chips.

Mr. and Mrs. Boston Smith (Kelly)

WALTER CAMP CRABMEAT DIP

6 ounces frozen crabmeat, thawed and
  strained
½ cup mayonnaise

¼ cup milk
1 (8-ounce) package cream cheese,
  softened
Dash onion salt

Shred crabmeat; set aside. Mix mayonnaise, milk, cream cheese and salt; blend until smooth. Stir in crabmeat. Spoon into a 1-pint casserole dish. Bake, uncovered, at 350° for 20 minutes. Serve hot with crackers.

Mr. and Mrs. Buddy Dike (Sara)
Cotton Bowl President 1976-1978

OFFICIAL SALMON LOG

16 ounces cream cheese
1 (1-pound) can salmon, drained, bones
  and skin removed
¼ teaspoon Liquid Smoke
½ teaspoon horseradish
1 teaspoon Worcestershire sauce

1 teaspoon salt
1 tablespoon lemon juice
1 tablespoon minced onion
1 cup chopped pecans
2 teaspoons parsley flakes
Paprika

Soften the cream cheese and mix with salmon, Liquid Smoke, horseradish, Worcestershire sauce, salt, lemon juice and minced onion. Refrigerate until cold, then roll mixture into a log. Roll the log into a mixture of chopped pecans and parsley flakes. Sprinkle with paprika. Serve with crackers.

Dixon Holman
Southwest Conference Referee

SAUSAGE SPREAD SECONDARY APPETIZERS

1 pound medium hot sausage
½ cup finely chopped onion
½ cup finely chopped green pepper
1 pound Velveeta cheese, cubed

½ teaspoon garlic powder
1 teaspoon Worcestershire sauce
2 packages party bread (pumpernickel or rye)

Brown sausage, drain grease, reserving a small amount in pan. Sauté onion and green pepper in grease. Add sausage and cheese. Continue cooking until cheese melts. Add garlic powder and Worcestershire sauce. Spread mixture on bread slices. May be frozen on cookie sheet, then placed in plastic bags. Bake at 400°.

Tracy Rowlett
WFAA-TV, Channel 8
Dallas-Fort Worth

FETA & CREAM CHEESE SADDLE TRAMP SPREAD

4 ounces feta cheese
1 cup cream cheese

1½ cups unsalted butter

Have all ingredients at room temperature. Stir feta cheese until smooth, then blend in softened cream cheese and butter until mixture is a smooth paste. Store in crock jar in refrigerator. Serve on breads or crackers.

Mr. and Mrs. Boston Smith (Kelly)

CHEESE BALL BACKFIELD

2 (8-ounce) packages cream cheese, softened
1 small can crushed pineapple, drained
¼ cup chopped chives
Dash garlic salt

Dash soy sauce
Chopped pecans
Chopped parsley

Mix cream cheese, pineapple, chives, garlic salt and soy sauce. Shape into a ball. Roll ball in chopped pecans and chopped parsley. Serves 8 to 10 people.

Keith Flowers

CLASSIC MILESTONE

1936 - In January of 1936, Sanford applied to copyright the name "Cotton Bowl," then entered into a agreement with the State Fair of Texas for the rental of its stadium the following January 1.

CHEESE SNAPPIES FOR THE CENTER

2 sticks margarine
2 cups flour
8 ounces extra sharp Cheddar cheese,
   grated

1 to 3 teaspoons cayenne pepper
Salt, to taste
2 cups Rice Krispies

Cut margarine into flour until mixture resembles coarse meal. Mix in cheese, cayenne pepper and salt. Stir in Rice Krispies. Shape into small balls and place on ungreased cookie sheet. Flatten with fork. Bake at 350° for 15 minutes. For variation, you may add ½ to ¾ pound Owens sausage (spicy).

HASHMARK HAM BALLS

1 pound ham, ground
1½ pounds pork, ground
2 cups soft bread crumbs

2 eggs, beaten
1 cup milk

Mix ground ham and pork with bread crumbs. Add eggs and milk, blending well. Form into balls or small loaves. Pour sauce over meat balls, basting occasionally. Bake at 350° for 1 hour.

SAUCE
1 cup brown sugar
1 teaspoon dry mustard

½ cup vinegar
½ cup water

Blend ingredients.

Mrs. Otto H. Eisenlohr (Nell)
Wife, Cotton Bowl President 1952-1954

CHILI BISCUITS TEXANA

Pepperidge Farm party rolls
Your favorite canned chili

Cheddar cheese, grated

Pinch a nickel-sized hole in the top of each roll. With your finger, mash the dough down inside the roll. Fill with chili, spooned right out of the can. Top with grated cheese. Bake at 350° for a few minutes until warmed and cheese is melted. Serve immediately. Serves 12.

Mrs. James C. Wright, Jr. (Betty)
Wife, U.S. Congressman

CLASSROOM CAVIAR SUPREME

1 package unflavored gelatin   ¼ cup cold water

Line bottom of 1 quart soufflé dish with foil, extending 4 inches beyond rim of dish on 2 sides. Oil lightly or spray with Pam. Soften gelatin in water in measuring cup. Liquefy gelatin by setting cup in pan of hot water, or in microwave for about 20 to 40 seconds at lowest setting. This gelatin will be divided among 3 layers.

EGG LAYER
4 eggs, hard-boiled and chopped   ¾ teaspoon salt
½ cup homemade mayonnaise   Dash hot pepper sauce
¼ cup parsley leaves, minced   Freshly ground white pepper
1 large green onion, minced

Combine ingredients with 1 tablespoon of the dissolved gelatin. Adjust seasoning according to taste. Using spatula, spread egg mixture evenly into prepared dish, smoothing top. Wipe any egg mixture from foil with paper towel.

AVOCADO LAYER
1 (9-ounce) avocado, pureed just before   2 tablespoons fresh lemon juice
adding   2 tablespoons homemade mayonnaise
1 (9-ounce) avocado, diced just before   ½ teaspoon salt
adding   Dash hot pepper sauce
1 large shallot, minced   Freshly ground white pepper

Combine ingredients with 1 tablespoon of the dissolved gelatin. Adjust seasoning according to taste. Gently spread mixture evenly over egg layer.

SOUR CREAM AND ONION LAYER
1 cup sour cream   ¼ cup minced onion

Mix sour cream, onion and remaining 2 tablespoons dissolved gelatin. Spread carefully over avocado layer. Cover dish tightly with plastic wrap and refrigerate overnight.

TO SERVE
1 (3½ to 4-ounce) jar red/black caviar   Lemon slices
Lemon juice   Pumpernickel bread, thinly sliced

Just before serving, place caviar in fine sieve and rinse gently under cold, running water. Sprinkle with lemon juice; drain. Lift mold out of dish using foil "handles." Using wide spatula, transfer mold to serving dish. Spread caviar over top. Garnish with lemon slices and serve with dark pumpernickel bread. Serves 12 to 16.

SHRIMP AND ARTICHOKES

2 packages Italian dressing mix
½ cup vinegar
4 tablespoons water

1⅓ cups salad oil
2 pounds shrimp, boiled then chilled
2 cans artichoke hearts, drained

Mix Italian dressing mix with vinegar, water and oil. Pour over shrimp and artichoke hearts. Cover and refrigerate for 24 hours.

Mr. and Mrs. Billy Joe Smith (Georgia)

MELBA'S ABSOLUTELY FAMOUS ANTIPASTO DIP

⅔ cup white vinegar
⅔ cup olive oil
¼ cup minced dry onion

½ package Italian salad dressing
1 teaspoon each of salt, seasoning salt,
   MSG, garlic salt and sugar

Then mix, drained and chopped.

8 ounce can mushrooms
14/16 ounce can artichoke hearts
1 jar salad olives

1 can ripe olives
1 green pepper
½ cup celery

Pour on dressing and chill.

Melba Todd

SHRIMP DIP LINEMAN

1½ pounds shelled shrimp or 3 cans
   broken shrimp
1½ cups Miracle Whip salad dressing
   (no substitute)
1 pint small curd cottage cheese, drained
½ teaspoon salt
1 teaspoon sugar
3 teaspoons lemon juice

3 teaspoons finely grated onion
1 large garlic clove, pressed
8 teaspoons minced celery
8 teaspoons minced fresh parsley
1 teaspoon paprika
¾ teaspoon cayenne pepper
1 teaspoon Mister Mustard

Mix all ingredients. Refrigerate for at least 8 hours (preferably 24 hours) before serving. Serve as a dip with seasoned crackers or stuffed tomatoes.

Cris Pye

SHRIMP SPREAD KICKOFF RETURN

½ cup margarine, softened
1 (8-ounce) package cream cheese, softened
2 teaspoons mayonnaise
Dash garlic salt
⅛ teaspoon pepper
⅛ teaspoon Worcestershire sauce

2 teaspoons lemon juice
1 small onion, finely chopped
½ cup finely chopped celery
2 (4½-ounce) cans shrimp, drained and chopped

Blend margarine, cream cheese, mayonnaise, garlic salt, pepper, Worcestershire sauce and lemon juice. Stir in onion, celery and shrimp. Serve with crackers or party rye. (You may use frozen or fresh cooked shrimp instead of canned.) Makes 2¼ cups.

Joy Westerhouse, R.D., L.D.
Director of Dietetics
Gaston Episcopal Hospital
Dallas

COTTON BOWL SHRIMP DIP

2 (8-ounce) packages cream cheese
1 cup Miracle Whip salad dressing
⅛ teaspoon garlic powder
1 small onion, finely chopped
1 tablespoon vinegar
½ cup Catalina French salad dressing
6 drops Tabasco sauce
1 tablespoon horseradish

3 tablespoons lemon juice
1½ tablespoons sugar
1 tablespoon Accent
1 tablespoon Worcestershire sauce
Salt, to taste
Pepper, to taste
1 to 2 pounds shrimp, cooked and cut into bite-size pieces

Combine all ingredients except shrimp and transfer to a blender. Process until smooth. Transfer mixture to a bowl and stir in shrimp. Refrigerate until ready to serve. Note: This recipe makes enough for a large group. Goes best with Fritos.

Cheryl Wilson

HOT BROCCOLI DIP

1 (6-ounce) roll jalapeño cheese
1 (6-ounce) roll garlic cheese
1 can cream of chicken soup

1 package frozen chopped broccoli, thawed

Cook until hot - serve warm with chips.

Kelly Houston

HOT SPICED CHRISTMAS PUNCH

1 qt. apple juice
1 qt. cranberry juice
3 cups water
1 orange (whole)
18 cloves
3 cinnamon sticks
2 cups orange juice

Mix apple juice and cranberry juice with water in a stainless steel pot. Bring to boil. Stick orange with cloves and add to liquid. Add cinnamon sticks to liquid. Simmer mixture 30 minutes. Add orange juice and let cool for 2 hours. remove orange and cloves and cinnamon. Bring to boil just before serving. Also can be served cold.

TEXAS CHRISTIAN UNIVERSITY
Fort Worth, Texas 76129

QUICK GOLDEN PUNCH

1 6 ounce can frozen orange juice concentrate
1 6 ounce can frozen lemonade concentrate
1 12 ounce can apricot nectar
1 No. 2 can (2 1/2 cups) pineapple juice
1 quart dry ginger ale (add at the last minute)

Add water to frozen concentrates as directed on cans. Combine
with apricot nectar, pineapple juice. Make the punch ahead of
time and freeze some of the punch in shaped molds. Add ginger
ale just before serving. Garnish with frozen punch molds, orange
slices and mint. Makes about 3 quarts.

Nell B. Robinson

BREAKFAST DRINK OF THE BEAR

1 small container plain yogurt (or your favorite flavor)
1 banana
¾ cup icy cold orange juice

1 raw egg
½ to ¾ cup fresh peaches, strawberries, melon or your favorite fruit

Combine all ingredients in blender and blend until smooth. Great for when you have very little time.

DRAMA DEPARTMENT FRUIT SMOOTHIES

1 bag frozen strawberries
2 ripe bananas

1 cup orange juice (or substitute club soda)
6 large ice cubes

Combine all ingredients in blender and blend until smooth. This beats a soda with caffeine any day when you're by the pool.

GRAPE-CIDER PUNCH

4 sticks cinnamon
24 whole cloves
5 cups sweet cider or apple juice
4 cups grape juice

½ cup lemon juice
1 teaspoon each of lemon rind and orange rind
2 quarts ginger ale or 7-UP

Combine spices and 2 cups cider in a saucepan; place over low heat, bring to boiling point and simmer about 5 minutes. Remove from heat and let stand ½ hour. Strain. Add remaining cider, grape juice, lemon juice, lemon and orange rind. Chill. When ready to serve pour into punch bowl and add ginger ale or 7-UP. Garnish with orange or lemon slices. Makes 35 to 40 servings.

Mrs. Helen Woldt

OLD FASHIONED LOUISIANA LEMONADE

½ cup sugar
½ cup very hot water
Juice of 3 lemons

½ lemon, sliced very thin
1 quart very cold water

In pitcher, stir sugar with hot water, until sugar completely dissolves. Stir in lemon juice, lemon and cold water. Stir and pour into tall glasses over ice.

Karen Haram
San Antonio Express and News

MARY KAY'S SPICE TEA

2 rounded tablespoons Lipton's tea
1 cinnamon stick
1 teaspoon whole cloves
1 teaspoon whole allspice

2 tablespoons Sweet 'N Low or 1 cup
sugar
6 ounces frozen orange juice
½ cup lemon juice

Stir tea, cinnamon stick, cloves and allspice into a quart of boiling water. Steep 1 hour. Pour into a container with 1 quart of water and Sweet 'N Low or sugar. Mix orange juice with 3 cans of water; add lemon juice. Pour juice mixture into tea mixture. Heat to serve. Can be kept in refrigerator for indefinite lengths of time. Can be served iced if desired. Using Sweet 'N Low instead of sugar reduces the calories to 20 per cup. Serves 15 to 20.

Mary Kay Ash
Mary Kay Cosmetics

HOSPITALITY DRINK HOME TEAM

1 (18-ounce) jar Tang
1 cup instant tea with sugar and lemon
2 teaspoons cinnamon

2 packages lemonade mix
2 cups sugar
1 teaspoon cloves

Mix ingredients and store in a jar. To serve, stir 1 to 2 teaspoons of the mix into a cup of hot water. May be served iced.

Mr. and Mrs. Stearns H. Gardner (Mary Lou)

CALICO CHRISTMAS TEA

2 cups Tang
1 package dry lemonade mix - not
Kool-Aid- this is individual foil
package
½ cup instant tea

1 cup sugar
1 teaspoon cinnamon
½ teaspoon allspice
½ teaspoon cloves

Mix well with fork in bowl. Store in airtight jars. Use 1 teaspoon to 1 cup boiling water.

Mrs. Henry Houston (Dana)

RUSSIAN TEA MIX

½ cup instant tea
2½ cups sugar
2 scant cups Tang

2 small packages Twist lemonade
2 teaspoons cinnamon
1 teaspoon cloves

Mix ingredients and store in jar. To serve, mix 2 teaspoons with 1 cup hot water. Keeps indefinitely.

Mrs. Glynn Gregory (Virginia)
Cotton Bowl Committee

ANNAPOLIS ALMOND TEA
Hot or cold.

3 tablespoons instant tea
2 cups cold water
2 cups hot water
1½ cups sugar

2 small cans frozen lemonade
2 quarts water
3 teaspoons almond extract
3 teaspoons vanilla

Mix tea and cold water; set aside. In a saucepan, mix hot water and sugar; boil for 5 minutes. Combine the mixtures and stir in lemonade, 2 quarts water, almond extract and vanilla. Makes 1 gallon. Wonderful served over cracked ice and garnished with a mint leaf.

PRESS BOX PARTY PUNCH

1 quart pineapple sherbet
1 (6-ounce) can frozen lemonade
  concentrate

2 (5-ounce) bottles ginger ale, chilled
1 (12-ounce) can pineapple juice, chilled

Set sherbet out to soften. Reconstitute lemonade according to can directions. Stir in chilled ginger ale and pineapple juice. When sherbet begins to soften, add to punch mixture and stir until blended. For Pink Punch, use frozen pink lemonade and raspberry sherbet instead of pineapple. Serves 25.

Nell B. Robinson
Texas Christian University

CLASSIC MILESTONE

1936 - On December 10, Marquette accepted Sanford's invitation as the visiting team for his January 1 game. Southwest Conference runnerup TCU was selected as the host team on December 14. TCU received a $10,000 guarantee for appearing in the first Classic, Marquette received a minimum guarantee of $6,000.

SPICED TEA FORMATION

1 cup lemon-flavored instant tea
2 cups Tang
3 cups sugar

1 teaspoon cloves
1 teaspoon cinnamon

Mix ingredients and store in a jar. To serve, stir 2 teaspoons mix into 1 cup boiling water.

V.I.P.
It's impressively tasteful...and diplomatically smooth! And oh so easy to mix!

4 ice cubes
1 jigger vodka
2 jiggers Dr Pepper

½ jigger lime juice
Twist of lemon
Orange slices, to garnish

Put ice cubes in a highball glass. Pour in vodka, Dr Pepper and lime juice. Add twist of lemon. Decorate with half an orange slice, if desired.

Dr Pepper Company

MOLLY HOGANS
Great for a crowd.

6 eggs
1 tablespoon vanilla
1 (12-ounce) can frozen orange juice
1 (6-ounce) can frozen limeade

1 cup sugar
1 quart gin
1 (32-ounce) bottle 7-Up

In blender, mixing a little at a time, whip eggs with vanilla, orange juice, limeade and sugar. Blend well. Pour into large container and stir in the gin. Let mixture stand at least 1 hour. To serve, pour 2 ounces of gin mixture in a large glass. Fill with ice and 7-Up. Serves 12.

Mrs. Richard E. Miles (Karen)

THE ALAMO
Conquer that thirst with this refreshing, cool drink.

3 ice cubes
1 jigger Kahlua

2 jiggers Dr Pepper
Lime slice, to garnish

Put ice cubes in an old fashioned glass. Pour in Kahlua and Dr Pepper. Decorate with lime slice.

Dr Pepper Company

CHRISTMAS BREAK EGGNOG

Eggs	1½ pints half and half or whipping
Sugar	cream
Whiskey	Nutmeg

Separate eggs. In 1 bowl, beat egg whites until stiff; set aside. In another bowl, beat yolks, gradually adding 2 scant tablespoons of sugar for each egg. Slowly mix in whiskey and cream. Fold beaten egg whites into mixture. Sprinkle with nutmeg.

Mr. and Mrs. Theodore Pibil (Lenora)

PERUVIAN BOMB
A strawberry fizz.

½ cup freshly made strawberry juice	2 teaspoons sugar
1½ ounces vodka per serving	1 teaspoon egg white
Juice of half an orange	Cracked ice

One pint strawberries will yield 1 cup fresh juice. To prepare, pick over the berries and remove the stems. Rinse berries in cold water and drain. Put the prepared berries in the container of an electric blender and blend, stirring down as necessary. Put the ½ cup of fresh juice in a bar glass. Add vodka, orange juice, sugar and egg white. Fill with cracked ice and shake well. Strain and serve. Yields 1 serving. Note: This drink was originally made with pisco brandy instead of vodka. The white eau de vie called framboise could also be substituted for the vodka.

Craig Claiborne
New York Times Food Editor

PEPPER MINT PERUNA
It's the cool, cool drink to serve! Ladies will love this one.

Shaved ice	Dr Pepper
1 jigger creme de menthe (white)	Cherry, to garnish

Fill old fashioned glass with shaved ice. Add creme de menthe. Top with Dr Pepper. Decorate with cherry.

Dr Pepper Company

SCOTCH IRISH SOURS
Even those who do not like Scotch love these!

1 (6-ounce) can frozen lemonade
1 lemonade can of Scotch
1 lemonade can of orange juice
2 lemonade cans of 7-Up

10 ice cubes
Cherries, to garnish
Orange slices, to garnish

Combine lemonade, Scotch, orange juice, 7-Up and ice cubes in a blender; process on high speed until thoroughly mixed. Pour over cracked ice in short highball glasses. Garnish each glass with a cherry and orange slice. Serves 6.

John "Scotty" Galvin

WILD CAT
It'll be the pet drink of your party. Don't snarl, just mix . . .

3 ice cubes
1 jigger whiskey
1 jigger Dr Pepper

Dash of bitters
Orange slice, to garnish
Cherry, to garnish

Put ice cubes in an old fashioned glass. Pour in whiskey, Dr Pepper and bitters. Decorate with orange slice and cherry.

Dr Pepper Company

KILLER FROG

½ ounce blue Curacao
½ ounce grenadine
1 ounce Myers's rum

Ice
Coconut, to garnish

In blender container, add Curacao, grenadine, rum and ice; process to mix. Serve in beer mug. Garnish with coconut.

R.J. Sandoval
Vice President
All Saints Episcopal Hospital

Breads

UNIVERSITY OF ARKANSAS

UNIVERSITY OF ARKANSAS

Founded in 1871 as the Arkansas Industrial University, the University of Arkansas began classes in 1872 with eight students and three faculty members.

The university has come a long way in 114 years. Arkansas is now the home of approximately 14,500 students and more than 800 full-time faculty. Students can pursue baccalaureate degrees in more than 95 fields, master's degrees in more than 86 fields, and doctorates in 27 fields.

There are nine colleges and schools on the Fayetteville campus. These are the School of Architecture, the College of Agriculture and Home Economics, the J. William Fulbright College of Arts and Sciences, the College of Business Administration, the College of Education, the College of Engineering, the Graduate School, the School of Law, and the Associate Degree Nursing Program of the School of Nursing.

Key figures in Arkansas athletics include university president Ray Thornton, SWC faculty representative Al Witte, athletic director Frank Broyles, and head football coach Ken Hatfield.

David Wade

KRLD RADIO
NEWS - SPORTS
INFORMATION
1080 AM

FRIED LIGHT BREAD

1 yeast cake or 1 package active dry yeast
1 cup milk
1/2 cup hot water
3-4 cups sifted flour
4 tablespoons shortening
4 tablespoons sugar
1 teaspoon salt

Mix milk and hot water, dissolve yeast cake. Add melted shortening, sugar and salt. Add flour, beating until smooth. Continue adding flour until mixture can be turned out on floured board. Knead until elastic. Turn into greased bowl, let double in size. Work down and place into refrigerator until ready to use. Pinch off amount of dough needed and place on floured surface. Knead for a few minutes then roll out as if preparing a pie crust. Let rise. Cut into strips or pieces of your configuration and drop dough into hot (350 degrees) oil. Fry just until strips are light golden brown.

For making rolls with this same dough, after doubling in size in greased bowl, work down then make into buns in muffin tin. Let rise and bake at 450 degrees until done.

Serve fried bread with butter, honey, and any fruit preserves or sprinkle tops with powdered sugar. Can be used as bread with main course or as dessert bread.

TEXAS CHRISTIAN UNIVERSITY
Fort Worth, Texas 76129

SWEET DOUGH YEAST BREAD

BASIC SWEET DOUGH

This basic sweet dough recipe may be used to make luncheon or dinner rolls or to make cinnamon rolls, coffee cake, etc. The dough may be refrigerated, but for best results, it should be used within a week.

½ c. water
2 pkg. yeast (dry or compressed yeast may be used)
1½ c. scalded milk
½ c. shortening
½ c. sugar
2 t. salt
2 eggs
7 c. sifted flour

Dissolve yeast in warm (not hot) water. Dissolve shortening, sugar, and salt in scalded milk. Add eggs and combine with yeast mixture. Add sifted flour small amounts at a time. Beat well after each addition of flour. When the mixture has more flour than one can stir, turn onto lightly floured pastry cloth and knead until dough is smooth and elastic. Knead dough about five minutes being careful not to add more flour than the recipe allows. Place in a greased bowl. Cover with a damp cloth, and allow to rise in a warm place (85 degrees) until double (about 1½ hours). Punch down; allow to rise again until double (about 45 minutes). Shape rolls and place on a lightly greased pan. Allow to rise until light (15 to 20 minutes). Bake at 400 degrees for 12 to 15 minutes. Serve hot. Makes approximately 4 dozen small rolls.

CINNAMON ROLLS

Roll dough into 15" x 9" sheets. Spread with 2 T. melted butter and sprinkle with a mixture of ½ c. sugar and 2 t. cinnamon. Roll tightly beginning at wide side. Seal by pinching edges of roll together. Cut roll into 1" slices. Place ½" apart on a greased pan. Cover, allow to rise until double in size (35 to 40 minutes). Bake at 375 degrees for 25 to 30 minutes. Makes 3 dozen cinnamon rolls.

Nell B. Robinson, Ph.D., R.D.
Chairman
Department of Nutrition and Dietetics

KIM DAWSON AGENCY, INC.

Artists Manager

RECIPE......KIM DAWSON

ONION SHORTCAKE

Slice and sautee large sweet onion.....in ¼ cup butter....
Combine 1½ corn muffin mix (1 small prepackaged variety), 1 beaten egg,
 1/3 cup milk, 1 cup cream style corn, 2 drops tabasco sauce,

Put in an 8" buttered square pan.....add 1 cup dairy sour cream and
 ¼ teaspoon salt and ¼ teaspoon dill weed and ½ cup grated cheddar
 cheese that has been added to the sauteed onion

Spread the mixture over the batter of corn meal and sprinkle with
 an additional ½ cup of grated cheddar cheese..

Bake 25-30 minutes at 425 degrees....Cut and serve warm

Variations: Use Mexican corn muffin mix....or add chopped green chilis
 or pitted ripe olives.

NANA'S CORNBREAD
(Elizabeth's Favorite)

1 Cup White regular corn meal
1/3 Cup flour
1 teaspoon baking powder
1/2 teaspoon soda
1/2 teaspoon (scant) salt
Scant 1 tablespoon sugar
2 or 3 tablespoons bacon drippings
1 1/4 cup buttermilk
1 egg

Heat your bacon drippings in 9" or 10" skillet.
Mix all other ingredients to make a thin batter.
Pour about 1/2 of hot bacon drippings into cornbread mix. Then pour into hot skillet and bake
about 15 minutes in 400 or 450 degree oven.

Linda Gale

SOUTHWEST ATHLETIC CONFERENCE

UNIVERSITY OF ARKANSAS
BAYLOR UNIVERSITY
UNIVERSITY OF HOUSTON
RICE UNIVERSITY
SOUTHERN METHODIST UNIVERSITY
THE UNIVERSITY OF TEXAS AT AUSTIN
TEXAS A&M UNIVERSITY
TEXAS CHRISTIAN UNIVERSITY
TEXAS TECH UNIVERSITY

May 15, 1985

Mr. Jim Brock
Executive Vice President
Cotton Bowl Athletic Association

Dear Hoss:

It is certainly exciting to look forward to 1986 as it brings the State of
Texas Sesquicentennial, and the 50th Anniversary of the Cotton Bowl. The SWC
is proud to share in the rich tradition of the Cotton Bowl, and also, of the
long friendship the SWC and the CBAA have enjoyed.

To honor the 1986 Cotton Bowl Classic, please consider the following recipes
for the Cotton Bowl 50th Anniversary Cookbook:

JACK ROBERTS' SOUR DOUGH FLAP-JACKS

Sour dough starter:
a. Boil some potatoes and save the potato water
b. Use 2 cups of luke warm potato water with
    enough flour to make a thick dough.
c. Put this mixture into a crock, cover it up,
    and set it in a warm place to ferment for a
    few days.

To make Flap-Jack batter:
note: always make more flap-jack batter than you
need so you can return left over batter to the
starter in the crock.
a. Return to the starter crock as much batter as
    you remove.
b. If very little batter is left, make up
    difference with flour and canned evaporated
    milk.
c. Mix left over batter gently, by hand, into
    remaining starter in crock and return it to a
    warm place.

Mix:
1 cup sour dough starter
1 cup f our
2 tablespoons bacon grease
1/4 cup canned evaportaed milk

Blend in:
1 teaspoon baking soda
2 tablespoons sugar
pinch of salt

Let mixture bubble a minute, and then drop spoon fulls onto a hot griddle.
Warm syrup, boil a big pot of coffee, and invite the neighbors in.

Best wishes for the 1986 Cotton Bowl Game, and the Cotton Bowl 50th
Anniversary Cookbook.

Dutch Baughman

TEXAS HOT CHEESE TOAST

8 bacon slices
⅓ cup mayonnaise
1 cup grated sharp Cheddar cheese
1 small onion, grated
1 egg, lightly beaten
Freshly ground black pepper

⅛ teaspoon dry mustard
½ teaspoon Worcestershire sauce
⅛ to ¼ teaspoon Tabasco sauce
8 slices day-old white bread
Paprika

Cook bacon until crisp. Drain and crumble. Mix remaining ingredients except bread and paprika. Trim crusts from bread; toast bread on both sides. Cut each slice into 6 squares. Spread each square generously with cheese mixture and sprinkle with paprika. Place on baking sheet, cover with waxed paper and refrigerate. Remove from refrigerator 30 minutes before baking. Bake at 350° for approximately 20 minutes or until light brown and puffy. Serve hot. Yields 48 squares.

Tim Brookshire
Brookshire Grocery Company

AUDIBLE APPLE BREAD

½ cup margarine, softened
1 cup sugar
2 eggs
2 cups flour
½ teaspoon salt

1 teaspoon soda
2 tablespoons buttermilk
1 teaspoon vanilla
2 cups peeled, diced apples

In a large mixing bowl, cream margarine and sugar until light and fluffy. Add eggs and mix well. Stir in flour and salt. Dissolve soda in buttermilk; add to batter, mixing well. Stir in vanilla and apples. Spoon into a greased and floured 9x5x3-inch loaf pan. Sprinkle with topping, then bake at 325° for 1 hour and 10 minutes or until bread tests done. Yields 1 loaf.

TOPPING
2 tablespoons margarine, softened
2 tablespoons sugar

2 tablespoons flour
1½ teaspoons cinnamon

Combine all ingredients in a medium mixing bowl; mix with pastry blender until consistency of coarse crumbs.

Mrs. John W. Carpenter III (Cele)
Wife, Cotton Bowl Director

AUSTIN APPLESAUCE MUFFINS

2 teaspoons soda
1½ cups applesauce, heated
⅔ cup melted margarine
1 cup sugar

2 cups flour
1 teaspoon cinnamon
½ teaspoon cloves
½ teaspoon allspice

Stir soda into hot applesauce. Mix applesauce and melted margarine; set aside. Mix sugar, flour, cinnamon, cloves and allspice. Add to applesauce mixture. Bake at 350° for 10 to 12 minutes. Note: For variation, you may add 1 cup raisins that have been plumped in simmering water. You may also add 2 cups finely chopped pecans.

Governor and Mrs. Mark White

APRICOT NUT BREAD

1 package dried apricots, washed, dried
   and finely cut
1½ cups hot milk
2 tablespoons butter
1 cup sugar
1¼ teaspoons salt

2 eggs, beaten
1 cup whole wheat flour
1½ cups white flour
1 teaspoon soda
1 cup chopped nuts
1 teaspoon orange rind

Mix apricots, milk, butter, sugar, salt and eggs. In a separate bowl, mix whole wheat flour, white flour and soda; stir in nuts and orange rind. Add the liquid mixture to the dry mixture and stir together (25 strokes or less) until dry ingredients are just mixed.

Mary Ellen Durrett
Chairman, Department of Home Economics
The University of Texas at Austin

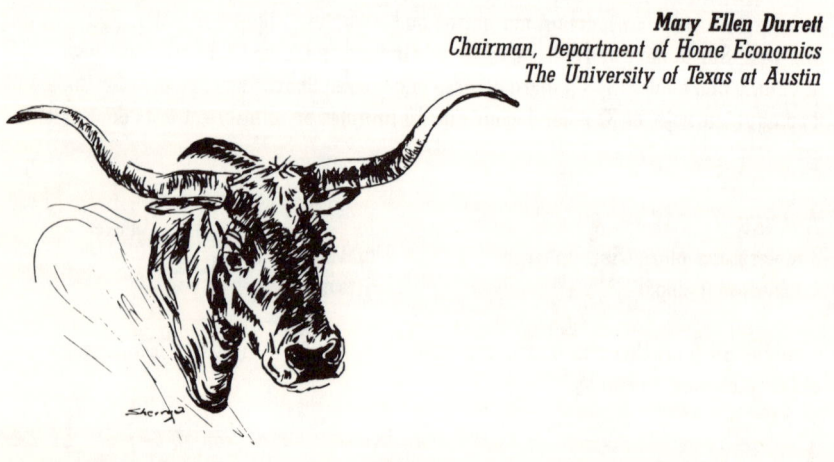

DATE NUT BREAD

2 cups boiling water
1 pound dates, cut up
2 teaspoons soda
½ cup margarine
2 cups sugar

2 large eggs
4 cups flour
½ teaspoon salt
1 cup pecan pieces

Pour boiling water over dates. Add soda to water and let cool. In a mixing bowl, cream margarine and sugar. Add eggs, flour, salt, the date mixture and pecan pieces. Mix well. Grease and lightly flour 6 or 7 (#303-size) cans. Fill with batter and bake at 350° for 20 minutes or until browned. Note: Delicious spread with cream cheese. Perfect for dainty occasions.

Joy Westerhouse, R.D., L.D.
Director of Dietetics
Gaston Episcopal Hospital
Dallas

HOLLAND HALF-TIME CARROT BREAD

2 cups flour
2 teaspoons soda
2 teaspoons cinnamon
½ teaspoon salt
1½ cups sugar
1½ cups oil

3 eggs
2 teaspoons vanilla
2 cups grated carrots
½ cup chopped nuts (optional)
½ cup raisins (optional)

Sift flour, soda, cinnamon and salt into a large bowl. Make a well in the center and into it add the sugar, oil, eggs and vanilla. Beat at medium speed. Fold in carrots. If desired, stir in nuts and raisins. Turn mixture into 2 well-greased and floured loaf pans and bake at 300° for 1 hour.

Linda Gray
Actress

CLASSIC MILESTONES

1936 - Sixteen days before the game, Dr. George I. Bennett, a blind man and a practicing Dallas chiropractor, purchased the first Cotton Bowl tickets, two seats on the 50-yard line.

1937 - January 1, 1937, the first Cotton Bowl, featuring the nation's top two collegiate passers-Slingin' Sammy Baugh of TCU and Ray "Buzz" Buivid of Marquette. The Frogs posted a 16-6 victory over the Golden Avalanche.

GIG 'EM GINGERBREAD

½ cup shortening
½ cup sugar
½ cup molasses
2 cups flour
½ teaspoon salt

1 teaspoon ginger
1 egg
1 teaspoon baking powder
1 teaspoon soda
1 cup hot water

Mix all ingredients except soda and hot water. Dissolve soda in hot water and mix into batter. Bake in moderate oven until done. While gingerbread is still warm in baking pan, spread with icing.

ICING
3 tablespoons butter, melted
5 tablespoons brown sugar

2 tablespoons cream or milk
Shredded coconut or chopped nuts

Mix ingredients and pour over the slightly cooled gingerbread in baking pan. Broil until icing bubbles.

Mrs. Lucy Morgan Venable

END ZONE ZUCCHINI BREAD

3 cups wheat flour
1 tablespoon baking powder
½ teaspoon soda
1 teaspoon salt
2 teaspoons cinnamon
1 teaspoon nutmeg
½ teaspoon cloves

1 cup milk
2 eggs, beaten
½ cup vegetable shortening, melted
½ cup honey
2 cups zucchini, shredded raw
1½ cups chopped walnuts

Preheat oven to 350°. Grease and flour 2 (8x4-inch) pans. Stir flour with baking powder, soda, salt, cinnamon, nutmeg and cloves; set aside. Combine milk, eggs, shortening, honey and zucchini in mixing bowl. Add dry ingredients and beat until batter is blended. Stir in walnuts. Bake 50 to 60 minutes. Remove from oven, cool 5 minutes, then turn out on rack to cool.

Meriam (Meri) Calabria

CLASSIC MILESTONE

1937 - L.D. (Little Dutch) Meyer, the nephew of TCU coach Dutch Meyer, scored the Cotton Bowl's first points on a 33-yard field goal to push the Frogs to an early 3-0 lead over Marquette. When the day was done, Meyer had accounted for each of TCU's 16 points.

ZUCCHINI BREAD BONFIRE

3 cups flour
2 cups sugar
3 teaspoons cinnamon
1 teaspoon soda
1 teaspoon baking powder
¼ teaspoon salt

2 cups grated zucchini
1 cup cooking oil
3 eggs
2 teaspoons vanilla
½ cup chopped walnuts
½ cup chocolate chips (optional)

Preheat oven to 350°. Grease and flour 2 (9x5-inch) loaf pans. In large bowl, combine all ingredients except nuts and chocolate chips. Mix with a spoon until batter is just moistened. Beat 1 minute with electric mixer at medium speed. Stir in nuts and chocolate chips. Divide evenly and pour into prepared pans. Bake at 350° for 45 to 55 minutes. Cool 10 minutes, then remove from pans.

Mr. and Mrs. Buddy Dike (Sara)
Cotton Bowl President 1976-1978

FT. PITT ZUCCHINI MUFFINS

1 egg
½ cup oil
1 cup sugar
1 cup grated zucchini
1 teaspoon vanilla
1½ cups flour

½ teaspoon soda
⅛ teaspoon baking powder
¼ teaspoon salt
1½ teaspoons cinnamon
½ cup walnuts

In mixing bowl, mix egg, oil, sugar, zucchini and vanilla; set aside. In a separate bowl, mix sifted flour with soda, baking powder, salt and cinnamon. Combine the 2 mixtures, stirring to mix. Stir in walnuts. Fill greased muffin cups ⅔ full. Bake at 350° for 25 minutes.

Mary McVay

CLASSIC MILESTONE

1938 - Rice spotted Colorado and its Rhodes Scholar and Heisman Trophy runnerup Byron "Whizzer" White, now a United States Supreme Court Justice, a 14-0 first quarter lead. But, the Owls' outstanding sophomore back Ernie Lain came off the bench to spark a Rice comeback that produced a 28-14 victory.

SOUR DOUGH STARTER FOR THE TIMEKEEPER

2 cups lukewarm potato water
2 cups flour

1 tablespoon sugar

(To prepare potato water, boil 2 medium potatoes, cut up, in 3 cups water, until potatoes are very tender. Measure out 2 cups of water for the Sour Dough Starter.) Blend water, flour and sugar into a smooth paste; set mixture in a warm place until it has doubled in bulk. Before sour dough is used, remove 1 cup of the mixture, then stir in equal amounts of flour, lukewarm water and a little sugar to replenish the starter.

SOUR DOUGH BISCUITS
Flour, sifted
1 cup sour dough starter
1 teaspoon soda

1 teaspoon salt
1 teaspoon sugar
1 heaping tablespoon shortening

Sift flour into a large bowl; make a well in the center of the flour and put in the sour dough starter. Stir in soda, salt and sugar. Add the shortening. Gradually pull in the flour, mixing as it is added until there is a stiff dough. Pinch off dough for 1 biscuit at a time, roll in melted shortening in biscuit baking pan. Crowd the biscuits in the pan for baking. May be allowed to "set" for 20 to 30 minutes before baking, if desired. Bake at 425°.

Melba Tompkins

ANGEL BISCUITS
They are heavenly!

1 package yeast
2 tablespoons warm water
5 cups flour
1 teaspoon soda
3 teaspoons baking powder

1 teaspoon salt
¼ cup sugar
1 cup shortening
2 cups buttermilk

Dissolve yeast in water; set aside. Mix flour, soda, baking powder, salt and sugar. Add dissolved yeast, shortening and buttermilk. Mix well. Roll dough into ¼-inch thickness and cut into circles. Dip each biscuit in butter and place on cookie sheet. Bake at 400° for 15 minutes. Note: This is a favorite family recipe handed down from a few generations, so the exact wording and increments may be a tad one side or the other. Experiment!

Angel Hightower
Miss Dallas USA 1986

THE DEAN'S DILL BREAD

2 packages dry yeast
½ cup warm water
3 tablespoons sugar
2½ cups creamed cottage cheese
2½ tablespoons dry onion
2½ tablespoons dill weed

1 teaspoon baking powder
2 teaspoons salt
2 eggs
4½ cups flour
½ stick butter, melted

Dissolve the yeast in water. Add 1 tablespoon of the sugar, and set aside. Mix cottage cheese, onion, dill, baking powder, salt, remaining 2 tablespoons sugar and eggs. Add the yeast mixture, stirring to mix well. Add flour; knead the dough. Place into greased bowl, turn dough over, and cover. Allow to rise until doubled. Punch down. Knead. Immediately shape into loaves and place into greased pans. Brush with melted butter and bake at 350° for 20 to 25 minutes. Makes 12 demi-loaves or 2 regular loaves.

Sharon Bailey Nelson
Director, Food and Nutrition Services
The University of Texas Health Center at Tyler

GERMAN ROLLS ROLLOUT

1 package dry yeast
1 teaspoon salt
1½ cups warm water

Flour
Butter, melted

Dissolve yeast and salt in warm water. Add flour until dough can be kneaded smooth and elastic. Let rise until doubled. Punch down and shape into rolls. Let rise. Bake at 425° until golden brown. Brush with butter.

Mr. and Mrs. Doug Carpenter (Theda)

MRS. FITCH'S NEVER FAIL BRAN ROLLS

1 cup shortening
½ cup sugar
1 cup bran buds
1½ teaspoons salt
1 cup boiling water

2 eggs
2 packages dry yeast
1 cup lukewarm water
6 generous cups sifted flour

Combine shortening, sugar, bran buds and salt in large bowl of mixer. Pour boiling water over the mixture and beat until dissolved. Add eggs, 1 at a time. Dissolve the yeast in the lukewarm water. Stir yeast mixture into batter. Gradually beat in the flour. Cover and refrigerate overnight. Transfer mixture to a greased pan. Let rise for 2 hours. Bake at 425° until browned.

John Kimbrough

Commemorating the 50th Anniversary
of the Cotton Bowl Classic.

INSTANT SKILLET CORN BREAD MATADOR

2 cups stone ground cornmeal
1 teaspoon baking powder
½ cup nonfat dried milk
½ teaspoon salt (optional)

2 eggs
1½ cups water
1 to 2 tablespoons oil or bacon grease

Mix cornmeal with baking powder, dried milk and salt in a bowl. In a separate bowl, mix eggs with water and oil. Mix liquid and dry ingredients, stirring to make a smooth batter. Pour into a 10-inch skillet which has been heating on a burner or electric unit which is the same size as the bottom of the skillet. Cover with fitted lid, lower the heat to medium low and "bake" the bread for 10 minutes. Check the top of the corn bread to determine if the top is dull, dry and firm to the touch. Also check the sides to see if they are turning golden brown. When the top is firm to the touch with none sticking to the finger, take a long pancake turner, loosen the edges and flip the whole round corn bread over, with the brown bottom side up. Leave uncovered on the heat for about 10 minutes and serve piping hot at the table. Either side may be up, depending on your taste. Lightly "butter" the upper crust to enhance the appearance and flavor. (The whole kernel, stone ground cornmeal gives the best flavor and texture with maximum nutrient content. The leavening baking powder is kept low to reduce sodium content.)

Mina W. Lamb
Professor Emeritus
Texas Tech University

BUTTER FLAVORED LOW SODIUM CORN BREAD

2 tablespoons butter flavored shortening
¾ cup white cornmeal
¼ cup yellow cornmeal
1 tablespoon flour
1½ teaspoons baking powder

⅛ teaspoon soda
2 eggs
1 cup buttermilk
¼ cup water

Preheat oven to 450°. Using a black iron skillet, heat the shortening in the oven while mixing the batter. Mix cornmeal, flour, baking powder and soda. In a separate bowl, mix eggs, buttermilk and water. Combine the 2 mixtures; mix well. Pour half the melted shortening into batter; stir to mix well. Pour batter into very hot skillet. Bake for 10 to 12 minutes, or until bread is firm in the center. Move skillet to top rack and continue baking for 5 minutes. Cut into serving pieces and serve immediately. Serves 6 to 8.

Mrs. Otto H. Eisenlohr (Nell)
Wife, Cotton Bowl President 1952-1954

CORN BREAD DRESSING

4 packages corn bread mixture, or 12
  crumbled toast slices
2 medium onions, chopped
1½ cups chopped celery
1 stick butter

5 eggs
Salt, to taste
Pepper, to taste
1 to 1½ top rubbed sage
Swanson's chicken broth

Mix corn bread, onions, celery and butter in a bowl. Add eggs. Season to taste with salt and pepper. Add sage and hot chicken broth, stirring to mix well. Transfer mixture to greased pan and bake at 350° for 30 minutes, or until top turns golden brown.

Sandra Fox
Live Oak Ranch

BENA'S GEORGIA BULLDOG HUSH PUPPIES

1 cup cornmeal
1 teaspoon salt
½ teaspoon sugar

1 tablespoon bacon drippings
1 cup boiling water
Fat for frying

Sift together cornmeal, salt and sugar. Stir in bacon drippings and water. Drop by spoonfuls into hot fat and fry until done. Serves 4 to 6. Note: This recipe endures from years ago when I was a small child growing up in East Texas.

Ellen Terry
Realtor

COKE'S OKRA CAKE

1 tablespoon baking powder
3 cups buttermilk
1 teaspoon salt
1 tablespoon pepper
6 egg whites
1 cup flour

1 cup cornmeal
16 cups sliced fresh okra
Red cabbage (optional)
Pimento (optional)
Jalapeños (optional)
1 quart vegetable oil, for frying

In a large bowl, mix baking powder, buttermilk, salt, pepper, egg whites, flour and cornmeal. Stir in okra by hand. If desired, add cabbage, pimento and jalapeños. Heat oil and deep fry batter until brown. Turn in 1 piece upside down on plate when cool. Decorate and serve.

Coke Gage
Coke Gage, whose family pioneered Wise County, is the former mayor of Decatur. He is an oilman/ rancher and a true gourmet and gourmand of world renown.

Soups
Sauces
Salads

BAYLOR UNIVERSITY

BAYLOR UNIVERSITY

Chartered by the Republic of Texas in 1845, Baylor University is the oldest university in continuous existence in the state and the largest Baptist institution of higher education in the world. Its 350-acre main campus in Waco offers facilities for an enrollment of about 10,500 students.

Baylor offers 50 major areas of concentration and approximately 35 different degree programs. The university is comprised of the College of Arts and Sciences and six schools: business, education, graduate, law, music, and nursing. Baylor also operates the Medical Center in Dallas and has affiliated degree programs at the Academy of Health Sciences in San Antonio and the Baylor College of Dentistry in Dallas.

Dr. Herbert H. Reynolds is president of the university. Key athletic department personnel include SWC faculty representative David Guinn, athletic director Bill Menefee, and head football coach Grant Teaff.

COLD SPINACH SOUP
(also great hot!)

(serves 6)

1 pkg. frozen chopped spinach (cooked)
4 cups light cream
4 chicken bouillon cubes
1/4 cup dry vermouth
1/2 tsp. ground mace
2 hardcooked eggs (chopped)
1 tbsp. grated lemon rind

Put cooked spinach into blender and reduce to
pulp. Put bouillon cubes into cream and scald,
stirring until cubes are dissolved. (I put in
cream in top of double boiler - easier and keeps
from burning!!) Remove from heat. Stir in
spinach, vermouth, lemon rind and mace. Chill.

Top with egg or serve piping hot with croutons.

Barbara Bush

TEXAS A&M UNIVERSITY

COLLEGE STATION, TEXAS 77843-1246

FRANK E. VANDIVER
PRESIDENT

Let's start with a Creole gumbo, a dish which originated in la Belle Nouvelle Orleans. A gumbo is something unique to the Creole cuisine that developed out of the specialties of this area. One of the greatest of these, actually termed the king of the gumbos, is GUMBO Z'HERBES, the gumbo of herbs or green gumbo -- a sort of revivification or rejuvenation given by this conglomeration of greens. Legend had it that for every green that was put into the gumbo, a new friend would be made during the succeeding year.

GUMBO Z'HERBES

1 pkg frozen spinach
1 pkg. frozen mustard greens
1 pkg. frozen turnip greens
1 pkg. frozen collard greens
1/2 cabbage, shredded
2 qts. water
stick butter
2 onions, chopped
1 cup chopped celery
1 cup chopped bell pepper
2 tbsp. oil
1 lb. stew meat, cut into small pieces
3/4 lb. ham, cut into small pieces

4 cloves garlic, chopped
1 bunch shallots, chopped*
4 bay leaves
1 tsp. basil
1 tsp. powdered thyme
1/8 tsp. allspice
1/8 tsp. cloves
1/2 cup chopped parsley
1/4 tsp. Tabasco
5 tbsp. flour
salt and pepper to taste
1 doz. oysters (optional)
file (if desired)

*When the Creoles refer to "shallots," they mean green onions or scallions.

Into the water place the spinach, turnip greens, mustard greens, collard greens, cabbage, bay leaves, basil, thyme, allspice, and cloves. Bring to a boil, lower the heat, and let simmer, covered.

In a frying pan melt 1/2 stick butter and saute the onions, bell pepper, and celery. When limp, add to the greens. In the same frying pan, fry the stew meat and ham in the oil. When brown, add to the pot. Let this mixture simmer for 1 hour and then add the green onions (shallots), parsley, garlic, Tabasco, salt, and pepper. Mix well.

At this point, if you wish, you may take about a quart of the gumbo out of the pot and run it into a blender to puree it. Return it to the pot. Now allow to simmer for another 2 hours.

About 1/2 hour before the gumbo is finished, take the 1/4 stick of butter (at room temperature), add to it the flour, and work it into a paste. When the paste is smooth, slice a bit at a time and add to the pot. The lumps will soon disappear as you stir.

Five minutes before serving, if you wish, add the oysters and their water. Cook until the edges of the oysters begin to curl.

The gumbo is now ready to serve over rice in soup bowls. A pinch or two of file powder may be added to the gumbo in the bowl, if desired. Serves eight. File is served in a small open dish (as a salt-dish).

*File, a favorite of Creole cooks, was an herb given to the Creoles by the Indians; the Indians used it for seasoning as well as for medicinal purposes. It was prepared by taking young, tender sassafras leaves, drying them, grinding them into a fine powder, and then sifting the powder through a hair sieve. File literally means "to make threads," and anyone who has misused this seasoning knows very well how appropriately it was named. File has to be added at the very end of the cooking process -- not boiled in the gumbo -- because it gets thready or gummy. When gumbo has file added to it, it is not a good idea to reheat.

Frank Hardin

PACIFIC 10 CONFERENCE

THOMAS C. HANSEN, *EXECUTIVE DIRECTOR*

STEAK SOUP

1 pound chopped round steak
1/2 pound butter
1 cup flour
8 cups water
fresh ground pepper
omit salt
1 large carrot, diced
1 medium onion, diced
1 stalk celery, diced
1 package frozen mixed vegetables
1 large can tomatoes
1 tbsp. beef base granules
    (Spice Island's Beef Stock Base is good)

Melt butter, stir in flour and gradually add 2 cups of the water. Stir until smooth. Add all other ingredients except steak. Set aside. In another pan saute steak in 2 tbsp. butter until browned. Drain off grease. Add meat to first mixture and simmer, stirring occasionally for 2 hours or until the vegetables are tender. Yields one gallon. If possible, make the day before serving to let soup season. Soup bones add very good flavor. Freezes well.

This is a hearty winter dinner soup. A delicious combination served with this soup is a loaf of San Francisco Sour Dough French Bread and a bottle of California Cabernet.

Best regards,

Tom

Tom Hansen

DEPARTMENT OF THE NAVY
UNITED STATES NAVAL ACADEMY
OFFICE OF THE SUPERINTENDENT
ANNAPOLIS, MARYLAND 21402

NAVY BEAN SOUP

1	Pound Navy Beans
1	Smoked Ham Hock
1	Medium Potato, Finely Diced
1	Onion, Diced
½	Cup Diced Celery
½	Cup Diced Carrots
2	Cloves Garlic, Minced
1	Bay Leaf
	Salt and Pepper
	Chopped Parsley

Soak beans overnight in quart of water. (Or bring beans to a boil in the water; boil for 2 minutes, cover and let stand for 1 hour.) Drain beans, reserving water. Add enough water to make 2 quarts.

Place beans, water and ham hock in kettle. Cover and simmer 2 hours. Add potato, onion, celery, carrots, garlic and bay leaf. Simmer another hour. Remove ham hock and cut meat. Remove one cup of boiled beans and puree in blender. Return meat and pureed beans to soup. Reheat. Season to taste with salt and pepper. Sprinkle with chopped parsley for serving.

Makes 6 servings.

Best wishes,

C. R. LARSON
Rear Admiral, U.S. Navy
Superintendent

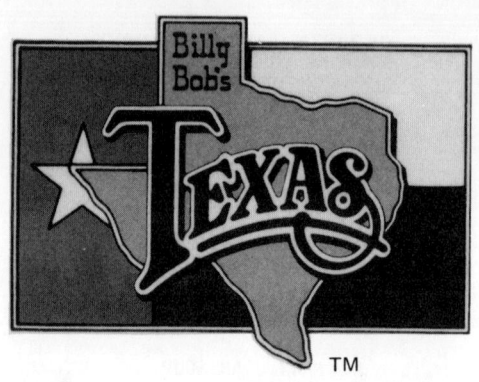

TM

BILLY BOB'S TEXAS

HONKY TONK CLAM CHOWDER

5 Gallons

5 lbs.	Canned Clams
1 lbs.	Salt pork - run through grinder
3 lbs.	Celery - diced not too small and not too large
3 lbs.	Ground Pepper - diced not too small and not too large
3 lbs.	Leeks
3 lbs.	Onions - diced not too small and not too large
3 lbs.	Potatoes - diced not too small and not too large
12 oz.	Olive Oil
5 qts.	Whipping Cream
6 #5 cans	Clam Juice

Boil Salt Pork. Add canned clams, celery,pepper,leeks onions,olive oil, potatoes, (make sure these are added last). Add Whipping Cream. Make Roux (butter & flour) in a skillet. Cook till medium consistency. Not too thick or thin. Have ready ahead. With whip add Roux to stock to desired consistency.

BILLY BOB BARNETT

Office of the
Head Football Coach

ODRE'S SHRIMP GUMBO

3 - 4 tablespoons flour
4 tablespoons shortening
1 medium onion, chopped
1 medium bell pepper, chopped
3 stalks celery, chopped
3 cloves garlic, chopped
2 - 2½ pounds cleaned shrimp, uncooked
1 pound fresh crabmeat
Salt & pepper to taste
6 - 8 cups water

Make a dark brown roux by stirring flour into melted shortening
over low heat. Add bell pepper and onion, browning these. Add
4 cups of water and simmer 5 - 10 minutes. Add celery and garlic,
simmering 10 minutes, adding more water. Keep roux at a medium
thickness, adding water as needed. Simmer covered over low
heat 10 minutes. Add shrimp and simmer 10 minutes. Depending
on preference, add water. Some prefer "soupy" gumbo while others
prefer thick gumbo.

This "secret" recipe was given to Diane Akers by the late
Odre Speyrer, father of Longhorn player Cotton Speyrer.

CREAM OF CUCUMBER SOUP

Excellent at a cold football game, served hot out of a thermos

1½ pounds cucumbers (3–about 8 inches long)

½ cup minced shallots, or a combination of shallots, scallions, and/or onions

3 tablespoons butter

6 cups liquid: light chicken stock, or canned broth and water

1½ teaspoons wine vinegar

¾ teaspoon dried dill weed

4 tablespoons quick-cooking farina (cream of wheat) breakfast cereal

1 cup sour cream

1 to 2 tablespoons minced fresh dill or parsley

Salt/pepper

More liquid, if necessary

A heavy-bottomed stainless steel or enameled saucepan with cover
A food mill with mediumdisk, or an electric blender
Soup bowls

Peel the cucumbers. Cut 18 to 24 paper-thin slices and reserve in a bowl for later. Cut the rest of the cucumbers into half-inch chunks; you will have about 4½ cups.

Cook the shallots, scallions, or onions slowly in butter for several minutes until tender but not browned. Add the cucumber chunks, chicken broth, vinegar, and herbs. Bring to a boil, then stir in the farina. Simmer, partially covered, for 20-25 minutes. Purée, and return the soup to the pan. Thin out with more liquid if necessary; season carefully with salt and pepper.

NOTE:
*I use 4 cans of Swanson's Chicken Broth.
2 bunches of green onions are adequate.
White wine vinegar is used.
2 teaspoons of white pepper.
Salt to taste.
I use the blender; pour the soup through a strainer to remove the cucumber seeds and the return the entire quantity of soup to its original cooking vessel, into which I then add the salt and pepper. Stir the salt and pepper with a wire whisk to blend.
If you are not serving at this point, stop here and set aside.
Bring to simmer just before serving, and beat in ½ cup sour cream. Ladle into bowls, place a dollop of sour cream in each bowl, float slices of cucumber on top of cream, and decorate with sprinkling of herbs.

*I have never had to thin out with more liquid.

Jack Miller
Cotton Bowl Director

CLASSIC MILESTONE

1938 - Dan D. Rogers was named in July as Chairman of the Board of the Cotton Bowl Athletic Association, a position he held until his death in 1952. Rogers helped lead the campaign for the Southwest Conference's involvement with the Cotton Bowl.

BROCCOLI SOUP
Diet Version

1 head broccoli, cut into pieces
2 cups chicken broth
¼ cup chopped onion
2 tablespoons butter (or diet Butter Buds)

1 teaspoon salt
1 to 2 teaspoons curry powder
1 cup lowfat buttermilk
1 tablespoon lemon or lime juice

Mix broccoli, chicken broth, onion, butter, salt and curry powder in large saucepan. Cover and simmer for 8 to 12 minutes, or until broccoli becomes tender. Puree in blender in batches. Add buttermilk and lemon or lime juice. Chill.

Ara Parseghian

BIG "D" BROCCOLI SOUP
Delicious.

½ cup chopped onion
¼ cup chopped green pepper
2 tablespoons margarine
1 (10-ounce) package frozen chopped broccoli, thawed

1 can cream of chicken soup
1 can milk
¾ pound Velveeta cheese, cubed

Sauté onion and green pepper in margarine. Add broccoli and remaining ingredients. Cook in microwave approximately 6 minutes, or on top of the stove until cheese melts. Serve in small cups.

Mr. and Mrs. Walter Coughlin (Ann)
Cotton Bowl Director

QUICK COLD SOUP

1 can stewed tomatoes, chilled
Jane's mixed up salt

Curry powder
½ cup sour cream

Combine ingredients in blender and blend until smooth. For diet version, substitute about 1 cup of lowfat buttermilk for the sour cream.

Ara Parseghian

COLD CUCUMBER SOUP I

2 large cucumbers
Butter
1 small Spanish onion, sliced
1 pint chicken stock
¼ cup flour
½ cup milk

½ cup heavy cream
Salt, to taste
Cayenne pepper, to taste
½ teaspoon lemon juice
Fresh chives, chopped, to garnish

Peel the cucumbers, slice them in half lengthwise, remove the seeds and cut them into 1-inch pieces. Heat the butter until bubbly. Add the onions, and sauté until they are transparent. Add the cucumbers and cook gently for 2 minutes, stirring occasionally. Add the chicken stock. When the stock boils, reduce the heat and simmer until the cucumbers are mushy. Blend the flour with the milk until smooth, then stir into the soup. Let the soup boil for 10 minutes, then strain it through a colander and refrigerate until chilled. Add the cream, salt, cayenne pepper and lemon juice to taste. Garnish with fresh chives. Serves 4.

Walter Kaufmann
Owner/Executive Chef
Old Swiss House

COLD CUCUMBER SOUP II

4 medium cucumbers
4½ ounces butter
1 small onion, peeled and diced
2 medium leeks, chopped (white part
    only)
1 bay leaf, halved
2 ounces flour, sifted

½ quart chicken stock
Salt, to taste
Pepper, to taste
1 pint heavy cream
Fresh mint, to garnish

Peel cucumbers, halve lengthwise, remove seeds and slice thinly. Set aside. In a saucepan, heat the butter until bubbly. Add onions and leeks and sauté until transparent. Add cucumbers and bay leaf; cook gently for 5 minutes. Add flour and continue cooking, stirring, for 1 minute. Stir in chicken stock. Bring to a boil, then simmer for 5 minutes. Remove bay leaf, add salt and pepper to taste, then puree in a blender until the soup is smooth. Cool the soup, then add heavy cream. Serve in individual bowls or soup plates set in crushed ice. Garnish each serving with a fresh mint sprig. Serves 6 to 8.

Mrs. C.E. Seal, II (Crickett)
Wife, Cotton Bowl Committee

GAZPACHO

4 large very ripe tomatoes, peeled and
diced
1 green pepper, finely chopped
1 large cucumber, peeled and diced
1 cup tomato juice
1 medium onion, finely chopped
1 celery stalk with top, finely chopped

3 tablespoons Italian salad dressing
1 pinch garlic salt
Salt, to taste
Pepper, to taste
Dash hot pepper (optional)

Combine tomatoes, green pepper, cucumber, tomato juice, onion, celery, salad dressing
and garlic salt. Season to taste with salt and pepper. Add hot pepper, if desired. Mix well
and chill. Serves 8.

Mrs. Kenneth P. Dowell (Jo)
Wife, Cotton Bowl President 1970-72

NAVY BEAN SOUP
A perfect winter time meal.

1 pound dried navy beans
1 fresh or leftover ham bone, fat
removed
1 onion, chopped
1 cup mashed potatoes
1 cup chopped celery with leaves

1 garlic clove, minced
1 carrot, chopped
3 tablespoons catsup
Salt, to taste
Pepper, to taste

Rinse beans. Add beans to 3-quart saucepan and cover with water. Add ham bone.
Simmer approximately 2 hours. Stir in onion, potatoes, celery, garlic and carrots. Simmer
1 more hour. Prior to serving, stir in catsup, salt and pepper. Thin, if necessary, with
water or milk. Serves 8.

Tom Forrestal, Jr.

HAM AND LENTIL SOUP INVOCATION

4 bacon slices
½ cup chopped onion
5½ cups water
2 cups diced cooked ham
1 cup dried lentils

1 (8-ounce) can tomatoes, chopped
1 (6-ounce) can tomato paste
¼ cup snipped parsley
2 chicken bouillon cubes
¾ teaspoon thyme

Fry bacon until crisp. Crumble and set aside. Add onion to drippings and sauté until
tender. Add remaining ingredients. Cover and simmer for 30 minutes or until lentils are
tender. Stir in crumbled bacon and simmer for 10 minutes. Serves 6.

GREEN CHILI AND RICE SOUP

½ cup chopped onion
1 garlic clove, minced
2 tablespoons butter
2 cups chicken stock
1 cup milk
½ cup raw rice
6 ounces diced green chilies
2 cups whipping cream

½ cup grated Monterey Jack cheese
½ cup process American cheese
Salt, to taste
Cayenne pepper, to taste
Comino, to taste
Tomatoes, diced, to garnish
Avocado, sliced, to garnish
Tortilla chips, to garnish

Sauté the onions and garlic over low heat for 10 minutes. Add stock, milk and rice and cook for 20 minutes. Add remaining ingredients and heat thoroughly. Adjust seasoning according to taste. Green chilies have a wonderful flavor. They are a little hot, so go lightly with the cayenne. Yields 6 cups.

Shelby Volk
The Buffet
Kimbell Art Museum
Fort Worth

CHICKEN GUMBO GOAL LINE

1 (4-pound) hen
Salt, to taste
Pepper, to taste
4 cups cut okra (fresh or frozen)
2 cups chopped green onions with tops

2 cups chopped celery
1½ cups flour
1½ cups chicken fat or vegetable oil
8 drops Tabasco sauce
2 tablespoons filé (ground sassafrass leaf)

Cover the hen with water, season with salt and pepper, and boil until tender. Let chicken cool in broth. Remove and bone the chicken. Skim fat from broth and set aside. Add okra, onions and celery to skimmed broth; simmer. In a heavy skillet, stir flour into oil or fat and sauté very slowly, stirring constantly, until mixture turns dark brown. (Back in Louisiana they call this a roux!) Carefully add roux to simmering vegetables. Season to taste with salt, pepper, Tabasco sauce and filé. Simmer for 1 hour and serve with rice.

Mr. and Mrs. Gus E. Lehmann (Frances)

IVY LEAGUE TURKEY VEGETABLE SOUP

Turkey bones
2 whole celery stalks
1 onion, quartered
1 bay leaf
1 tablespoon salt
1 tablespoon pepper

2 celery stalks, finely chopped
1 onion, finely chopped
1 can tomatoes, cut up
2 medium potatoes, chopped
2 carrots
1 package onion soup mix

Boil turkey bones with the whole celery stalks, quartered onion, bay leaf, salt and pepper. Cook for 2 hours over medium heat. Remove from heat and drain the stock. To the stock, add chopped celery, onion, tomatoes, potatoes, carrots and onion soup mix. Boil over medium heat for 1 hour or until all vegetables are tender.

John White's Ranch Style Cooking
J.A. Mathews Ranch Co.

TOMATO SOUP

2 pounds tomatoes, quartered or 2
  pounds (3-ounce) canned Italian
  tomatoes, including juice
1 bunch celery, sliced
2 large onions, chopped
½ cup unsalted butter (1 stick)
8 cups water
1 teaspoon minced fresh thyme or a
  pinch of dried

1 teaspoon minced fresh basil or a pinch
  of dried
1 teaspoon minced fresh tarragon or a
  pinch of dried
Pinch of sugar
Salt, to taste
Pepper, to taste

Cook tomatoes, celery and onions in butter over low heat until soft. Add water, bring to a boil and simmer for 1 hour. Puree mixture thoroughly, using fine disc of Cuisinart into a steel or enamel pan. Stir in thyme, basil, tarragon, sugar, salt and pepper. Simmer for 10 minutes and serve.

Mrs. Finley Ewing, Jr. (Gail)
Wife, Cotton Bowl Director

CLASSIC MILESTONE

1939 - J. Curtis Sanford turned the Classic over to the Cotton Bowl Athletic Association for the 1940 Boston College vs. Clemson matchup, but still played the key role in staging the fourth Cotton Bowl.

FILET OF BEEF WITH WINE AND MUSHROOM SAUCE

2 whole tenderloins (2½ to 3 lbs each)

Marinade

½ cup soy sauce
½ cup dry vermouth
1 tblspn dry mustard
1 tspn ginger
1 tsp thyme crushed

Sauce

1 cup sliced mushrooms
4 tblspns butter
1½ cup beef broth
½ cup sliced onions
2 tblspns flour
½ cup Madeira wine
Salt & pepper to taste

Marinate tenderloins for 2 to 6 hours. Do not pierce meat.

To prepare sauce, saute mushrooms and onions in butter until tender. Sprinkle on flour and stir well. Add beef broth and Madeira wine. Stir until mixture is thickened. Simmer for ten minutes. Season with salt, pepper and paprika.

Remove tenderloins from marinade and roast on rack in 400° oven until desired doneness. (Best on rare side) When done, slice tenderloin and place on meat platter. Spoon some sauce over the sliced meat. Pour remaining sauce in gravy boat for serving at the table.

JOHN J. CLUNE, Colonel, USAF
Director of Athletics
U.S. Air Force Academy
President, NACDA

WHITE SAUCE

Medium—can be made thicker or thinner by adding more flour or milk.

2 tablespoons butter or margarine
2 tablespoons flour
½ teaspoon salt

¼ teaspoon pepper
1 cup milk

Melt butter or margarine in top of double boiler; add flour, salt and pepper. Stir until well blended. Remove from heat. Gradually stir in milk and return to heat. Cook, stirring constantly, until thick and smooth. Makes about 2 cups.

A good addition to this for Cheese potatoes is ½ cup of Velveeta cheese added just at the end of cooking and melted. Also can by used on vegetables, fish loaf, macaroni or hard cooked eggs.

Mrs. Carroll Woldt (Helen)

JEZEBEL SAUCE

18 ounces pineapple preserves
18 ounces apple jelly
1 (5-ounce) jar fresh horseradish

1 tablespoon dry mustard
1 tablespoon cracked peppercorns
3 drops red food coloring

Mix pineapple preserves with apple jelly in a mixing bowl. Blend in horseradish. Stir in dry mustard and cracked peppercorns. Mix together until blended. Store in jar in refrigerator. Makes a delicious accompaniment to all meats. It has a sweet, hot taste that is not for every palate.

J.R. Martin

CHICAGO BEAR BARBECUE SAUCE

3 small cans Hunt's tomato sauce
1 tablespoon Liquid Smoke
1 tablespoon Worcestershire sauce

3 tablespoons vinegar
¾ cup brown sugar (packed)
Tabasco sauce, to taste

Mix ingredients in a saucepan and simmer until mixture reaches desired consistency.

Ross Montgomery

CLASSIC MILESTONES

1941 - The Cotton Bowl Classic came under the sponsorship of the Southwest Conference with the 1941 Classic.

1941 - The Classic's first sellout of more than 45,000 witnessed Texas A&M, coached by Homer Norton, score a one-point victory over Jim Crowley's Fordham Rams, 13-12.

SADDLE TRAMP "SOPPIN" SAUCE FOR BEEF

2 garlic cloves, coarsely chopped
1 small dried hot red pepper
½ teaspoon chopped fresh cilantro or ¼ teaspoon dried coriander
¼ teaspoon ground comino
½ teaspoon anise seed

½ teaspoon salt
2 tablespoons brown sugar
1 tablespoon Worcestershire sauce
1 cup cider vinegar
2 cups catsup
Hot pepper sauce (optional)

In a blender or food processor, combine garlic, red pepper, cilantro, comino, anise seed, salt, brown sugar and Worcestershire sauce. Process until smooth. Place mixture in a medium saucepan and add vinegar and catsup. Heat to boiling; reduce heat and simmer, uncovered, for 30 minutes. Add hot pepper sauce, if desired. Yields about 3 cups.

Darla Tinsley
Gaylen's Bar-B-Q

RED RAIDER OUTDOOR MATADOR MARINADE

1 stick real butter
Juice of 2 large limes
1 (6-ounce) glass dry white wine

1 tablespoon Worcestershire sauce
1 teaspoon fines herbes (Spice Islands)

Melt butter and mix with remaining ingredients. Marinate meat for 15 to 20 minutes before cooking, then baste with marinade while cooking. The butter tends to make the charcoal flame, so watch out. This recipe is marvelous for almost everything you cook on your charcoal or gas grill except red meat. Try it on chicken, game hens, pork ribs, pork chops, firm white fish such as sword fish, amberjack, grouper, shrimp, etc.

Tim Johnson
Mac's House

RAZORBACK "MOPPIN" SAUCE FOR PORK

1½ cups cider vinegar
1 tablespoon dry mustard
2 teaspoons cayenne pepper

1 tablespoon Worcestershire sauce
1 tablespoon oil

In a medium saucepan, combine ingredients. Heat slowly to just below the boiling point. Remove from heat and let stand for 2 hours before serving. Yields about 1½ cups.

Darla Tinsley
Gaylen's Bar-B-Q

WILD BILL'S RED SAUCE

2 cups water
½ cup sugar
Lemon juice
1 teaspoon salt
1 teaspoon paprika
1 tablespoon celery seed

3 teaspoons cayenne pepper
¼ cup vegetable oil
2 large bottles spicy catsup
¼ cup grated onion
⅛ cup onion flakes

Boil water. Measure the ½ cup sugar, then add lemon juice until cup is full. Add remaining ingredients. Simmer for 35 to 45 minutes. Pour into 3 catsup bottles to store. Excellent with baked beans, as a hot sauce, or to cook with as a barbecue sauce.

William B. "Wild Bill" Forrester
Trinity Insurance Company

FULLBACK FUDGE SAUCE

2 tablespoons butter
2 squares unsweetened chocolate
¾ cup sugar

½ cup evaporated milk
1 teaspoon vanilla

Mix all ingredients in a double boiler. Heat thoroughly. Note: I use this sauce to prepare Chocolate Surprises. Spoon the sauce over pear halves to make this delightful dessert.

Mrs. Margaret Lowdon

RASPBERRY SAUCE

1 cup fresh raspberries
¼ cup tarragon vinegar

1 teaspoon Dijon mustard

Combine ingredients in a blender container; process until well mixed.

Mrs. C.E. Seal, II (Crickett)
Wife, Cotton Bowl Committee

CLASSIC MILESTONE

1942 - The Southwest Conference prohibited its champion from playing in any bowl other than the Cotton Bowl.

CHINESE CHICKEN SALAD

Serves 2

2 chicken breasts (marinade for 1 hour, discard
                   marinade or save for future use)
Marinade:
    1 oz. Soy sauce
    1 oz. Teriyaki sauce
    1 oz. Seasame oil
    ½ oz. Ginger
    1 tsp. Seaseme seeds

Grill chicken breast and let cool

Vegetables:

2 oz. carrots   1 oz. bean sprouts
2 oz. Daikon   ½ oz. ginger ⎤
4 each Scallions   ¼ oz. garlic ⎦ mince
½ red bell pepper   1 oz. Seaseme oil
½ green bell pepper   ¼ red onion
2 oz. Snow peas

Julienne all vegetables and mix saute pan. Add
sesame oil, garlic, and ginger. Add vegetables and
stir fry and let cool. Julienne chicken and mix
with stir fry and serve in lettuce cup. Garnish
with fried cellophane noodles and chives.

                    Executive Chef - Jean-Marie Josselin

CBS SPORTS

Peter A. Lund, President

This Is A Lund Favorite

-And-

One We Are Pleased To Submit For
The Cotton Bowl 50th Anniversary Cookbook

CURRIED CHICKEN SALAD

-- Serves 4 --

4 cups cooked chicken breasts - cubed
1/4 cup thinly sliced celery
1/3 cup raisins
2/3 slivered almonds
1/3 cup diced apples
2/3 cup mayonnaise
1 tablespoon dijon mustard
1-2 teaspoons curry powder
salt and white pepper

Combine chicken, celery, raisins, apples, and
1/3 cup almonds. In small bowl, mix mayonnaise,
mustard, and curry. Season to taste with salt and
pepper. Combine all and refrigerate.

To serve: Place on bed of lettuce, garnish with
fresh strawberries and pineapple slices. Sprinkle
with remaining 1/3 cup almonds.

THE **STOCK YARDS**

FORT WORTH, TEXAS ™

MATTIE MAY'S MAYONNAISE

Keep all ingredients <u>cold</u>...

```
  4      egg yolks
  3 cups Mayzola (1 sm. bottle, 24 oz)
  3 tbl. lemon juice
1/2 tsp. paprika
  1 tsp. salt
1/2 tsp. red pepper
  2 tsp. grated onions
```

Start with 4 egg yolks in small bowl.
Mix well. Start adding your oil, 1 cup
at a time. Then 1 tbl. of lemon juice
(pushing the ingredients to center with
spatula at all times). Add Mazola Oil
by pouring slowly from bottle into the
beaters. Add salt, paprika and red pepper
at one time. Then 1 tbl. lemon juice,
onions, then more oil. Then 1 tbl. lemon
juice & onions, then finish up with oil.

Hub Baker

HUB BAKER

STATE OF ARKANSAS
OFFICE OF THE GOVERNOR
State Capitol
Little Rock 72201

Bill Clinton
Governor

CHINESE CHICKEN RICE SALAD

1/4 cup soy sauce
2 teaspoons prepared mustard
2 1/2 cups cooked chicken,
    cut in thin strips
1 tablespoon oil
1/4 cup sliced green onions,
    with tops

1/2 cup sliced celery
1/4 cup chopped green pepper
2 hard cooked eggs, diced
3/4 cup salad dressing
1 can (3 oz.) chow mein noodles

Blend soy sauce, mustard, and oil. Add chicken (turkey or tuna may be substituted) and toss to coat. Let stand 30 minutes. Stir in rice, vegetables, eggs and salad dressing. Spoon onto beds of lettuce. Top with noodles. Serves 6-8.

Bill Clinton
Governor

BAYLOR UNIVERSITY
DEPARTMENT OF ATHLETICS

POLAR BEAR SALAD

Ingredients: Small box of Jello (strawberry, cherry, etc.)
3 bananas; 1 box strawberries; 1/2 cup of nuts; 1/2 pint
sweetened whipping cream.

Mix one small box red (strawberry, cherry, etc.) Jello, as
directed.

Immediately add:

        3 chopped bananas

        1 box thawed strawberries or
        1/2 pint fresh, sliced strawberries

        1/2-1 cup chopped nuts

Fold In:

        1/2 pint whipped sweetened
        whipping cream

Freeze in a 9 x 12 container.

To serve, remove from freezer 15 minutes before serving.
Slice and serve on lettuce leaf.

Grant Teaff
Head Football Coach
Baylor University

Texas Tech University
Texas Tech University Health Sciences Center

Office of the President

DUTCH POTATO SALAD

(6 servings)

6 medium potatoes
1/3 cup sliced scallions
1/2 cup diced, peeled cucumbers
1/3 cup Miracle Whip Salad Dressing
1/3 cup sour cream
4 teaspoons horseradish

4 teaspoons vinegar
1 teaspoon salt
1/4 teaspoon sugar
1/8 teaspoon pepper
1 teaspoon caraway seeds

1. Boil potatoes in their jackets until soft. Peel and cube them.

2. Combine potatoes with scallions and cucumbers.

3. Mix all remaining ingredients, pour over potato mixture and toss lightly. Chill before serving.

from the desk of Joe Paterno

ANTIPASTO

Mrs. Joe Paterno
Penn State University

Dice or chop the following vegetables:

4 raw carrots	1 stalk celery
4 green peppers	1 lb. fresh mushrooms
2 large onions	1 cauliflower (fresh)

In one cup olive oil cook the above as follows:

Cook the carrots for 5 min., add onions, mushrooms and cauliflower for 2 minutes. Add celery and green peppers and cook for three minutes.

Mix the following in a large bowl:

2 small bottles catsup (or 28 oz.)
3 tsp. salt
2 bottles chili sauce (small)
2 tsp. Accent
2 cloves garlic (optional
juice of 2 lemons.

Chop or break up and add the following to the sauce:

1 can tuna (drained)
1 lb. frozen king crab meat, defrosted and drained
2 jars artichoke hearts, drained
½ cup pitted green olives
½ cup ripe olives

Add the cooked vegetables to the above. Mix everything together & let it marinate in the refrigerator for 24 hours. May be served hot or cold.

NOTE: A whole recipe makes at least three quarts.

KILGORE COLLEGE RANGERETTES

BIOLOGICAL SCIENCE
BUSINESS ADMINISTRATION
COMMUNICATIONS
ENGINEERING-SCIENCE
EVENING SCHOOL
FINE ARTS
FOREIGN LANGUAGE
MATHEMATICS
PHYSICAL EDUCATION
SOCIAL SCIENCE
TECHNICAL-VOCATIONAL

EMPHASIS EXCELLENCE

1935

FROZEN FRUIT SALAD

2 No. 2 cans crushed pineapple (drained
  so there is no juice left).
1 cup chopped pecans.
1 small jar maraschino cherries (drained
  and diced)
1/2 pkg. miniature marshmallows (halved)

Place in bowl
1 large pkg. Phil. cream cheese (creamed with
2 tablespoons salad dressing
2 tablespoons lemon juice

Add sugar to taste
1/2 pint cream whipped, adding enough sugar
  to make it as sweet as if used for a
  topping

Mix Phil. cheese and whipped cream together.
Pour other ingredients into this and place
in ice tray that has been lined with wax
paper. Can also be eaten immediately.

Deana Bolton

Ms. Deana Bolton, Director
Kilgore College Rangerettes

PINK MAJORETTE SALAD

1 can Eagle Brand sweetened condensed
   milk
1 small can crushed pineapple
1 (9-ounce) container Cool Whip

¼ cup lemon juice
¼ teaspoon almond extract
1 cup chopped pecans
1 can cherry pie filling

Mix milk, pineapple, Cool Whip, lemon juice, almond extract and pecans. Stir in cherry pie filling. Freeze or refrigerate until serving time.

Mr. and Mrs. Buddy Dike (Sara)
Cotton Bowl President 1976-1978

PARTY APPLESAUCE CONGEALED STRONGSIDE SALAD

⅔ cup cinnamon Red Hots
1 cup boiling water
1 small package lemon gelatin
2 cups applesauce

8 ounces cream cheese, softened
½ cup mayonnaise
1 cup diced celery
1 cup chopped nuts

Melt Red Hots in boiling water, add gelatin and dissolve. Fold in applesauce. Pour half the gelatin mixture into a 10x6-inch glass dish. Refrigerate until firm. Combine remaining ingredients. Spoon over firm gelatin and add remaining gelatin mixture on top. Cut into squares and serve on a bed of lettuce. Serves 12.

Mr. and Mrs. Charles Mayberry (Cathy)

APRICOT ORANGEMAN SALAD

2 (16-ounce) cans apricot halves
Dash salt
2 (3-ounce) packages orange gelatin

1 (6-ounce) can frozen orange juice
2 tablespoons lemon juice
1 (7-ounce) bottle of lemon-lime (TEEM)

Drain apricots, reserving 1½ cups syrup. Puree the apricots. In a saucepan, mix the syrup and salt; bring mixture to a boil. Add the gelatin and stir until completely dissolved. Remove from heat. Mix in the apricot puree, orange juice and lemon juice. Slowly add the lemon-lime TEEM, pouring the liquid onto the side of the saucepan. Gently fold into the gelatin mixture. Pour into a ring mold. Very good served with ham or ham loaf.

Mary McVay

LEXINGTON LIME-PEAR SALAD

1 large can pears
1 package lime gelatin
½ pound package Philadelphia cream
   cheese, softened

½ pint Cool Whip
Maraschino cherries (optional)
Walnuts (optional)

Drain pears, reserving juice. Boil 1 cup pear juice. Stir gelatin into hot juice to dissolve. Mash pears well with a fork. Mix a little pear juice with cream cheese. Add the pears and cream cheese to the gelatin mixture. Let the mixture cool. Fold in Cool Whip, cherries and walnuts.

Mary McVay

CONTINENTAL CLEMSON SALAD

1 (3-ounce) package lemon gelatin
½ cup boiling water
1 can chicken rice soup
1 (6½-ounce) can white water-packed
   tuna
½ cup blanched almonds

½ cup chopped celery
½ cup whipping cream, whipped
   creamy but not stiff
½ cup mayonnaise

Combine all ingredients; pour in mold or dish. Refrigerate until set.

Mrs. Richard E. Miles (Karen)

FIVE CUP FUMBLE SALAD (AMBROSIA)

1 cup mandarin oranges, drained
1 cup pineapple chunks, drained
1 cup grated coconut

1 cup miniature marshmallows
1 cup Cool Whip or sour cream

Combine all ingredients; chill. Just before serving, you may add well-drained maraschino cherries.

NEW YEAR'S DAY FRUIT BOWL

1 (1-pound) can pitted dark sweet
   cherries
1 (13½-ounce) can pineapple chunks
1 (11-ounce) can mandarin orange
   segments

1 (8¾-ounce) can seedless green grapes
1 tart apple

Have all fruit chilled. Just before serving, drain canned fruit thoroughly. Cut unpeeled apple into quarters. Core and slice into thin wedges. Mix apple slices with canned fruit in a large bowl. Pour dressing over fruit, tossing until fruit is well coated. Serves 7 to 8.

SOUR CREAM-HONEY DRESSING
½ cup sour cream
1 tablespoon honey

1 tablespoon orange juice

Blend ingredients.

WATERBOY'S WATERGATE SALAD

3 cups whipped cream
2 cups pineapple chunks, with juice
1 package instant pistachio pudding

½ cup chopped pecans
2 cups small marshmallows

Combine ingredients in a large salad bowl, stirring to mix well. Refrigerate until set.

Vance Godbey

LEMON GELATIN SALAD

2 cups boiling water
1 cup Campbell's tomato soup
1 (8-ounce) package cream cheese,
   softened
2 packages lemon gelatin

2 cups chopped celery
½ cup chopped green pepper
½ cup grated onion
1 cup Miracle Whip salad dressing

Mix all ingredients. Refrigerate until set.

Mrs. O.M. Lynch (Annie)

AVOCADO SALAD MOLD

1 cup boiling water
1 (6-ounce) package lime gelatin
2 tablespoons lemon juice
1 tablespoon chopped parsley

2 cups pureed avocado
¼ cup whipping cream, whipped
¾ cup mayonnaise

Pour boiling water over gelatin in large bowl. Stir constantly until gelatin dissolves. Stir in lemon juice. Set bowl in larger bowl of ice, stirring occasionally until mixture reaches the consistency of unbeaten egg white. This takes about 15 to 20 minutes. Add parsley, avocado, whipped cream and mayonnaise. Pour into a 5-cup decorative mold or ring mold. Refrigerate overnight. Unmold and fill center with seafood or chicken salad, if desired. Serves 8.

Mrs. Gordon R. Miller (Rita)

FRESH SPINACH SPECIAL TEAMS SALAD

DRESSING

3 celery stalks, chopped
1 large onion, sliced and divided into
   rings
1 garlic clove, minced
2 tablespoons sugar
1 tablespoon Worcestershire sauce

2½ tablespoons dry mustard
½ cup vinegar
⅔ cup oil
½ cup chili sauce
Paprika

Mix ingredients and marinate in refrigerator for at least 8 hours. The longer the better.

SALAD

1 package fresh spinach, washed and
   drained
10 large fresh mushrooms, sliced

2 to 3 eggs, hard-boiled and sliced
6 crisp bacon slices, crumbled

Toss ingredients and serve with Dressing.

Mr. and Mrs. Walker Harman (Elaine)
Cotton Bowl Director

CLASSIC MILESTONE

1942 - This was the first war-time Classic that saw 31 Texas, Oklahoma and Alabama men take the oath of enlistment into the Naval Air Corps at halftime. Among them were Texas A&M's great tackle Martin Ruby, Sam Porter, a reserve Aggie back, and Alabama's Paul Spencer.

24-HOUR LAYER SLANT IN SALAD

Iceberg lettuce, torn into bite-sized pieces
½ green pepper, chopped
½ red pepper, chopped
½ cup chopped celery
½ sweet red Spanish onion (other onions are too strong)
1 package frozen peas (2 if making larger salad)

1½ cups mayonnaise
2 tablespoons sugar
Pepper, to taste
4 ounces Cheddar cheese, grated
12 crisp bacon slices, crumbled

Line a 13x9x2-inch glass dish with lettuce. Sprinkle with green and red pepper. Add a layer of celery, then a layer of red Spanish onion, then uncooked frozen peas. Combine mayonnaise with sugar and pepper. Spread over peas. Sprinkle with grated cheese and top with crumbled bacon. Refrigerate overnight. Serves 10 to 12.

Suzy Ellis

CREAMY COLE SLAW WHEN CLIPPING

1 head cabbage
1 carrot
1 green pepper
1 purple onion
½ red pepper
1 can Eagle Brand milk

⅓ cup oil
⅓ cup cider vinegar
1 teaspoon celery seed
1 teaspoon dry mustard
½ teaspoon salt
¼ teaspoon pepper

Shred cabbage and carrot. Chop green pepper, onion and red pepper; mix with cabbage and carrot. In a separate bowl, blend milk, oil, vinegar, celery seed, mustard, salt and pepper. Pour mixture over vegetables and toss. Chill until ready to serve.

Carol Godbey

CLASSIC MILESTONE

1944 - The Classic encountered a unique twist when Randolph Field became the first and only military installation to play in the Cotton Bowl. The Ramblers and Texas battled to the Classic's first tie, 7-7.

FESTIVE LIMA SALAD

1 package frozen lima beans, cooked and
    drained
1½ cups halved cherry tomatoes
1 medium purple onion, sliced and
    separated into rings
1 medium green pepper, cut into strips
½ cup sliced black olives

½ cup olive oil
½ cup red wine vinegar
¼ teaspoon crushed basil
1 garlic clove, minced
Salt, to taste
Black pepper, to taste

In large bowl, combine beans, tomatoes, onion, pepper and olives. Blend oil, vinegar, basil, garlic, salt and pepper; pour over vegetables. Cover and refrigerate for 2 hours before serving.

Mr. and Mrs. Burt Shryock (Judy)
Cotton Bowl Director

PALM SALAD

2 avocados, peeled and coarsely chopped
Lemon juice
1 (14-ounce) can hearts of palm, drained
    and sliced
1 (14-ounce) can artichoke hearts,
    drained and chopped
2 large tomatoes, coarsely chopped

2 cucumbers, thinly sliced
⅔ cup oil
¼ cup vinegar
2 tablespoons water
1 (0.6 ounce) package Italian dressing
    mix
Lettuce (optional)

Sprinkle avocado with lemon juice, tossing to coat avocado. Combine avocado with next 4 ingredients; toss gently. Refrigerate until serving time. Combine oil, vinegar, water and salad dressing mix in a jar. Cover tightly and shake. Chill. Toss salad with dressing just before serving. Serve on lettuce, if desired. Serves 6.

Mrs. John W. Carpenter, III (Cele)
Southland Financial Corporation
Wife, Cotton Bowl Director

CLASSIC MILESTONE

1944 - Randolph Field's Martin Ruby became the only player to star for two different Cotton Bowl teams. In 1942, Ruby was named Texas A&M's outstanding player in the Aggies' 29-21 loss to Alabama. Two years later, he returned to Cotton Bowl action as a member of Uncle Sam's team, playing for Randolph Field, the San Antonio airbase. Again, Ruby was voted as one of the game's outstanding players.

MACARONI SALAD

2 cups salad macaroni, uncooked
8 green onions, chopped
½ cup chopped green peppers
1 cup chopped sweet pickles

2 tablespoons chopped pimento
½ pound sharp Cheddar cheese, diced
6 eggs, hard-boiled and chopped

Cook macaroni; drain and place in large bowl. Mix in green onions, green peppers, pickles, pimento, cheese and eggs. Toss with dressing and refrigerate for several hours before serving.

DRESSING
1½ cups mayonnaise
1 cup sweet pickle juice
1 tablespoon salt

1 tablespoon Lawry's Season-All
1 tablespoon prepared mustard
½ teaspoon Accent

Combine ingredients in a blender; process until smooth.

Mary Ellen Durrett
Chairman, Department of Home Economics
The University of Texas at Austin

MOM'S WAR EAGLE POTATO SALAD

4 cups cooked, peeled, cubed potatoes (5 or 6 medium)
1 cup chopped hamburger dill pickle slices
½ cup chopped onion
2 eggs, hard-boiled and chopped
1 cup chopped green pepper

¼ teaspoon lemon pepper
1 teaspoon salt
1 tablespoon white vinegar
2 tablespoons vegetable oil
½ cup mayonnaise

Mix together well. Cover and chill. Makes about 5 cups.

Mrs. William R. Gardner (Mary Ann)

TOMATO SALAD

3 to 4 large tomatoes, peeled and seeded
1 large purple onion
Fresh basil, chopped

Fresh pepper
Homemade basil vinegar

Mix tomatoes, onion, basil and pepper. Marinate in homemade basil vinegar for several hours or overnight. Serve on lettuce leaves.

Mrs. C.E. Seal, II (Crickett)
Wife, Cotton Bowl Director

RELISH SALAD

1 can French style green beans, drained
1 large can Le Seur peas, drained
1 large can white shoe peg corn, drained
1 large can baby green lima beans, drained

1 large green pepper, chopped
1 large sweet onion, chopped
1½ cups chopped celery
1 large jar chopped pimentos, drained

Combine ingredients in large salad bowl, tossing to mix. Pour dressing over salad, toss to mix and refrigerate for 24 hours. Drain well before serving.

DRESSING
1 teaspoon salt
1 teaspoon seasoned pepper
1 cup sugar

½ cup oil (not olive oil)
¾ cup red wine vinegar
1 tablespoon water

Mix ingredients well.

Mrs. Jane Ray Dietrich
Cotton Bowl Director

ARTICHOKES AND RICE
CHICKEN SALAD FOR THE VANQUISHED

1 package Chicken Rice-A-Roni
4 green onions, finely chopped
1 large green pepper, finely chopped
½ cup sliced Spanish olives
4 large chicken breasts, cooked, boned and cubed

1 jar marinated artichoke hearts, chopped, reserving juice
½ cup mayonnaise
¼ teaspoon curry powder

Cook Chicken Rice-A-Roni according to package directions; cool. Transfer to a mixing bowl. Stir in onions, green peppers, olives, chicken and artichokes. Mix artichoke hearts with mayonnaise and curry powder; stir into rice mixture. Chill. Serve on lettuce leaves. Serves 6.

Lee Angle
Lee Angle Inc. Photography

CHICKEN BREAST SALAD

Boneless, skinless chicken breasts
Soy sauce (low sodium)
Baslamic vinegar
Raspberry vinegar
Lemon zest
Oregano (optional)

Dijon mustard (optional)
Bay leaf (optional)
Lettuce, shredded
Lowfat cheese (optional)
Tomatoes (optional)

Use equal parts of chicken breasts, soy sauce, vinegars and lemon zest. Add oregano, mustard and bay leaf, if desired. Marinate chicken for 2 to 3 hours. Put on grill just to "mark" it on both sides. Then transfer to a 500° oven for 5 minutes. Cut chicken in small pieces and sprinkle over shredded lettuce. Top with cheese or tomatoes, if desired.

Mrs. C.E. Seal, II (Crickett)
Wife, Cotton Bowl Director

SHRIMP AND PASTA SALAD

DRESSING
¾ cup olive oil
¼ cup wine vinegar
½ teaspoon salt

¼ teaspoon pepper
½ teaspoon dry mustard
2 garlic cloves, minced

Combine all ingredients in a jar with a tight-fitting lid. Shake vigorously to mix well.

SALAD
1 pound pasta noodles
1 green pepper, finely chopped
3 green onions with tops, finely chopped
1 tomato, peeled and seeded, chopped
2 celery stalks, chopped

1 pound shrimp, cooked, cleaned and
  chopped
¼ cup chopped ripe olives
½ cup chopped parsley

Cook noodles until barely tender; drain well. Immediately pour dressing over warm noodles. Add remaining ingredients and toss well.

Ms. Karen Haram
San Antonio Express and News

MARYLAND SEAFOOD SALAD

1 to 1¼ cups cooked shrimp, crabmeat
   or lobster
1 cup thinly sliced celery
⅓ cup mayonnaise or salad dressing

1 tablespoon minced green onion
¼ teaspoon salt
Dash pepper

Combine seafood and celery in bowl. Mix mayonnaise, onion, salt and pepper; pour over seafood and celery, tossing to mix. Cover and chill for at least 2 hours. Serves 3 to 4.

SAM'S SEAFOOD SALAD SCREEN PASS

1 (8-ounce) package corkscrew noodles
1 (8-ounce) package frozen green peas
2½ pounds frozen crab legs, thawed
16 ounces mayonnaise

2 tablespoons lemon juice
2 tablespoons fresh dill
2 tablespoons grated onion
2 cups sliced celery

Cook noodles; drain and chill. Blanch and chill green peas. Combine with remaining ingredients. Toss and chill. For variation, add P&D salad shrimp. A more economical variation, for instance, on a self-serve bar, could be achieved by extending the basic recipe by adding another raw vegetable—cucumber, especially.

Sam Samuels

HOT FRUIT SALAD

1 (20-ounce) can of pineapple chunks
   (drained)
1 (20-ounce) can of sliced peaches
   (drained)

10 maraschino cherries

Set fruit aside and mix the following and pour over fruit.

¼ cup brown sugar
1 teaspoon cornstarch
½ teaspoon cinnamon
¼ teaspoon curry powder

¼ teaspoon nutmeg
½ teaspoon brandy extract
1 teaspoon vanilla

Vivie Rowan

ROQUEFORT DRESSING

1 cup mayonnaise
1 garlic clove, grated
1 tablespoon anchovy paste
½ cup sour cream
¼ cup vinegar
1 tablespoon lemon juice

¼ pound Roquefort cheese
Salt, to taste
Pepper, to taste
⅛ cup chopped green onion
¼ cup parsley

Mix mayonnaise, garlic, anchovy paste and sour cream. Thin the mixture with vinegar and lemon juice. Crumble the cheese and beat into the dressing. Season with salt and pepper. Refrigerate. Before using, mix in green onion and parsley.

Mrs. Finley Ewing, Jr. (Gail)
Wife, Cotton Bowl Director

OLD SWISS HOUSE SALAD DRESSING

2 eggs
⅓ cup red wine vinegar
½ teaspoon salt
1 teaspoon Accent
2 teaspoons chopped chives

1 soupspoon Creole mustard
1 soupspoon chopped shallots
Pinch ground black pepper
3 cups peanut oil

Heat a pan of water to boiling; add eggs and cook for 1 minute. Mix the soft-boiled eggs with remaining ingredients except oil. When well mixed, slowly add peanut oil and whip until creamy.

Walter Kaufmann
Owner/Executive Chef
Old Swiss House

CLASSIC MILESTONE

1945 - Led by sophomore sensation Bob Fenimore, Missouri Valley champion Oklahoma A&M scored the Classic's most lopsided victory ever, defeating TCU 34-0.

Pasta
Eggs and Cheese

UNIVERSITY OF HOUSTON

UNIVERSITY OF HOUSTON

Founded on 1927, the University of Houston encompasses four separate, but inter-related campuses.

University Park, the central campus, is located in southeast Houston and serves an enrollment of approximately 30,000 students. Students may choose from 13 colleges and schools offering undergraduate and graduate degrees in over 100 major fields of study.

The UH Downtown College, with a current enrollment of some 5,000 students, emphasizes liberal arts and teach courses for freshmen and sophomores. UH's other two campuses are the Clear Lake City Campus and the Victoria Center.

Dr. Richard L. Van Horn is the university chancellor. Leading figures in the athletic program include SWC faculty representative and conference president Mike Johnson and head football coach Bill Yeoman.

Clemson University Athletic Department

FRANK JOHNSTONE JERVEY ATHLETIC CENTER
CLEMSON, SOUTH CAROLINA 29633

June 26, 1986

FETTUCCINE WITH ZUCCHINI AND MUSHROOMS

In a large deep skillet saute' ½ lb. mushrooms, trimmed and thinly sliced, in ½ stick butter over moderately high heat for 2 minutes and add ¼ lb. zucchini, scrubbed and cut into julienne strips, 1 cup heavy cream and 1 stick butter, cut into bits. Bring the liquid to a boil and simmer the mixture for 3 minutes.

In a kettle, bring to a boil 7 qts. water and 2 T salt and 1 T olive oil, add the fettuccine and boil it 3 mins. (if fresh) or 7 mins. (if dried). Drain pasta, then add to skillet with 3/4 cup freshly grated Parmesan or Romano Cheese and ½ cup chopped parsley on top of mixture with wooden forks, lifting pasta and mixing well.

Serves 6 - Homemade pasta makes all the difference

Submitted by Coach Danny Ford
              Head Football Coach

SPINACH RAVIOLI STUFFED WITH PUMPKIN

SERVED WITH SPICY WATERCRESS VINAIGRETTE

Serves 6

Ingredients:

For the pasta:

    3 oz. Semolina
    3 oz. All Purpose Flour
    5 Eggs
    3 Tablespoons Water
    3 Tablespoons Virgin Olive Oil
    2 oz. Cooked Spinach, Press and Puree
    Salt to taste

For Pumpkin Stuffing:

    2 oz. Chopped White Onion
    3 Tablespoons Dry White Wine
    Salt
    Pepper
    8 oz. Pumpkin

For Dressing:

    2 Tablespoons White Wine Vinegar
    Salt and Pepper to taste
    4 Tablespoons virgin olive oil
    One lemon juice
    ½ teaspoon Chili Flakes
    2 Tablespoon Chopped Basil
    1 Tablespoon Chopped Oregano

SPINACH RAVIOLI STUFFED WITH PUMPKIN

SERVED WITH SPICY WATERCRESS VINAIGRETTE

Method:

For the pasta:

1. Mix simoulina and all purpose flour.
2. Add 5 eggs, water, slowly by slowly and then your olive oil.
3. Add your 2 oz. of cook, pressed, pureed spinach.
4. Kneed the dough for 20-25 minutes.

For the pumpkin:

1. Sweat your onions slowly with a little butter.
2. Add pumpkin.
3. Salt and pepper to taste.
4. Add white wine and let reduce slowly.
5. Cook about ten minutes and puree.
6. Add 3 tablespoons heavy cream and cool down.

For the ravioli:

1. Roll out until very thin - put on ravioli mold.
2. Stuff ravioli.
3. Poach in boiling water for 3 minutes and cool down.
4. Mix with vinaigrette.
5. Season to taste.

--At the spa, it is served with diced red bell pepper on top.
  In the middle of the plate, some red oak leaves are placed.

Executive Chef - Jean-Marie Josselin

PESTO PASTA SCAMPI LON

PESTO SAUCE

¼ cup fresh minced parsley
¼ cup minced basil
⅛ cup garden mint

¼ cup grated Parmesan cheese
½ cup olive oil

Combine parsley, basil, mint and Parmesan cheese in blender, adding just enough olive oil to make the sauce thick yet pasty. Puree the mixture for a few seconds. You may need to use a spatula to scrape the mixture down from the sides of the blender jar. Transfer to a small bowl or jar and set aside.

SCAMPI

¾ to 1 pound medium raw shrimp
⅓ cup sherry
Pepper
Basil, minced

¼ lemon
3 garlic cloves, minced
Butter
Flour

Shell, devein and rinse shrimp. In large skillet over medium flame, heat the sherry with the shrimp. Season lightly with pepper, then generously with basil. Stir. Squeeze fresh lemon liberally over shrimp. Cook for approximately 3 to 4 minutes, stirring occasionally. Sprinkle in minced garlic (the more the better). Maintain medium high heat, shake skillet and stir shrimp until done (pink). If liquid in skillet is too thin, a butter flour mold made of 1 to 2 tablespoons of butter molded with flour can be added to the mixture to thicken. (Takes 7 to 10 minutes.)

VEGETABLES

¼ to ½ stick butter or margarine
⅛ cup olive oil
4 garlic cloves, minced
2 medium zucchini, sliced and quartered
1 medium onion, chopped
3 to 4 carrots, sliced
1 pound broccoli flowerets
¼ cup white wine

Lemon
1 teaspoon salt
1 teaspoon seasoned pepper
1 teaspoon onion powder
1 teaspoon oregano
½ teaspoon garlic powder
½ teaspoon basil
½ pound fresh mushrooms, sliced

In a separate large skillet, melt butter. Add olive oil. Add 1 tablespoon of garlic and heat for a minute. Add zucchini, onion, carrots and broccoli; stir well. Splash in white wine. Liberally squeeze in fresh lemon. Add salt, seasoned pepper, onion powder, oregano, garlic powder and basil. Cover and cook for about 8 minutes. Add mushrooms, cover, reduce heat and simmer for another 8 to 10 minutes. (Takes 12 to 15 minutes.)

PASTA

½ cup olive oil

¼ lemon

1 to 1½ pounds spaghetti, fettucine or other desired pasta

In a large pan boil approximately 3 to 4 quarts of water. Add olive oil. Squeeze lemon juice into water then drop in the rind. Add pasta and cook al dente. (Takes 12 to 14 minutes.)

COMBINE

Try to have all elements of the dish come together at about the same time. Drain the pasta well. (Rinsing in cold water is not necessary. It is better to keep the noodles hot.) Transfer pasta to a large bowl. Pour in enough pesto sauce so that the pasta has a glossy green spotted appearance. Mix well. Add in total scampi and veggie skillet mixtures. Stir and mix thoroughly. Serve with a good Italian or French bread, toasted with melted garlic butter and Italian seasonings. Serves 4 to 6.

Lon Lowenthal
Mama's Pizza

DUKE FETTUCINE AL FREDO

4 ounces fettucine noodles

2 egg yolks

1 pint heavy cream

3 tablespoons butter

Coarsely ground black pepper, to taste

½ cup grated imported Romano cheese

2 garlic cloves, finely chopped

Parsley, chopped

Cook noodles al dente. Rinse with cold water and set aside. Mix egg yolks with cream; set aside. Melt butter in a 14-inch sauté pan. Add noodles and toss to distribute butter throughout. Sprinkle with pepper; toss again. In a saucepan on medium heat, stir half the cream mixture with the Romano cheese. Heat until mixture begins to bubble. Let simmer for 1 minute or until mixture begins to thicken. Add garlic. Remove from heat, top with chopped parsley and serve immediately. Note: If noodles are too dry, add more cream mixture.

Ray Petta

CLASSIC MILESTONE

1946 - Bobby Layne of Texas recorded one of the most unforgettable performances in Classic history, accounting for all 40 Longhorn points. Texas defeated the Missouri Tigers 40-27 as Layne rushed for three touchdowns, passed for two others, was on the receiving end of a 50-yard bomb, and kicked four extra points.

TRAINERS TALLERINE

1 medium onion, minced
2 tablespoons butter
1 pound ground round steak
1 can tomato soup
1 cup water

2 heaping cups wide noodles
Salt
1 can whole kernel corn
1 can ripe olives, chopped
1 cup grated cheese

Mince and fry onion, add meat and cook until brown. Add soup and water. Add noodles. Stir and cook until noodles are tender, adding more water if needed to keep the mixture moist. Add salt, corn and olives. Transfer to a greased baking dish. Sprinkle with cheese and bake at 350° for 45 minutes. Turn off heat and let stand 15 minutes before serving.

Jan Walker
Kim Dawson Model

COLORADO DAIRY NOODLE PUDDING

16 ounces medium egg noodles
½ pound margarine
1 cup sugar
6 eggs, separated

1 (8-ounce) package cream cheese,
 softened
16 ounces small curd cottage cheese
16 ounces sour cream
1 tablespoon vanilla

Cook noodles according to package directions. Preheat oven to 350° and grease casserole. Cream margarine, sugar and egg yolks. Add cream cheese, cottage cheese, sour cream and vanilla. Stir in noodles. Beat egg whites until stiff and fold into noodle mixture. Pour into a greased 12x9x2-inch casserole dish and bake for 40 to 45 minutes. Remove from oven and sprinkle with topping. Return to oven and bake for 10 minutes.

TOPPING
½ cup corn flake crumbs
¼ cup sugar

1 teaspoon cinnamon
4 tablespoons margarine, melted

Mix ingredients well.

Zella Sobel

TIGHT END TORTELLINI IN MUSHROOM & GARLIC SAUCE

1 (7-ounce) package tortellini
1½ cups sliced mushrooms
4 tablespoons butter
4 garlic cloves, finely chopped
1 pint whipping cream

1 chicken bouillon cube
1 pint sour cream
Freshly ground pepper, to taste
Grated Parmesan cheese

Prepare tortellini according to package directions; set aside. Sauté mushrooms in butter and garlic. Over low heat, stir in whipping cream and chicken bouillon cube. Slowly bring to a boil, making sure chicken bouillon cube is completely dissolved. Add sour cream and bring to a boil. Season with pepper. Pour over well-drained tortellini and stir to coat well. Sprinkle each serving with grated Parmesan cheese. Serves 4.

Hunter Wilcox

QUICK CLAM LINGUINI

1 stick margarine
¼ cup white wine
Salt, to taste
Pepper, to taste
Garlic powder, to taste
1 tablespoon lemon juice

½ teaspoon fines herbes
1 can minced clams, reserving juice
2 ounces cream cheese
½ pound linguini, cooked
Grated Parmesan cheese (optional)

Melt margarine in a large pan. Add wine, salt, pepper, garlic, lemon juice and fines herbes; simmer. Blend the clam juice with the cream cheese. Combine with the margarine mixture. Stir in clams. Spoon over cooked linguini. Top with grated Parmesan cheese, if desired.

Ara Parseghian

FRESHMAN PASTA IN CREAM

4 to 5 tomatoes, peeled, seeded and
  drained
3 tablespoons olive oil
1 pound fresh fettucine
4 tablespoons butter
1¾ cups heavy cream

¾ cup milk
1⅓ cups freshly grated Parmesan
  cheese
1 teaspoon parsley
3 tablespoons freshly chopped basil
  leaves

Quarter sections of tomatoes and heat through in olive oil. Toss and set aside. Boil pasta until al dente; drain. Remove from pot. Add butter to pot and sauté garlic briefly. Add pasta; toss to coat. Add cream, milk and cheese. Toss until cheese melts and sauce boil for 1 minute and begins to thicken. Add parsley and basil. Transfer to serving dish. Reheat tomatoes, then use as garnish for top of pasta. Serves 4.

Duke University
Durham
North Carolina 27706

Terry Sanford, President

My favorite breakfast recipe, especially for a cold morning, is Cheese Grits Souffle and Creamed Chip Beef, the latter not cooked like it was by the Army during World War II

Cheese Grits Souffle

½ cup dry grits, cooked according to directions on box
2 ounces sharp cheddar cheese, grated or in small cubes
2 eggs
1 cup milk

To hot grits, melt in cheese. Beat eggs with milk and add slowly, stirring.

Turn into a greased, deep baking dish, and bake 45 minutes @ 375°F.

Creamed Chip Beef

This probably should be called Chip Beef Gravy, since it does not follow the recipes that provide for a cream sauce.

4 or 5 ounces sliced, dried beef, jar or package
4 Tbl. corn oil, or ½ stick margarine or butter
¼ cup flour (4 Tbl.)
1½ cups milk

Break or cut dried beef into small pieces. Fry in butter or corn oil until pieces begin to get crisp. While stirring, slowly add flour to absorb grease and coat beef. Turn heat high. Allow flour to brown. Quickly add the milk to all parts of pan, and bring to a boil.

Add pepper to taste. To get the right consistency, either add additional milk, or allow to boil.

Terry Sanford

CHEESE/NOODLE BAKE
Serves 4-6)

1 pound tomato sauce
1 1/2 pound chopped beef
8 oz. cottage cheese
8 oz. sour cream
8 oz. wide noodles
8-10 oz. SHARP cheddar cheese

Blend sour cream and cottage cheese in large bowl.   Add
cooked noodles and set aside.

Fry loose chopped beef and add to the tomato sauce.

Shred (not too fine) cheddar cheese.

Wet bottom of deep 2-qt. baking dish (Corning ware is good)
with tomato sauce mix.   Add 2" layer of noodle mix, cover
with some tomato-beef mix and sprinkle with cheddar chedse.
Repeat noodle layer, cover with remaining sauce and top off
with heavy layer of cheddar cheese as topping.

Mix will be warm from hot sauce.

Bake in 325° oven 24-35 minutes.

If flat casserole dish is used, use only single
layer of noodles and do not heat as long.

When cooking noodles remember they will be
cooked further during baking.

Jane White

Gordon S. White, Jr.

NATIONAL
CUTTING
HORSE
ASSOCIATION

CUTTER'S CAMPFIRE EGGS

Serves eight.

2 doz   fresh eggs
1 tsp   dill weed
1/4 lb grated cheddar cheese
        garlic salt to taste

Mix eggs and add ingredients. Use low fire and
DO NOT OVERCOOK.

Zack T. Wood Jr.
Executive Director

July, 1986

President Reagan's Favorite Macaroni and Cheese

½ lb. macaroni
1 t. butter
1 egg, beaten
1 t. salt

1 t. dry mustard
3 C. grated cheese, sharp
1 C. milk

Boil macaroni in water until tender and drain thoroughly. Stir in butter and egg. Mix mustard and salt with 1 tablespoon hot water and add to milk. Add cheese leaving enough to sprinkle on top. Pour into buttered casserole, add milk, sprinkle with cheese. Bake at 350° for about 45 minutes or until custard is set and top is crusty.

Quick and Creamy Eggs

Individual servings:

    2 eggs beaten

    butter

    farmer's cheese

    honey or chutney

Scramble the eggs in a pat of butter in a small non-stick skillet. Remove.

Add a slice of farmer's cheese to the skillet, place the scrambled eggs on top, put a spoon of honey or chutney on top. Cover and heat for a minute. Serve with sliced fruit and dry toast. A perfect late-night snack.

PREGAME BUFFET EGGS

My favorite brunch eggs.

3 tablespoons butter
3 tablespoons flour
Dash salt
Dash pepper
2 cups milk
1 cup grated American cheese
16 eggs

3 tablespoons butter
1 (3-ounce) can chopped mushrooms, drained
¼ cup finely chopped green onion tops
3 bread slices, diced
4 tablespoons butter

Melt 3 tablespoons butter, blend in flour, salt and pepper. Stir in milk to make a white sauce. Stir in cheese and cook until thick; set aside. Scramble eggs in 3 tablespoons butter until barely set. Stir eggs into cheese sauce. Add mushrooms and onion tops. Pour into a 13x9-inch baking dish. Brown diced bread in 4 tablespoons butter. Refrigerate overnight. Sprinkle bread over egg mixture and bake, uncovered, at 350° for exactly 30 minutes. Makes 10 to 12 generous servings. Note: Serve with bacon, sausage, etc. A nice hot curried fruit goes well with hot blueberry muffins.

Ray Underwood

EGG DISH

10 eggs
½ cup unsifted flour
1 teaspoon baking powder
1 pint small curd cottage cheese

1 pound Monterey Jack cheese, grated
¼ cup butter, melted
2 small cans diced green chilies

Combine ingredients, mixing well. Transfer to a 13x9-inch baking dish. Bake at 350° for 35 minutes or until firm. This can be reheated or frozen.

Mr. and Mrs. Buddy Dike (Sara)
Cotton Bowl President 1976-1978

CLASSIC MILESTONES

1947 - Arkansas and LSU played in snow and ice and posted the Cotton Bowl's first scoreless tie.

1948 - The Cotton Bowl's upper west side was added in 1948 just in time for the 13th Classic. With the addition, the stadium's capacity rose from 45,507 to 67,431. SMU and Penn State played to a 13-13 tie.

BARNHILL BREAKFAST CASSEROLE

10 eggs
2 cups milk
1 teaspoon salt
7 bread slices, cubed
1 pound sausage, browned

1 (8-ounce) package grated mozzarella
  cheese
1 cup grated Cheddar cheese
2 cups grated Velveeta cheese

Beat eggs with milk and salt. Add remaining ingredients, stirring to mix. Pour into a greased 13x9-inch casserole dish. Refrigerate overnight. Bake at 350° for 45 to 50 minutes.

Mrs. Guy Ramsey Carter (Debbie)

CHICKEN SOUFFLÉ

2 pounds chicken
Chopped onion, to taste
Chopped celery, to taste
Bay leaves, to taste
Salt, to taste
Pepper, to taste
1 teaspoon dry mustard
6 tablespoons butter or margarine,
  melted

10 white bread slices, crusts removed
1 (12-ounce) package yellow cheese,
  grated (4 cups)
5 eggs, lightly beaten
1 quart milk, at room temperature or
  slightly warmed

Boil chicken until tender with onion, celery, bay leaves, salt and pepper. Cool in broth. Bone and chop chicken. Stir dry mustard into melted butter and spread mixture on bread slices. Stack bread and cut into cubes. Mix bread with chicken. (If desired, add a small amount of chopped parsley.) Pour any remaining mustard-butter mixture over chicken mixture. Layer half the chicken in a 9½ x 9½ x 2½-inch casserole dish. Add half the grated cheese. Cover with remaining chicken mixture. Top with remaining cheese. Mix eggs and milk, and pour over casserole in dish. Sprinkle with paprika. Place casserole dish in large pan of very hot water. Bake at 350° for 1 hour.

Mrs. Otto H. Eisenlohr (Nell)
Wife, Cotton Bowl President 1952-1954

CLASSIC MILESTONE

1949 - Doak Walker of SMU became the first Heisman Trophy winner to play in the Cotton Bowl and led the Ponies to a 21-13 win over Oregon.

BOSTON COLLEGE BROCCOLI SOUFFLÉ

2 packages frozen chopped broccoli
¼ cup margarine
¼ cup flour
1½ cups milk
Onion, chopped, to taste

¾ cup grated sharp Cheddar cheese
1½ cups cottage cheese
6 eggs
1½ cups corn flakes
¼ cup grated cheese

Cook broccoli in salted water; drain and arrange in bottom of 2½ or 3 quart baking dish. Melt margarine and stir in flour. Add milk and stir until mixture begins to thicken. Stir in onion and Cheddar cheese. In a separate bowl, beat cottage cheese with eggs. Mix into cheese sauce. Pour over broccoli and top with corn flakes and grated cheese. Bake at 350° for 40 minutes or until knife inserted in center comes out clean. Serves 12.

Ms. Paula Zahn

GRIDIRON CHEESE GRITS

1½ cups grits
6 cups water
2 teaspoons salt
2 teaspoons seasoned salt
Dash Worcestershire sauce

1 pound Velveeta cheese, cut into several
   slices
1½ sticks butter
3 eggs, well-beaten

Cook grits in water until done. Add salt, seasoned salt, Worcestershire sauce, cheese and butter. Stir until cheese and butter melt. When slightly cooled, mix in eggs. Bake at 350° for 45 to 60 minutes. This freezes very well, but must be cooked before freezing. Reheat in a very low oven. Serves 8 to 10.

Mr. and Mrs. Sam S. Stollenwerck (Carol)
Cotton Bowl Director

CLASSIC MILESTONE

1949 - Following the 1949 Classic, construction began on the Cotton Bowl's east side upper deck which increased the stadium's capacity to today's 72,032.

EGG AND ARTICHOKE CASSEROLE
Great for brunch!

1 bunch green onions
2 (6½-ounce) jars marinated artichoke
hearts
1 garlic clove

4 eggs, beaten
8 ounces mild Cheddar cheese, grated
6 saltine crackers, rolled

Finely mince onions, including half the tops. Cut artichokes in thirds and reserve marinade from jar. Mix onions, artichoke hearts, garlic, eggs, cheese and crackers. Transfer to a greased 9x9-inch glass baking dish and bake at 350° for 40 minutes. Serves 4 as a main dish. Triple the recipe to serve 30 for brunch. To serve as a brunch dish, cut into 2-inch squares. The casserole does not have to be kept hot to serve. May be prepared a day ahead and refrigerated or frozen. Thaw and rewarm at 350° for about 15 to 20 minutes. This recipe was given to me by a friend from Mississippi.

Mrs. John Stuart, III (Barbara)
Wife, Second Vice President
Cotton Bowl Athletic Association

RON RIDGEWAY'S STOW AWAY
BREAKFAST CASSEROLE

7 slices bread, crust removed, cubed
and buttered
1 pound sausage, loosely fried and
drained
1 pound grated Cheddar

1 teaspoon salt
1 teaspoon dry mustard
2 cups milk
9 eggs

Layer bottom of greased 3 quart casserole with cubed bread. Put sausage over bread; mix other ingredients and pour over all. Top with Cheddar. Cut five additional slices of bread in half, remove crust, and butter one side. Put buttered side up on top of cheese.

Refrigerate overnight. Bake at 350° for 45 minutes. Note: If freezing, leave in refrigerator overnight, and then freeze. Defrost before baking.

Ron Ridgeway
President
Braniff Airlines

Meats
Chicken
Seafood
Game

RICE UNIVERSITY

RICE UNIVERSITY

Located just three miles from the center of Houston, Rice University opened its doors to higher education in 1912. The faculty of 10 assembled for opening classes in 1912 has expanded to a corps of nearly 400, and the original student population of 77 might be lost among the 3,500 graduate and undergraduate students of today.

The facilities and resources available at the private university are among the top in the nation. The student-faculty ration remains a low nine-to-one. One out of five students admitted are National Merit Scholars. The enrollment includes men and women from all 50 states and over 60 foreign countries.

The university consists of seven academic divisions—the School of Architecture, the George R. Brown School of Engineering, the School of Humanities, the School of Social Sciences, the Shepherd School of Music, the Wiess School of Natural Sciences, and the Jesse H. Jones Graduate School of Administration. Within these divisions are 32 departments.

The President of Rice University is Dr. George Rupp. Dr. James Castaneda is the SWC faculty representative. A.E. "Augie" Erfurth serves as executive athletic director while Jerry Berndt is both Athletic Director and head football coach.

Boston College Football

JACK BICKNELL
Head Coach

STROMBOLI

1/2 Lb Ham - Sliced Thin
1/4 Lb Genoa Salami - Sliced Thin
1 C. Grated Monterey Jack Cheese
1 C. Grated Cheddar Cheese
Onions
Peppers
Mushroom - optional
Fresh Bread Dough - Frozen or Hot Roll Mix
Olive Oil
1 Tsp Oregano
1 Tsp Parsley

Foll out fresh or thawed bread dough or prepare hot roll mix as directed on package and roll out into large circle. On half of rolled dough layer Ham, then Genoa Salami and sprinkle with cheeses. Add vegtables if desired. Gently fold remaining dough over prepared half (turnover style). Pinch edges to seal. Lightly spread olive oil over top - sprinkle with oregano and parsley. Transfer to cookie sheet. Bake at 400° for approximately 20 min.

Kenneth G. Germann
Commissioner

June 27, 1985

My Favorite Recipe:

SPECIAL VEAL SCALLAPINE

3 lbs. of veal cut thin for scallapine
3 cans sliced mushrooms
2 7½ oz. jars fried pepper and onions
½ cup white wine
½ cup chicken broth
Garlic powder
Flavored bread crumbs
Salt & pepper

Sprinkle veal with garlic powder, dip in bread crumbs and brown in pan.
When brown, remove veal and place in baking dish.
Put rest of ingredients in pan used for veal, mix, and heat.
When heated pour over veal and bake at 350° for 45 minutes.

Serves 8.

Best regards,

Kenneth G. Germann
Commissioner

 THE SOUTHLAND CONFERENCE

Office of the Commissioner

DOW GORK SOONG
(serves 6)

1½ pounds lean boneless pork, cut in one-inch cubes
4   teaspoons oil
1 small can water chestnuts, finely chopped
1 large onion, finely chopped
1½ pounds green beans, washed, drained, and sliced on
          two-inch diagonal

1 cup water
Salt and pepper

Heat oil, add pork and fry slowly until lightly browned.
Add water chestnuts and water. Mix well, cover and simmer
10 minutes. Add salt and pepper to satisfy taste. Bring a
pot of water to boil, add beans, return to boil and cook
no longer than 5 minutes; drain and add to meat mixture.

Mix: 2 tablespoons soy sauce
     1 teaspoon sugar
     2 tablespoons cornstarch
     2 tablespoons bourbon or brandy
     1 cup water

Add to first mixture, stir and heat just until thickened.
(Do not cook!). Serve over cooked rice with extra soy
sauce as desired.

Dick Oliver

MARCUS

BOILED BEEF BRISKET
(For 10 to 12)

*Ingredients

*   1 5- to 6-pound piece of brisket
1 large onion stuck with 2 cloves
1 bay leaf
1 piece celery with leaves
2 carrots
Few sprigs of parsley
6 peppercorns
1 bottle of beer (you may omit)
1 tablespoon salt

Place the beef in a kettle and cover with boiling water.
Add rest of ingredients. Bring to a boil; reduce heat
to simmer, and cook for 3 to 4 hours or until meat is
tender. Add 1 tablespoon salt after 1 hour's cooking.
Do not overcook or meat will be stringy and will not
slice properly. Remove, and keep warm. Cut off any
excess fat before serving, but leave on while cooking.
If you wish brisket for an entrée, strain the juices left
from cooking, skim off the fat, and for each cup of liquid,
add:

*   1 cup whipping cream
¼ cup grated horseradish or
   horseradish sauce
1 teaspoon chopped chives
½ teaspoon dry mustard
¼ cup diced apple

Cook until reduced to a thin sauce. Serve over thinly
sliced meat.

From Helen Corbitt Cooks for Company by Helen Corbitt.
Copyright 1974 by Helen Corbitt.
Reprinted by permission of Houghton-Mifflin Company.

J. L. Huffines, Jr.
Chairman of the Board

RACK OF LAMB WITH MINT AND HONEY

This rack of lamb is absolutely succulent. The honey and mint coating not
only gives it a look of glazed perfection but imparts a slightly sweet flavor. This is sheer inspiration!

Roast Lamb:

Rack of Lamb, Six to Seven Bones (About 2½ Pounds)
½ teaspoon of salt
¼ teaspoon of black pepper
2 tablespoons honey
1 tablespoon chopped fresh meat

Have the butcher trim the rack of excess fat, as well as partially crack the
back bone for easier serving.
Preheat oven to 325°. Season the lamb with a mixture of salt and pepper. Place
lamb on a rack in a shallow roasting pan-put lamb in preheated oven and roast
approximately one hour or until it reaches an internal temperature of 140° on a
meat thermometer. The lamb will be rare.
Mix honey with mint and spread over lamb. Lower oven to 250°-roast additional
fifteen minutes to set glaze. Remove lamb from oven and let rest several minutes before crowing-Serve with mint jelly.

SOUTHWEST ATHLETIC CONFERENCE

HAM LOAF

```
2 lbs. ground lean ham
1 lb. ground lean pork
2 eggs beaten
1 green pepper, finely chopped
1 C. soda crackers, crushed
1 8 oz. can tomato sauce
3/4 C. milk
1 tsp. parsley
1 tsp. horseradish
pepper
```

Mix together well. Form 2 medium sized loaves. Bake at 350 degrees for 1 hour. Baste with topping last half hour.

Topping
```
3/4 C. brown sugar         )
1 1/2 T. prepared mustard)   Mix together
1/4 C. water               )   and boil for
1/4 C. vinegar             )   10 minutes.
```

Best regards,

Fred Jacoby
Commissioner

University of Notre Dame
Notre Dame, Indiana 46556

Office of the Executive Vice-President

Cable Address "Dulac"

BEEF BURGUNDY STEW

This is a simple way to prepare an old favorite.

2 lb. chuck or round steak - cut in 1-inch cubes

2 large onions - cut up

1 sm. bunch celery - cut in chunks

6 sm. carrots - cut in chunks

4 med. potatoes - cut in chunks

1 can stewed tomatoes

1 can beef bouillon

1 teaspoon sugar

1/2 cup Burgundy wine

Mix tomatoes, bouillon, sugar and wine together. Pour over other ingredients in large heavy pan with lid. (I use a Dutch oven.) Bake in 250 degree oven for 5 hours.

Edmund P. Joyce, C.S.C.

(Rev.) Edmund P. Joyce, C.S.C.

University of Pittsburgh

PRESIDENT OF THE UNIVERSITY

MARINATED SHISH KEBAB

2 pounds tender lamb
2 large lemons
4 tablespoons olive oil
2 tablespoons grated onion
2 tablespoons ground chili peppers
1 teaspoon coriander
1 teaspoon powdered ginger
1 clove garlic, crushed
2 teaspoons turmeric
2 teaspoons curry powder*
3 teaspoons salt

Cut lamb into 1½" squares. Squeeze the juice from 2 large lemons and combine with rest of ingredients. Marinate the lamb for not longer than 2 hours.

Put lamb onto skewers and alternate meat with similarly sized pieces of tomato, onion, mushroom caps and green pepper. Charcoal broil the Kebabs, turning to brown and basting often with melted butter.

* I suggest Crosse & Blackwell curry or any good Indian curry.

Wesley W. Posvar

Gene F. Jankowski, President
CBS/Broadcast Group

CBS Television Network
CBS Entertainment
CBS Sports
CBS News
CBS Television Stations
CBS Radio
CBS Theatrical Films
CBS Operations and Engineering

POLISH SAUSAGE WITH MUSHROOM GRAVY

Makes 5 pounds

5 lbs., pork butt
1 heaping tablespoon plus 1 heaping teaspoon, marjoram
1 clove garlic, minced
3/4 level teaspoon, pepper
1 level tablespoon plus 1 level teaspoon, salt
1 cup hot water

Cut pork butt in small pieces; add all other ingredients. Soak
sausage casings in lukewarm water until soft. Stuff mixture into
casings. Cover with water and bring to a boil. Then reduce heat
and simmer 1 to 1 and 1/2 hours. Pour off liquid and brown the
sausage. Serve with mushroom gravy.

MUSHROOM GRAVY

1 chopped onion
1/4 chopped green pepper
1/2 stick butter
1 medium can mushrooms
2 tablespoons flour
  Kitchen Bouquet
  Beef or chicken juice

Saute onion and pepper in butter. Drain mushrooms but save the juice.
Cook mushrooms with onion and pepper until golden brown. Add juice
and some water. Cook for about 5 minutes. Thicken with flour. If
it is not dark enough, add a little Kitchen Bouquet. If you have any
beef or chicken juices, add them to the gravy.

Gene F. Jankowski

Gene F. Jankowski

TEXAS HASH

1 Lb. Ground Beef	1/2 Cup Uncooked Rice
1 Large Onion (diced)	2 Teaspoons Salt
1 Large Bell Pepper (diced)	1 to 2 Teaspoons of Chili Powder
1 Can of Tomatoes	
1 Cup Cheddar Cheese (grated)	1/8 Teaspoon Pepper
	Sour Cream (optional)

Heat oven to 350 degrees. In large skillet, cook and stir meat, onion, and bell pepper until meat is brown and vegetables are tender. Drain off fat. Stir in tomatoes, rice, salt, chili powder, and pepper. Heat thoroughly.

Pour mixture into ungreased 2-quart casserole dish. Cover. Bake for 1 hour.

When removed from oven, top with cheese. If desired, top with sour cream when served.

Billy Prince

Billy Prince
Chief of Police

May 1986

BAYLOR UNIVERSITY

STUFFED TENDERLOIN

1 (3 lb.) beef tenderloin	1½ c. soft bread crumbs
1 (4 oz.) can sliced mushrooms	½ c. butter
½ c. onion, chopped	Salt and pepper
½ c. celery, diced	4 slices bacon

Split tenderloin within ½ inch of edge. Lightly
brown onion and celery in butter; add mushrooms
and bread crumbs. Salt and pepper meat to taste.
Stuff sauteed mixture into tenderloin. Fasten
edges with toothpicks or wrap meat with string.
Place bacon slices over top of meat. Roast covered
at 350° for 1 hour. Uncover and roast 1 more hour
for well done.

When roast is done, let stand 15 minutes before
slicing. For each cup of pan drippings, add 1½
teaspoons cornstarch diluted in 2 tablespoons cool
water. Cook until thick. Makes 6 servings.

Herbert H. Reynolds
President

BEEF, BEANS & RICE

(Serves 6 - 8)

1 lb. ground beef
1 medium onion, chopped
1 cup uncooked rice
2 tsp. salt
¼ tsp. garlic powder
1 - 15oz. can Ranch-Style beans
1 - 15oz. can tomatoes with juice

Saute' ground beef until no longer pink. Add onions and rice. Brown slightly. Add remaining ingredients and place in 4 quart casserole. Cover with lid or foil. Bake at 325 degrees for about 35 to 40 minutes or until rice is done. May be cooked and frozen, if desired, for later use.

This is one of my favorite recipes.

Jim Ray Smith

Bob Lilly's Favorite Dish: Beef Stew

Ingredients:

    ½ to 1 lb. stew meat
    1 tsp. Beef Bouillon granules
    12-oz. can tomato juice
    2 16-oz. cans tomatoes, chopped
    2/3 of an onion, chopped
    2 stalks celery, sliced
    1 bay leaf
    2 small potatoes, diced
    2 carrots, diced
    1/3 cup peas
    1/3 cup corn
    salt, pepper
    water, as needed

Directions:

   Boil the stew meat with the beef bouillon
granules in 4 cups water for 2 to 4 hours.
Optional: refrigerate until cool, then take
fat layer off. Add vegetables and seasonings;
simmer 2-3 hours. Add water as needed.

Bob Lilly

DAN JENKINS

TRUCK STOP CHEESEBURGER

Slap, mash and squeeze the meat thin. Sprinkle fine chopped onions on top of the thin meat. Slap the onions into the meat with a spatula, like you're killing a roach. If you smoke a lot, use more salt and pepper than normal.

A bun with no seeds holds the most grease. Sliced tomato, lettuce, hamburger dill chips, mustard and mayo.

Double cheese. Two slices of American. Put the top side of the bun on top of the cheese and press down occasionally with the spatula. When the cheese melts and starts to run into the skillet, it's ready.

A thin meat pattie means you can eat more than one at a time.

If the grease don't run down your wrist after the first bite, you've screwed up.

Dan Jenkins

University of Notre Dame

Football Office

Lou Holtz
Head Football Coach

L O U   H O L T Z   C H I L I

IN BLENDER: 28 oz. can tomatoes
                 15 oz. tomato sauce
                  8 oz. V-8 vegetable juice
                  2 T. chili powder
             1/2 cup water

SAUTE: in olive oil
        $1\frac{1}{2}$ lb. lean ground beef
        2 cloves garlic (crushed)

SIMMER all ingredients over low heat 1-$1\frac{1}{2}$ hours. Stir often.

ADD: (the last 20-30 minutes)
      One 15 oz. kidney beans

SERVE: with grated cheese, chopped onions, chips, etc.

Bill Clements ★▬

MORE
A one-dish dinner

2 onions, diced
1 green pepper, diced
1 can mushrooms, diced
2 small garlic cloves, diced
Salad oil
1 1/2 pounds ground round beef
1 tablespoon chili powder
Salt
Pepper
1 can tomatoes
1 can tomatoe sauce
1 package frozen English peas
1 can whole kernel corn
1 1/2 cups cooked shell macaroni
Sharp Cheddar cheese, grated

Saute onions, green pepper, mushrooms and garlic in a
small amount of salad oil; add ground meat and chili
powder. Salt and pepper to taste. Add tomatoes and
tomato sauce and let simmer for awhile. Then add peas,
corn and cooked macaroni. Pour into a large Pyrex dish
and sprinkle with sharp Cheddar cheese. Bake at 350
degrees for 30 minutes. A wonderful family recipe.

COTTON BOWL ATHLETIC ASSOCIATION

FIELD SCOVELL
CHAIRMAN, TEAM SELECTION COMMITTEE

FIELD SCOVELL'S CHILI RECIPE

2 lbs. ground beef
1 tsp. shortening
2 tsp. ground cumin seed
1 small bottle of chili powder
2 tsp. chopped garlic (1 or 2 -- depends on whether you like garlic)
1 Tbs. salt
3 cups water
2 Tbs. flour
1/4 tsp. black pepper

Drop ground beef and garlic in hot grease; cook slowly 15 minutes, add chili powder, flour and cumin seed, stir and add water, salt and pepper, cook for 35 minutes.

The chili powder is small bottle of Gerhardt's or any other good brand, and the amount is 1/3 cup. We also add two large cans of brown beans or red beans, but do not use chili beans because they generally come in a chili sauce and this does not help the flavor. We also put 1/2 chopped jalapeno and 1/4 tsp. of red pepper into the chili. Do not add this unless you like it WARM.

SUE'S SAUSAGE & RICE
CASSEROLE

1 lb. Owens Country Sausage
1/4 cup chopped green pepper
1/2 cup chopped celery
1 large onion, chopped
4-1/2 cups boiling water
2 pkgs. chicken noodle soup, dry mix
1 cup uncooked instant rice
1 2-oz. can mushrooms

Brown sausage, pepper, celery and onion together in a skillet.
Combine remaining ingredients, add the meat mixture, and bake
in a greased casserole at 350 degrees for one hour. Serves
eight generously. Delicious with chilled green asparagus!

Submitted by Jerry P. Owens
Owens Country Sausage, Inc.
Chairman of the Board

CHICKEN FRIED STEAK

2lbs. Tenderized Beef Cutlets

Dip into:
2 eggs (beaten)
3 TBLSP milk
1t. salt
1t. pepper

1/2 c. flour
Alternate dipping cutlets into egg mixture and flour

Deep fry in a skillet until golden brown. Drain cutlets on
a paper towel.

WHITE GRAVY

Pour off all grease used to fry cutlets except for 1/3c.
Add about 1/8c of flour to grease, stir until mixture looks like a ruex
Add more flour if necessary. As the ruex thickens and starts to bubble
add 2 cups of milk. Let mixture simmer stirring constantly until gravy
is thick. If gravy gets too thick, add more milk and stir. Salt and
pepper to taste. Willie likes a lot of pepper.

Serve cutlets smothered in white gravy, add several fresh vegtables,
green onions, sliced tomatoes and cornbread and you've got a meal.

Willie Nelson

Lee Meredith

LEE MEREDITH'S BEEF STROGANOFF

1 1/2 pounds round steak
1/4 cup flour
Salt, to taste
Pepper, to taste
2 tablespoons margarine or butter
1 large onion, chopped
12 ounces beef broth
6 ounces of sherry
1/2 cup water
3 tablespoons paprika
8 ounces fresh mushrooms, cleaned and sliced
8 ounces sour cream

Cut round steak into 1/2" x 3" strips. Dust
with flour, salt and pepper. Heat margarine
in skillet, add steak and cook until brown.
Add onion and continue to cook, stirring constantly, until onions are transparent. Add beef
broth, sherry, water and paprika. Cover and
simmer, stirring occasionally, for one hour and
15 minutes or until steak is tender. Check
often, adding water if needed. Stir in mushrooms
near end of cooking time. When done, gravy should
be thick. Mix in sour cream. Serve over brown
or white rice or noodles. Enjoy a Lite beer or 2
from Miller while it simmers and you cool down.

Lee Meredith (DOLL)

 **Associated Press**

Jim Brock, Executive Vice President
Cotton Bowl Athletic Association

Dear Hoss:

   Having had the pleasure of dining with you in so many gourmet
establishments from coast to coast, my taste for home cooking
is somewhat on the downside.

   I am happy to say that my favorite recipes include anything
on the menu at Gaylen's, Campisi's Egyptian Lounge and the Casa
Dominguez. My favorite ingredient would have to be the Rocky
Mountain spring water which I believe is essential to Colorado
Kool-Aid.

                                        Herschel Nissenson
                                        College Football Editor

EASY BEEF BARBEQUE

1 beef brisket (5 to 7 pounds)
⅔ of 8 ounces jar of Kraft Hickory
   Smoked Barbecue Sauce
½ cup vinegar

½ cup water
1 tablespoon prepared mustard
¼ cup brown sugar
1 onion chopped

Place whole brisket in heavy roasting pan. mix remaining ingredients and pour over meat. Roast covered in 300° oven for at least six hours. Turn meat at least twice. Do not let pot cook dry. When meat is done, slice across grain. Pour pan drippings over meat. If pan drippings are inadequate, add more bottled sauce or water to suit taste. Meat should be moist but not floating in sauce. May be used for sandwiches or main meal.

John J. Clune, Colonel, USAF
Director of Athletics
U.S. Air Force Academy
President, NACDA

VEAL WHATEVER

6 to 8 ounces fresh mushrooms, sliced
1 garlic clove, pressed
2 tablespoons butter
½ cup flour
½ to ¾ pound veal scallopini
3 tablespoons light oil
1 small can sliced black olives

1 small jar marinated artichoke hearts,
   halved, with liquid
¾ cup white cooking wine
¾ cup chicken broth
1 tablespoon chopped fresh parsley
Salt, to taste
Pepper, to taste

Sauté mushrooms and garlic in butter for 3 to 4 minutes; remove from pan. Lightly flour veal and sauté in oil in hot frying pan until just brown on both sides. Drain off oil. Add remaining ingredients, (including liquid from artichokes). Cook over high heat for 15 minutes or until sauce reduces and thickens. Adjust seasonings. Transfer to heated platter and serve immediately. Note: This is my favorite recipe to make for friends because it looks so pretty and takes so little time! Enjoy!

Laura Bellomy

GREEN PEPPER STEAK

2 tablespoons vegetable oil
1 to 2 green peppers, cut in ¼-inch strips
1 pound flank steak, cut in ¼-inch strips

2 tablespoons cornstarch
2 tablespoons water
1 cup chicken broth
3 tablespoons soy sauce

Heat oil and stir fry peppers for 1 to 2 minutes. Push aside, then add meat and stir fry for 3 to 4 minutes. Mix meat and peppers. Blend cornstarch with water; stir into pan with broth and soy sauce. Heat and stir until sauce is thick and clear. Serve at once with rice.

Mrs. Tim Lindgren (Fran)
Wife, Cotton Bowl Committee

SWISS STEAK SQUIBB KICK

3 tablespoons flour
2 teaspoons salt
⅓ teaspoon pepper
1 (2½ to 3 pound) bone-in chuck beef steak (center cut and about 1½-inches thick)
1 to 2 tablespoons oil

1 large onion, thinly sliced
1 large green pepper, seeded and thinly sliced
2 celery stalks
1 pound canned tomatoes, undrained
1 teaspoon sugar

Pound mixture of flour, salt and pepper into both sides of steak. In a 4 to 5-quart Dutch oven, heat oil and brown meat on both sides. Add onion, green pepper, celery, tomatoes and sugar. Bake, tightly covered, in a preheated 300° oven for 2½ hours. Skim fat from sauce.

Charles E. Henke

FLANK-ER STEAK

1 flank steak, cut in strips
Shortening
Salt, to taste
Paprika, to taste
Garlic, to taste
Onion salt, to taste

2 onions
1 green pepper
1 to 2 tablespoons Wishbone Italian Dressing
3 to 4 baking potatoes, peeled and sliced

Brown both sides of steak in small amount of shortening. Season lightly with salt, paprika, garlic and onion salt. Slice onions and green pepper; add to meat. Add Italian dressing. Cover and simmer for 30 minutes. Add potatoes. Cover and continue cooking for 45 minutes or until meat is tender. Uncover pan and increase heat to brown the potatoes during the last 10 minutes.

Dan S. Petty
President
Cotton Bowl Athletic Association

SKEWERED TENDERLOIN OUT OF BOUNDS SHISH-KA-BOBS

Tenderloin
Green pepper
Cherry tomatoes

Onions
Creamy French dressing

Cut tenderloin into bite-size chunks. Skewer meat alternately with green pepper, tomatoes and onions. Marinate overnight in creamy French dressing. Grill over hot coals.

Janice Godbey

BARBECUED RIBS REVERSE

1 tablespoon salt
3 tablespoons sugar
3½ tablespoons lemon pepper
1 tablespoon Accent

1 tablespoon paprika
1 tablespoon garlic salt
Beef ribs

Mix salt, sugar, lemon pepper, Accent, paprika and garlic salt. Roll beef ribs in mixture and let stand for at least 30 minutes. Meanwhile, prepare sauce.

SAUCE
1 cup black coffee
½ cup Worcestershire sauce
1 cup catsup
¼ cup butter or margarine

1 tablespoon pepper
⅓ tablespoon salt
1 tablespoon sugar

Mix ingredients in a saucepan. Simmer for 30 minutes. Baste ribs every 5 minutes. This recipe works equally well with chicken.

Tracy Rowlett
WFAA-TV, Channel 8
Dallas-Fort Worth

CLASSIC MILESTONE

1953 - On May 16, 1953, the Southwest Conference formally committed its champion to host the Cotton Bowl Classic on New Year's Day.

HOUSE MAJORITY LEADER JIM WRIGHT'S BAR-B-QUE RECIPE

4 to 5 pound brisket (if 6 pounds or more, brisket is likely to be tough)
Soy sauce
Lemon juice
Wine or beer
1 stick margarine
1 garlic clove
1 white onion, finely diced
2 jalapeño peppers, skinned, seeded and finely diced
1 can tomatoes or tomato sauce
Dash Tabasco sauce
Worcestershire sauce
1 can beer
Coffee
Salt, to taste
Lemon pepper, to taste
Paprika, to taste
Cayenne, to taste
Garlic powder, to taste

Marinate the brisket overnight in equal parts of soy sauce, lemon juice and wine or beer. (You may substitute up to ¼ part Worcestershire instead of all soy sauce.) After marinating, the marinade forms the basis for the bar-b-que sauce. Pour it into a large pan, add the margarine, garlic, onion, jalapeño peppers, tomatoes or tomato sauce, Tabasco sauce and Worcestershire sauce. Bring the mixture to a slow boil, then pour in the can of beer. Simmer slowly for at least 2 hours. Don't let it get too thick. Thin from time to time with beer or coffee (yes, coffee). It is important that the sauce be thin for basting. (The residue from the pot on the fire will thicken a bit for the table when meat is cooked.)

Make the fire, let it burn to even coals covered with white ash before putting brisket on the fire. Meat should be at least 12 and maybe 18 inches above the fire. Smoke for 2½ to 3 hours, depending on the size of the brisket. Use foil under the brisket to avoid burning and dripping of juices into fire which cause flaming. Make pan of the foil to hold basting sauce. If fire flames, use beer can or bottle of water to put it out.

Baste generously with thin sauce at the beginning and each time of turning. At beginning, turn every 15 minutes; then every 20 minutes. Sprinkle meat with salt, lemon pepper, paprika, cayenne and garlic powder, if desired. Sprinkle at least twice of turning for 2 times each side.

Important that top of pit be lowered with small enough vent to permit lots of smoke accumulation in pit. It is the smoke that makes the bar-b-que. If using charcoal, it is good to soak hickory or mesquite chips, or oak bark in a bucket of water for at least 30 minutes, then sprinkle from time to time on coals. This promotes the smoke, the flavor from which permeates the meat.

House Majority Leader Jim Wright
U.S. House of Representatives

ROULADES RULE BLOCKING

1 eye of round roast (ask the butcher to slice the roast into ¼-inch slices)
Salt, to taste
Pepper, to taste
Mustard
Chopped onion
Raw bacon slices, cut into 2-inch pieces

Dill pickles (cut each pickle into 6 lengthwise strips)
2 tablespoons oil
2 (10½-ounce) cans beef bouillon, undiluted
Sour cream
Fettucine

Spread waxed paper on counter. Lay each slice of roast on waxed paper so that all are single thickness. Salt and pepper each piece. With pastry brush, cover each meat slice with mustard. Sprinkle with chopped onion. Lay 1 bacon slice and then 1 pickle slice on each piece of meat. Roll up each meat slice and fasten with a round, wooden toothpick. In Dutch oven, slowly heat oil, then brown roulades on all sides. (Brown only as many as will fit in the bottom of the pan at 1 time.) As they brown, remove to another pan. Pour off oil. Return all roulades to Dutch oven and pour bouillon over all. Cover and bring to boiling. Reduce heat and simmer very slowly about 2 hours or until tender. Remove roulades to serving platter, remove toothpicks and keep them warm. Mix some of the hot liquid into the sour cream to prevent curdling; slowly add the sour cream to the liquid in the pan. Stir constantly over low heat; do not boil. Cook fettucine according to package directions; drain. Transfer fettucine to a 13x9-inch serving dish, cover with roulades and top with sour cream gravy. This dish goes very nicely with a Caesar salad, okra with tomatoes and hot rolls for a lovely dinner party.

Mrs. Ellenore Flynn

BRACIOLI BACKFIELD

½ cup Crisco or bacon fat
½ cup chopped parsley
1 tablespoon black pepper
2 large garlic cloves, pressed

1 pound round steak, thinly sliced, or 1 pound cubed steak
⅓ cup oil

Make a paste by blending Crisco with parsley, black pepper and garlic. Spread on each slice of meat, roll up and secure with round toothpicks or tie with string. Heat the oil in a pan then brown the rolls evenly. Cover the rolls with the following sauce to serve.

SAUCE
2 cans tomatoes
1 can sweet basil

Salt, to taste
Pepper, to taste

Mix ingredients and simmer slowly for 3 to 4 hours. Pour over meat rolls.

Andy Stasio

SMOKED BRISKET BATON ROUGE

1 (4-ounce) bottle Liquid Smoke
1½ teaspoons celery salt
½ teaspoon meat tenderizer
2 teaspoons Worcestershire sauce

Salt, to taste
Pepper, to taste
1 beef brisket

Mix Liquid Smoke, celery salt, meat tenderizer, Worcestershire sauce, salt and pepper; pour over meat. Wrap tightly in aluminum foil and marinate for 6 hours or overnight. Bake at 250° to 275° for 6 to 8 hours.

Nikki Smith

LIZ SMITH'S & 5 MILLION OTHER TEXANS' CHICKEN FRIED STEAK

Buy half a pound of round steak per person.

Ask butcher to slice it about ⅛th of an inch thin, say to him, "sliced thin for frying."

Lay steak on flat surface and sprinkle with black pepper. Beat it with a mallet, hammer or Coke bottle to tenderize it. (Both sides.) Trim off any fat. Cut into small pieces like veal piccata.

Beat about five eggs into a shallow bowl. Lay out flour on a flat plate. Heat Wesson or oil of preference in frying pan until fairly hot. Dip meat in egg, flour and place in skillet.

Fry fairly fast, turn, brown on both sides, remove onto paper towel. Salt AFTER cooking.

GRAVY: In the same fry pan—pour off excess grease leaving as many drippings as possible. Put over moderate heat, add a teaspoon or so of flour and stir into drippings to thicken. (If you use Wondra flour you can add flour later if you need it.) Now add a mixture of milk and water (if you fill up whatever gravy boat or pitcher you intend to put the gravy in, you'll have your measurement. You can use whole milk, skim milk or half and half—depends on how rich you want it. It will taste pretty much the same whatever you do.) Keep stirring the gravy and tasting it—because you need to salt and pepper it to taste while it makes. If gravy becomes too thick, add more milk or water. Don't panic. Pour gravy out into pitcher when it seems the right consistency to you. Serve instantly and if you have a candle warmer under it, so much the better. Pepper and salt are the secret of taste here.

Terrific meal with biscuits and potatoes, tomato and lettuce salad, or pineapple chunks, lettuce, Cheddar cheese bits, mayonnaise. Excellent cold and left-over.

Drink with chicken fried steak: Pearl, Coors, Lone Star, Puligny-Montrachet '71, Dr Pepper, Dom Perignon, Ne-Hi Grape or Orange, Chateau Lafite Rothschild '67.

Liz Smith

LINEBACKER BEEF STROGANOFF

2 pounds tenderloin steak
2 tablespoons margarine
½ cup chopped onion
½ pound sliced fresh mushrooms
2 tablespoons flour
2 beef bouillon cubes
1½ cups boiling water

1 tablespoon tomato paste
½ cup red wine
1½ teaspoons salt
1 teaspoon dry mustard
Dash pepper
½ cup sour cream

Cut tenderloin into ½-inch cubes and brown in butter in heavy frying pan. Remove meat, add onion and mushrooms and sauté until onion is transparent. Blend in flour, stirring until lightly browned. Slowly stir in bouillon cubes dissolved in water, continuing to cook until mixture is slightly thickened. Add tomato paste, wine, salt, mustard, pepper and meat. Cover and simmer over low heat for 30 to 35 minutes or until tender. Fold in sour cream and heat through. Serve over cooked, buttered noodles. Serves 6 to 8.

Kenneth Stone

CHILI CASSEROLE A LA KELLY GARRETT

5 pounds pinto beans
4 pounds ham hocks
1 tablespoon salt
Oil or bacon grease
4 garlic cloves
3 large white onions
5 pounds round steak, cubed

1 tablespoon flour
1 dozen Josie's Best Blue Tortillas
   (available only in Santa Fe, New
   Mexico)
2 pounds Longhorn cheese, grated
Flour tortillas

Soak beans for 4 hours; rinse and cover with cold water. Bring beans to a full boil and skim foam from top. Stir in ham hocks and salt. Lower heat and simmer for 4 hours or until tender. To prepare chili, heat oil or bacon grease and sauté garlic and onions. Stir in cubed round steak, and continue simmering. Brown flour in a little oil; add water. Stir into chili mixture to thicken. In a large stew pot, layer chili, then tortillas and cheese. Repeat layers until all ingredients are used, topping with cheese. Cover and bake at 250° for 2 hours or until done. Serve beans in a bowl. Top with chili casserole and serve with flour tortillas on the side.

Kelly Garrett

CHUCK WAGON CHARLIE'S TEXAS MESQUITE BEEF JERKY

Beef flank strip
½ pint salt

Lawry's seasoned salt
Coarse ground pepper

Buy beef flank strip, soak 10 to 12 hours in 5 gallons of water and ½ pint of salt. Cut the beef strips approximately ½-inch wide. Now add Lawry's seasoned salt and coarse ground pepper. Amounts will vary depending on how hot you like it. Put jerky in smoker at 120° to 140°. Smoke slowly for 2 to 3 days. 10 pounds of raw beef yields 3 to 4 pounds jerky.

Rusty Lancaster

COTTON BOWL STEW

2 pounds ground beef
2 medium onions, chopped
1 can Ro-Tel tomatoes
1 large can tomatoes
1 can whole kernel corn

1 can Ranch Style beans
2 to 3 red potatoes, cubed
1 teaspoon chili powder
Chopped sweet peppers (optional)

Brown meat with onions. Stir in remaining ingredients. Cook, uncovered, until the potatoes are done. (Do not drain any of the canned ingredients.) Serve with big chunks of crusty bread. For variation, substitute macaroni for the potatoes.

Mr. and Mrs. Norm Bulaich (Susie)

NO PEEK PENALTY STEW

1½ pounds beef stew meat
Carrots
Celery
Potatoes
Onions
1 tablespoon cornstarch

1 can beef bouillon soup
1½ tablespoons sugar
3 tablespoons wine or wine vinegar
1 bay leaf
1 can tomato paste or 2 cans tomatoes

Combine all ingredients. Bake, covered, at 325° and don't peek for 6 hours.

Kent Lawrence

GOURMET MEAT LOAF

1 pound ground round steak, fat
   trimmed
1 pound ground lean pork
1 cup softened bread crumbs
Celery

Onion
Green pepper
Red pepper
Butter
½ to 1 can peeled tomatoes

Mix round steak, pork and bread crumbs; set aside. Chop celery, onion, green pepper and red pepper; measure 2 cups chopped vegetables, mixing according to individual taste. Sauté in butter. Mix sautéed vegetables into meat mixture. Shape into a loaf and transfer to baking dish. Pour tomatoes over meat loaf. Bake at 350° for 1½ hours. Drain gravy, reserving it to serve with the loaf. Skim off fat. Can be divided into 2 casseroles, and can be frozen. Serves 4 to 6.

Mrs. George W. Bailey (Novella)

MEAT LOAF

2 bread slices
1 small can Pet evaporated milk
1 pound lean ground beef
½ cup chopped onion

2 tablespoons chopped green pepper
Salt, to taste
Pepper, to taste
1 small can Hunt's tomato sauce

Soak bread in milk for a few minutes, then pulverize with a fork. Add beef, onion, green pepper, salt and pepper. Mix well and shape into a loaf. Transfer to baking dish, pour tomato sauce over loaf and bake at 400° for 1½ hours. (You may substitute cracker crumbs and an egg for the evaporated milk and bread.)

Cris Pye

TUSCALOOSA TOASTED DEVILED HAMBURGERS
Nice for a crowd of young people.

1 pound ground chuck
⅓ cup chili sauce
1½ teaspoons prepared mustard
1½ teaspoons bottled horseradish
Dash pepper

1 teaspoon minced onion
1½ teaspoons Worcestershire sauce
Butter
8 hamburger buns

Mix meat with chili sauce, mustard, horseradish, pepper, minced onion and Worcestershire sauce. Butter hamburger buns. Spread meat mixture on buns. Arrange on cookie sheet and broil about 2 inches from heat until meat is done.

PLAY ACTION PASTECIO

1½ pounds hamburger
1 (16-ounce) can tomato sauce
⅓ of a (16-ounce) package Velveeta
 cheese, cubed
½ teaspoon oregano

1 teaspoon steak sauce
1 (1-pound) box ziti macaroni
8 American cheese slices
6 eggs
3 cups milk

Simmer hamburger until done. Add tomato sauce, Velveeta, oregano and steak sauce. Stir and simmer for 20 minutes. Remove from fire. Cook macaroni for 15 minutes; drain. Grease a 13x9-inch pan. Layer half the macaroni in the pan. Cover with the hamburger mixture. Add remaining macaroni. Cover with cheese slices. Beat eggs, add milk and pour mixture over casserole. Bake at 350° for 45 to 60 minutes.

Stephen Strachan
Boston College

KIBBEE KICKOFF
(kibbeh)

DOUGH

3 cups cracked bulgor (bulghur) wheat
 (fine grind)
2 cups flour
2 teaspoons salt
1 teaspoon pepper

½ teaspoon allspice or ¼ teaspoon
 cinnamon (not both)
1 pound ground meat
Water

Soak wheat in plain water about 20 minutes. Squeeze out water and place wheat in a dry bowl. Add flour, salt, pepper, allspice or cinnamon, and mix well. Work meat into mixture and add a little water at a time to make a medium stiff dough.

FILLING

3 large onions, chopped
2 pounds ground meat
Salt, to taste

Pepper, to taste
Pine nuts, to taste (optional)
Oil for frying

Sauté onions until golden brown. Add meat, salt and pepper. Cook and stir until well done. Pine nuts may be added and cooked with the other ingredients after meat has been lightly browned. Then cook all until well done. After filling is made, form a ball about 2 inches in diameter, using 2 heaping tablespoons of dough. Hollow out the center by pushing your finger in the middle and gently turning the dough until you have made a well with a medium thin shell. Place about 1 tablespoon or so of the filling and seal the end by molding the dough over the end. Deep fry in oil until lightly brown.

Al Sankary
Al's Formal Wear

ITALIAN SPAGHETTI SAUCE I-FORMATION

1½ pounds ground beef
1 medium onion, finely chopped
1 small green pepper, finely chopped
Salt, to taste
Pepper, to taste
2 tablespoons oil

1 (9 or 10-ounce) can peeled tomatoes
1 small can tomato paste
1 tablespoon sugar
1 teaspoon garlic salt
3 to 4 bay leaves

In a large skillet, simmer beef, onion, green pepper, salt and pepper in the oil until beef is partially brown. Add tomatoes, tomato paste, sugar, garlic salt and bay leaves. Cook over medium to low heat for about 1½ to 2 hours. Serve over thin spaghetti or vermicelli. Sprinkle with Parmesan cheese. This sauce can also be stored in containers and kept in the refrigerator for later use. Also, saccharin can be substituted for the sugar for those on a restricted diet. Use 6 to 8 tablets.

Mrs. E.B. Moyers

CHILI SPAGHETTI

2 pounds ground chuck
2 cups chopped onion
2 cups chopped celery
2 cups chopped green pepper
3 large garlic cloves, minced
3 to 4 tablespoons chili powder
1 tablespoon cumin
1 tablespoon salt

½ cup oil
1 large can tomatoes, mashed
1 (8-ounce) can tomato sauce
1 (6-ounce) can tomato paste
1 pound spaghetti, broken up
1 large can ripe olives with juice
1 large can mushroom pieces

Sauté meat, onion, celery, green pepper, garlic, chili powder, cumin and salt in the oil. Add tomatoes, tomato sauce and tomato paste. Cook for 1½ hours. Separately cook spaghetti; drain. Add spaghetti to mixture, then add olives and mushrooms. Cook for 30 more minutes. Serves 10.

Mrs. Jimmie E. Franklin

CLASSIC MILESTONE

1953 - The Cotton Bowl's first nationally televised audience saw Texas shutout Tennessee, 16-0.

OSSO BUCO PHI ALPHA

3½ pounds veal shanks or knuckle
¼ cup flour
2 tablespoons oil
2 ounces salt pork
¼ cup melted butter
½ pound onions, peeled and diced
1 large garlic clove, pressed
2 bay leaves, crumbled
1 teaspoon rosemary, crumbled
1 teaspoon salt

1 teaspoon freshly ground pepper
¾ cup white wine
2 tablespoons grated carrot
½ celery stalk with leaves
10 parsley sprigs
1 cup canned tomatoes or 2 large fresh
     tomatoes, chopped
1 heaping tablespoon tomato paste
½ cup warm water

Have the butcher cut the meat into 3 pieces. Sprinkle with flour. Heat oil and butter in a heavy skillet. Add onions and sauté until brown. Add the salt pork and veal and continue cooking until meat browns. Stir in garlic and cook until brown. Add bay leaves, rosemary, salt and pepper. Sauté for 10 more minutes. Stir in wine, cover and simmer for 5 minutes. Remove and discard garlic. Add carrot, celery, parsley and tomatoes. Stir tomato paste with water until blended, then add to the mixture. Cook for 40 minutes. Serve with rice or homemade noodles. Serves 6.

Andy Stasio
Stasio Family & Friends Cookbook

CHICKEN FRIED VEAL STRIPS SITUATION SUBSTITUTION

Veal cutlets
Egg
Buttermilk
Flour

Bread crumbs
Salt
Pepper

Slice veal cutlets into ½-inch strips. Soak in egg and buttermilk, roll in flour, bread crumbs, salt and pepper. Fry until crisp; drain well. Serve with Spicy Mustard Sauce as a dip.

SPICY MUSTARD SAUCE
1 teaspoon dry mustard
1 cup sour cream
1 tablespoon prepared mustard
¼ teaspoon onion salt
1 teaspoon horseradish

Dash cayenne pepper
Sprinkle of Tabasco sauce
Dash white pepper
½ teaspoon garlic powder

Blend ingredients.

C.K. Godbey

BARBECUED SPARERIBS

Chinese style.

3 pounds baby back pork ribs
3 scallions, cut into 2-inch pieces
3 garlic cloves, pressed slightly
3 tablespoons tomato catsup
3 tablespoons chili sauce

3 tablespoons dry sherry
3 tablespoons soy sauce
1½ tablespoons corn syrup
½ teaspoon salt
1½ tablespoons honey

Marinate ribs in flat pan with scallions, garlic, catsup, chili sauce, sherry, soy sauce, syrup and salt for 2 to 3 hours, turning and basting after each hour. Brush ribs on both sides with honey. Cook for 30 minutes at 275°, another 30 minutes at 300°, and last 10 minutes at 400°.

Mrs. Jane Ray Dietrich
Cotton Bowl Director

RAZORBACK RIBS WITH SAUERKRAUT

Try the Aggie version by omitting the ribs!

4 pounds small pork ribs
Salt, to taste
Pepper, to taste

1 cup water
2 quarts sauerkraut

Cut ribs into separate pieces and remove excess fat. Rub salt and pepper into the ribs and brown thoroughly in a heavy roaster on top of stove. Cover and simmer over medium to low heat for 1 hour. Remove ribs. Pour off fat, leaving the good brown stuff in the bottom. Stir the water and 2 cups drained sauerkraut in with the pan drippings. Put the ribs on top, cover and simmer for 45 minutes.

David Lehmann

OVEN PORK CHOPS SOOIE

8 center cut pork chops, ¾-inch thick
1½ cups graham cracker crumbs
Salt, to taste

Pepper, to taste
8 (¾-inch) fresh tomato slices (optional)

Trim chops, leaving a little fat around edges. Dip each chop in crumbs. Pat each side of chop to secure crumbs. Place on ungreased baking sheet. Season with salt and pepper. Bake at 350° for 35 to 40 minutes or until nicely browned. For company dinner, broil fresh tomato slices, season to taste, and place in center of chop just before serving.

Mrs. J. Herman Musick (Celeste)

BOULDER BAKED PORK CHOPS

4½ cups water
½ cup uncooked instant rice

1 envelope dry onion soup mix
4 or more pork chops

Pour water into a 13x9-inch baking dish. Sprinkle rice into water. Stir in onion soup mix. Top with pork chops. Cover with foil and bake at 350° for 1½ hours or until chops are done.

Mrs. Glynn Gregory (Virginia)
Wife, Cotton Bowl Committee

GRADE POINT PORK CHOPS SWEET AND SOUR

6 thick pork chops
2 tablespoons butter
1½ cups chicken broth
¼ cup cornstarch
¼ cup soy sauce
¼ cup brown sugar

2 tablespoons red wine vinegar
1 (15-ounce) can pineapple chunks, drained, reserving juice
1 green pepper, sliced
2 white onions, sliced

Brown the pork chops on both sides in butter. Add broth, cover and simmer for 30 minutes, or until tender. Blend cornstarch, soy sauce, brown sugar, vinegar and pineapple juice. Add to pan juices with the pork chops. Then throw in the green pepper, onions and pineapple; cover and simmer for about 10 minutes. Eat, then pat yourself on the back!

Brad Wright (Tish)
KXAS-TV
Ft. Worth/Dallas

CARD SECTION SAUSAGE CASSEROLE

1 (8-ounce) package brown and serve sausage
2 (8-ounce) cans seasoned tomato sauce
½ cup water
½ cup chopped onion

½ cup chopped green pepper
1 tablespoon brown sugar
1 teaspoon Worcestershire sauce
Salt, to taste
3 cups hot cooked rice

Brown sausage according to package directions. Remove sausage and pour off drippings. In same skillet, combine tomato sauce, water, onion, green pepper, brown sugar and Worcestershire sauce. Simmer, uncovered, for 20 minutes or until thick. Add sausage links and heat. Season with salt and serve over hot rice. Serves 5 or more.

Mrs. Sam Jackson (Faye)

SAUSAGE CASSEROLE

2 pounds bulk sausage (1 hot and 1 regular)
¾ cup chopped onion
1 cup chopped green pepper
2½ cups chopped celery
¼ cup butter, melted
4½ cups boiling water

2 (2½-ounce) packages chicken noodle soup mix (noodles & herbs)
1 cup uncooked rice (1 box Uncle Ben's half and half)
½ tablespoon salt
1 cup slivered almonds

Brown sausage in skillet; drain off fat. Sauté onions, pepper and celery in butter; set aside. Combine water, soup mix, rice and salt and cook for 20 minutes or until rice is tender. Combine the sausage and vegetable mixture with the soup and rice mixture, mixing well. If mixture seems dry, add a little water. Transfer to a greased casserole. Sprinkle with almonds and bake at 375° for 20 minutes. Serves 10 and can easily be doubled for a party. If prepared the day before (almost better if done so), store in refrigerator. Just before serving, add almonds and heat in oven.

Mrs. David O'Brien (Janie)

CRUNCHY SAUSAGE CASSEROLE
Wonderful side dish for brunch.

1 (6-ounce) package long grain and wild rice mix
1 pound bulk pork sausage
1 pound ground beef
1 large onion, chopped
1 (8-ounce) can sliced mushrooms
1 (8-ounce) can water chestnuts, drained and sliced (optional)

3 tablespoons soy sauce
1 (2¾-ounce) package sliced almonds (optional)
Lemon slice
Parsley sprigs

Cook rice according to package directions; set aside. Cook sausage, ground beef and onion over medium heat in a large skillet until meat is browned, stirring to crumble. Drain off drippings. Stir in rice, mushrooms, water chestnuts and soy sauce; mixing well. Spoon into an ungreased 2-quart casserole dish. Cover and refrigerate overnight. Remove from refrigerator and allow to sit at room temperature for 30 minutes. Sprinkle almonds on top. Bake, uncovered, at 325° for 50 minutes or until thoroughly heated. Garnish with a lemon slice and parsley sprigs, if desired. Serves 8 to 10. Note: Casserole may be baked without refrigeration. Bake, uncovered, at 300° for 20 minutes or until hot.

Mrs. John Stuart, III (Barbara)
Wife, 2nd Vice President
Cotton Bowl Athletic Association

FAYETTEVILLE FAVORITE HAM LOAF

2½ pounds ground smoked ham (not boneless or skinless type)
½ pound fresh ground pork

1 cup dried bread crumbs
1 cup milk
2 eggs

Mix ham, pork, bread crumbs, milk and eggs. Shape into 2 long, narrow loaves. Bake at 300° for about 1½ to 2 hours, basting with the following sauce.

SAUCE
1 cup brown sugar
½ cup vinegar

½ cup water
½ teaspoon dry mustard

In a saucepan, mix ingredients and heat thoroughly. Baste ham loaf while baking. Serve any remaining sauce with ham loaf. Note: For variation, serve the ham loaf with a fresh mushroom sauce.

PINEAPPLE-BEAN SUPPER SYRACUSE

6 bacon slices, diced
1 medium onion, chopped
1 pound frankfurters, cut in chunks
1 (17-ounce) can butter beans
1 (16-ounce) can barbecue beans

1 (13½-ounce) can pineapple chunks, drained
2 tablespoons vinegar
1 teaspoon prepared mustard
½ teaspoon salt

In large skillet over high heat, fry bacon until almost crisp; drain off fat. (Set electric skillet at 325°.) Add onion and frankfurters and simmer for 5 minutes. Add remaining ingredients and heat for 10 more minutes, stirring occasionally. Makes 6 generous servings.

Jan Walker
Kim Dawson Model

COTTON BOWL MILESTONE

1954 - Rice halfback Dicky Maegle set an all-time Cotton Bowl record, rushing for 265 yards on just 11 carries for an unbelievable 24.1 per play average. Maegle also rushed for three touchdowns, including the famous "bench tackle" play. Maegle was awarded a 95-yard touchdown run after Alabama's Tommy Lewis came off the bench to nail him at the 'Bama 40-yard line. Rice won 28-6.

THE
STAUBACH
COMPANY

BROCCOLI-CHICKEN CASSEROLE

Temperature: 350°

Cooking Time: 25-35 minutes

Total Preparation Time: 30-40 minutes - if you use microwave for
    Broccoli and Chicken

Yield: 6-8 servings

Ingredients:

2 - 10 oz. packages frozen broccoli
3 cups diced cooked chicken
2 - 10½ oz. cans cream of chicken soup
1/2 cup soft bread crumbs
1 cup mayonnaise
1 teaspoon lemon juice
1/2 teaspoon curry powder
1 - 8 oz. can sliced waterchestnuts - drained
4 oz. shredded sharp cheese
1 tablespoon melted butter

Procedure:

Cook broccoli and drain. Place in bottom of a buttered 7"x11" casserole.

Place chicken on top of broccoli. Mix soup, mayonnaise, lemon juice, curry

powder and water chestnuts and pour over chicken in casserole. Place shredded

cheese on top and cover with soft bread crumbs and drizzle melted butter on top.

Serve with a green salad and rolls.

Can be frozen or made ahead and refrigerated.

                        Marianne and Roger Staubach

David O'Brien

DAVEY O'BRIEN EDUCATIONAL AND CHARITABLE TRUST

BLACK BEANS AND CHICKEN

1 Medium size onion, chopped

2 Tablespoons unsalted butter

1 Pound black beans (Soaked overnight and boiled in salted water until tender)

3 cups of beef stock or canned beef broth

4 six to eight oz. boned chicken breast (sliced crosswise in strips about 1/2 inches wide)

Salt and Pepper to taste

1 Teaspoon oregano leaves

In a medium sauce pan, place the butter over a medium fire, add onions and oregano and fry until transparent, add the chicken and cook for about 5 minutes stirring occasionally. Add bean and stock, reduce the fire and simmer for about 20 minutes. Taste and adjust seasoning accordingly. Serve with french bread or melba toast.

Charles A. Ringler

HOTEL *Crescent Court* DALLAS

GRILLED CHICKEN BREASTS WITH TOMATO, CUCUMBER, MINT AND CRUSHED BLACK PEPPER VINIAGRETTE

Marinade:

Chicken, 4 boneless breasts, 6-8 ounces
Olive Oil, 1/4 cup extra virgin
Basil, 2 tablespoons, freshly chopped
Oregano, 2 tablespoons, freshly chopped
Thyme, 1 tablespoon, freshly chopped
Parsley, 1 tablespoon, freshly chopped
Garlic, 4 cloves, crushed
Lemon, 2 lemons
Salt & Pepper

Viniagrette:

2 medium cucumbers, peeled, seeded and diced
6 ripe tomatoes, peeled, seeded and diced
3 tablespoons fresh mint, chopped fine
1 tablespoon crushed black pepper
1/4 cup balsamic vinegar or red wine
3 tablespoons Olive Oil, extra virgin
2 tablespoons salt

<u>Method:</u>

Prepare marinade by combining all ingredients in a stainless
steel bowl. Squeeze lemons and add the rinds to the marinade.
Pour all the marinade over the chicken breasts in a shallow
glass baking dish. Refrigerate overnight or at room temperature
for 3-4 hours (covered). The longer you marinate, the stronger
the garlic and herb flavor. Prepare the viniagrette by first
peeling and seeding the tomatoes. Fill an 8-quart saucepan 3/4
with salted water and bring to a boil. Drop tomatoes in for
30-45 seconds only and remove. Let cool. Peel off the skin and
separate the tomato sections with your fingers, shaking out the
seeds. Remove the stem top with a knife. Then cut into 1/8"
dice. Peel the cucumbers. Split length-wise and with a spoon
scrape the seeds out. Cut the cucumber into 1/8" dice. Combine
cucumbers, tomatoes, mint, black pepper, vinegar, salt and olive
oil. This should be made 2-3 hours before so the flavors infuse.
I prefer to grill the chicken over mesquite or charcoal, but you
can also bake or broil. Use general instructions for broiling or
baking. When grilling, stoke the fire to its hottest potential
state (white hot coals). Salt and pepper the chicken and remove
from marinade. Place on hot grill (skin side down) and cook for
4 minutes. Turn the chicken over and continue cooking for another
4 minutes until chicken is done. During the cooking, baste each
breast with 2 tablespoons of the marinade. Remove the chicken from
the fire when done. Serve with a large dollop of the viniagrette
on the side. Garnish the plate with fresh cooked garden vegetables.
This dish can also be served cold the next day.

Executive Chef: Steve Singer

Bill Bates

This recipe is one of Bill's favorites! Especially after a long day at practice. And it's easy to make which is why I like it. ENJOY!!!

CHICKEN STROGANOFF

4 Chicken Breast
(cooked & cut into small pieces)
1/2 cup chopped celery
1/2 cup onions
1/2 cup mushrooms
2 TBLS. butter
1 can cream chicken soup
1/2 pint sour cream
1/2 cup sherry
Salt & Pepper to taste
1 pkg. med. egg noodles

Cook chicken breasts and chop into bite sized pieces, then set aside. In a large skillet , saute' mushrooms, onions and celery in butter until tender. Add cream of chicken soup (undiluted) and stir rapidly. When bubbly, add sherry and mix well. Then add chopped chicken pieces, reduce heat, cover and let simmer 10 minutes stirring occasionally. Cook egg noodles and drain. Just before serving, stir in sour cream and serve over noodles.

SERVES 4 OR 1 FOOTBALL PLAYER AND WIFE!!!

THE FORT WORTH CLUB

Established 1885

CHICKEN DELIZIOSO with PENNE
(Serves 4 to 6)

6	large chicken legs
1/4	cup olive oil
1/2	cup dry white wine
1	small onion, chopped
1	celery stick, chopped
2	tablespoons chopped parsley
1	clove garlic
2	ounces sliced mushrooms
28	ounces of canned tomatoes
1	teaspoon of salt
1/4 - 1/2	teaspoon of pepper
12	ounces Penne (pasta)

In a large saucepan brown chicken with olive oil, add wine, onion, celery, mushrooms, parsley, garlic and bay leafs.

Saute for 5 minutes. Add tomatoes, salt, pepper and cook for 40 - 45 minutes on low fire.

Cook pasta in boiling salty water. When ready, remove from burner and drain.

Place penne on a large platter and pour over sauce with chicken.

Tito y Sonia Giraei

Ara Parseghian Enterprises

CHICKEN CUTLETS

3 Chicken breasts (boned, split & skinned)
Flour
3 Eggs
¼ c. Parmesan Cheese
¼ c. Parsley
Salt and pepper - touch of garlic powder

Pound chicken thin to make 6 cutlets.
Dip in the flour, then into the 3 eggs beaten
with the parsley and Parmesan - (can thin with
a little water) plus a touch of garlic powder.

Saute' in hot oil till done - (3 to 5 minutes
on each side) Season with salt and pepper.

Place cutlets on large pan in 200° oven in a
single layer and cover loosely with foil to hold
till serving time. Can hold an hour or two.

Sauce to spoon over at serving time ---

Saute some mushrooms in a little butter. Remove
mushrooms. Add 1/3 c.white wine, 1½ c. chicken
broth, 1T.lemon juice and simmer. Reduce to a cup.

Melt 1T. butter, blend in ½ T. flour - add broth
and simmer till blended. Return mushrooms. Add
1 or 2 T. capers if desired.

Auburn Athletic Department

Pat Dye
ATHLETIC DIRECTOR
HEAD FOOTBALL COACH

DAWSON STEW

2 frying chickens (cut up in individual pieces)
3 medium onions (sliced)
3-6 oz. cans tomato paste
6 cans water (mixed with tomato paste plus 1 teaspoon ground red pepper)
1 stick margarine
Salt and pepper to taste

Sear chicken pieces in ¼ inch of bacon drippings; remove chicken pieces and drain grease from pot. Layer chicken pieces, sliced onions, mixture of tomato paste, water and pepper in pot; top with stick of margarine. Cover and simmer for about 45 minutes. Spoon gravy over fresh, steamed rice and serve with cornbread.

Auburn University
Auburn, AL 36849

HOT CHICKEN SANDWICHES

3 teaspoons butter
3 teaspoons flour
½ teaspoon salt
½ teaspoon prepared mustard
2 cups milk
1½ cups grated Cheddar cheese

1 chicken, cooked, boned and sliced
Toast
Paprika
Tomato slices
Cooked bacon
Chopped green chilies

Prepare sauce by combining butter, flour, salt, mustard and milk in top of double boiler; cook and stir until mixture thickens. Stir in cheese and cook until cheese melts. Place chicken on toast and pour sauce over chicken. Sprinkle with paprika. Bake at 450° for 10 minutes. Serve with tomato slices and bacon. If desired, garnish with chopped green chilies.

Mrs. Darrell Royal (Edith)

CHICKEN PUFFS

2 tablespoons butter or margarine
1 cup pecans, finely chopped
1 (3-ounce) package Philadelphia cream
 cheese
1½ cups cooked, finely cut chicken
⅓ cup Hellmann's mayonnaise

¼ teaspoon salt
¼ teaspoon ground nutmeg
½ teaspoon grated lemon rind
36 small puffs, either make or buy from
 bakery
Finely chopped parsley

Melt butter in skillet, add pecans and cook over low heat until lightly browned; cool. Add cream cheese, chicken, mayonnaise, salt, nutmeg and lemon rind. Mix the filling well. With this mixture fill the puffs. Garnish tops with parsley.

Jane Justin
From 'Mother Jane's Prescriptions for Hunger'
Copyright 1968 by Jane Justin

CHICKEN ORIENTAL OVERTIME

1 (3 to 4 pound) chicken or 6 split
   chicken breasts
Onion
Celery with leaves
1 carrot
Salt
Pepper
1 cup Minute Rice
3 to 4 teaspoons chopped fresh onion
1 teaspoon curry powder

1 teaspoon salt
1 teaspoon vinegar
2 tablespoons corn oil or Italian salad
   dressing
1 cup chopped celery
1 can tiny peas
1 cup mayonnaise
1 package sliced toasted almonds
1 cup Thompson seedless grapes, halved
Chopped pimento (optional)

Cook chicken in water seasoned with onion, celery and leaves, carrot, salt and pepper. When tender, remove from heat and allow chicken to cool in broth. Cook rice according to package directions. While rice is warm, add chopped onion, curry powder, salt, vinegar and corn oil or Italian dressing. Mix with a fork, cover and refrigerate overnight. Fluff rice with a fork and add remaining ingredients. Toss lightly and refrigerate until serving time.

Mrs. Dan Goldsmith (Grace)

GAME CLOCK CHICKEN SUPREME

2 packages dried sliced beef
4 chicken breasts, split and boned
8 bacon strips

1 cup sour cream
1 can cream of mushroom soup

Cover bottom of baking dish with sliced beef. Wrap each piece of chicken with bacon; arrange on top of sliced beef. Mix sour cream with soup and pour mixture over chicken. Bake at 300° for 3 hours. (Use no seasonings.)

Mr. and Mrs. Walter Coughlin (Ann)
Cotton Bowl Director

CLASSIC MILESTONE

1957 - The Cotton Bowl began its long-standing CBS television relationship with the telecast of TCU's electrifying 28-27 victory over the Orangemen of Syracuse and Jim Brown in the 21st Classic.

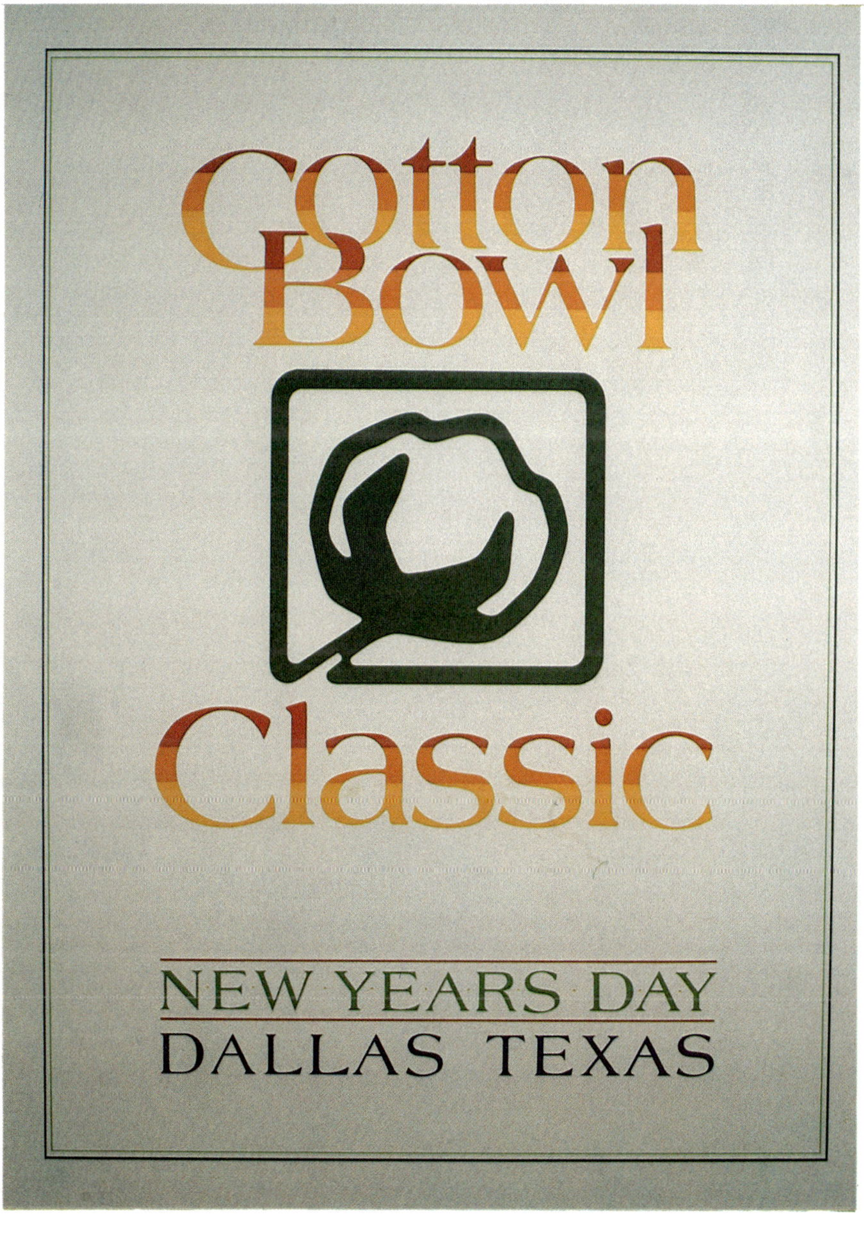
Cotton Bowl
Classic
NEW YEARS DAY
DALLAS TEXAS

"WELCOME TO BIG D!"

The Cotton Bowl Stadium, home of the annual Cotton Bowl Classic, with the skyline of Dallas, the nation's seventh largest city above.

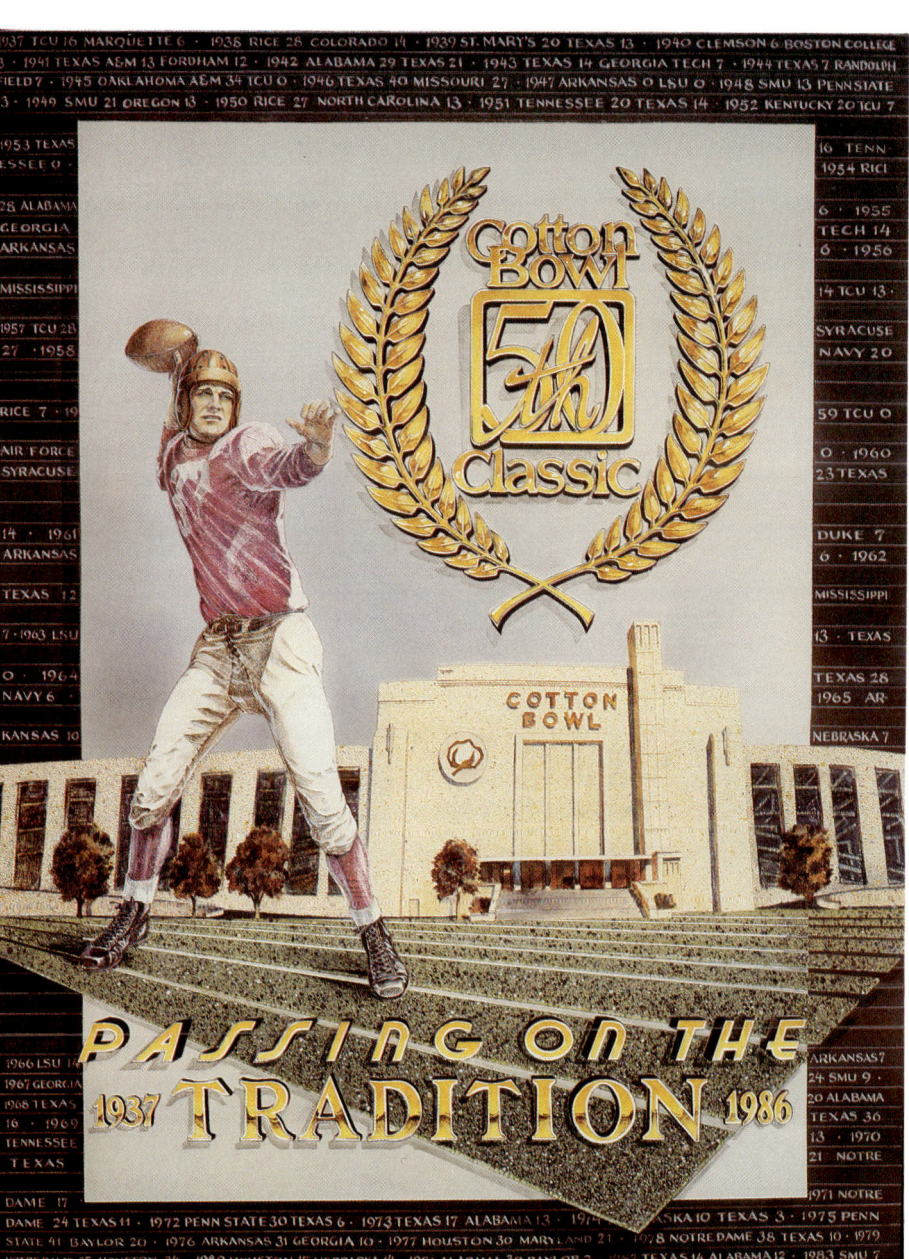

1937 TCU 16 MARQUETTE 6 · 1938 RICE 28 COLORADO 14 · 1939 ST. MARY'S 20 TEXAS 13 · 1940 CLEMSON 6 BOSTON COLLEGE 3 · 1941 TEXAS A&M 13 FORDHAM 12 · 1942 ALABAMA 29 TEXAS 21 · 1943 TEXAS 14 GEORGIA TECH 7 · 1944 TEXAS 7 RANDOLPH FIELD 7 · 1945 OKLAHOMA A&M 34 TCU 0 · 1946 TEXAS 40 MISSOURI 27 · 1947 ARKANSAS 0 LSU 0 · 1948 SMU 13 PENN STATE 13 · 1949 SMU 21 OREGON 13 · 1950 RICE 27 NORTH CAROLINA 13 · 1951 TENNESSEE 20 TEXAS 14 · 1952 KENTUCKY 20 TCU 7

Cotton Bowl 50th Classic

COTTON BOWL

PASSING ON THE TRADITION 1937 1986

1966 LSU 14 ARKANSAS 7 · 1967 GEORGIA 24 SMU 9 · 1968 TEXAS 20 ALABAMA 16 · 1969 TEXAS 36 TENNESSEE 13 · 1970 TEXAS 21 NOTRE DAME 17 · 1971 NOTRE DAME 24 TEXAS 11 · 1972 PENN STATE 30 TEXAS 6 · 1973 TEXAS 17 ALABAMA 13 · 1974 NEBRASKA 10 TEXAS 3 · 1975 PENN STATE 41 BAYLOR 20 · 1976 ARKANSAS 31 GEORGIA 10 · 1977 HOUSTON 30 MARYLAND 21 · 1978 NOTRE DAME 38 TEXAS 10 · 1979 NOTRE DAME 35 HOUSTON 34 · 1980 HOUSTON 17 NEBRASKA 14 · 1981 ALABAMA 30 BAYLOR 2 · 1982 TEXAS 14 ALABAMA 12 · 1983 SMU 7

"COTTON IS OUR GOAL"

The 1986 Southwest Conference head football coaches gather at August kickoff luncheon at the Dallas Hyatt Regency. Back row, left to right, Ken Hatfield, Arkansas; David McWilliams, Texas Tech; Jim Wacker, TCU; Grant Teaff, Baylor; and Jerry Berndt, Rice. Front row, left to right, Bill Yeoman, Houston; Bobby Collins, SMU; Jackie Sherrill, Texas A&M; and Fred Akers, Texas.

The 50th Anniversary Cotton Bowl Classic, January 1, 1986 served as the inaugural event of the Texas Sesquicentennial and the handsome Cotton Bowl Parade float signified the State's 150th birthday.

1. Auburn Players relax during 1986 Cotton Bowl Hat Ceremonies.

2. Texas A&M's Jackie Sherrill takes time out to visit with young admirers during the 1986 Cotton Bowl Week.

3. Auburn's Spirited Tigers represented the Southeastern Conference in the 1986 Cotton Bowl.

4. Texas A&M's 1986 SWC Champions gather on First day in Dallas.

1. (left to right) CBAA's Jim Brock and Brent Musburger of CBS Sports pause with wives Shirley (left) and Arlene during the 1986 Cotton Bowl Anniversary Dinner.

2. Former Baylor All-American, Mike Singletary.

3. Legend Roger Staubach says hello to some young fans.

4. (left to right), Auburn Coach Pat Dye, Jim Brock of CBAA and Texas A&M Coach Jackie Sherrill huddle before the 1986 Cotton Bowl.

5. Long time CBAA Team Selection Chairman Field Scovell, left, visits with close friend and director, Felix McKnight.

6. Brunch at Hyatt's Reunion Tower.

PROGRAM

6:00 P.M.   50TH ANNIVERSARY RECEPTION

7:15 P.M.   WELCOME
             JIM RAY SMITH, PRESIDENT
             COTTON BOWL ATHLETIC ASSOCIATION

             INVOCATION
             FRED JACOBY, COMMISSIONER
             SOUTHWEST ATHLETIC CONFERENCE

             MASTER OF CEREMONIES
             LINDSEY NELSON
             "VOICE OF THE COTTON BOWL FOR
                27 YEARS"

7:30 P.M.   FABULOUS FOOTSTEPS
             50 YEARS OF COTTON BOWL MEMORIES

8:15 P.M.   DINNER

9:15 P.M.   REMARKS
             PAT DYE, HEAD COACH AND ATHLETIC
                DIRECTOR
             AUBURN UNIVERSITY

             JACKIE SHERRILL, HEAD COACH AND
                ATHLETIC DIRECTOR
             TEXAS A&M UNIVERSITY

9:30 P.M.   CBS 50TH COTTON BOWL FEATURE

9:40 P.M.   BENEDICTION
             DR. MICHAEL JOHNSON, UNIVERSITY
                OF HOUSTON
             PRESIDENT, SOUTHWEST ATHLETIC
                CONFERENCE

COTTON BOWL CLASSIC
ADMIT ONE
MARQUETTE vs. T. C. U.
Price .. $1.82   Friday, January 1st, 1937 ... 2:00 P. M.
State Tax .19   SEAT CHECK
Fed. Tax .19   COTTON BOWL STADIUM
Total . $2.20   OF THE
GREATER TEXAS PAN-AMERICAN EXPOSITION
ROW 17 SECTION 3 SEAT 1
COTTON BOWL—DALLAS
EXLINE-LONDON CO.

MENU

Cajun Seafood Salad
With A Light Cajun Spice
On Melange Of Lettuce And Vegetable Garnish
Dendrobium Orchid
Russian Dressing

Petite Filet Mignon And
Noisette Of Veal
Bordelaise Sauce And
Dijon Mustard Sauce
Spinach And Tomato Pasta/Herb Butter
Rondelle Of Squash With
Green Beans

Chocolate Velvet Torte
Decorated With Miniature
Marzipan Football
Inscribed With "50"
Raspberry Glaze

Mini Croissants, French Rolls, Lahvosh

Coffee, Tea, Sanka

"A DAY AT THE DUDE RANCH"

Each year during the annual Cotton Bowl Classic, the participating teams are treated to some "real" Texas hospitality at a local Dude Ranch, where they ride horses, see a rodeo, and enjoy delicious prime Texas beef.

Top:
Willie Nelson and the Lone Star . . . in no where else but Texas.

Bottom:
Kilgore Junior College's famed Rangerettes have been featured in both pre-game and halftime pageantry at the annual Cotton Bowl Classic for more than a quarter of a century.

"ANNUAL NEW YEAR'S DAY COTTON BOWL PARADE"

Texas sized colorful floats along with many top high school and university bands highlight the annual New Years Day Parade televised nationally by CBS from downtown Dallas.

"DALLAS' MOST EXCLUSIVE NEW YEARS' EVE PARTY"

"GAME DAY IN THE COTTON BOWL JANUARY 1"

1. Texas A&M Athletic Director and Head Coach Jackie Sherrill, left, visits with former University of Texas famed athletic director and coach, Darrell Royal, during Cotton Bowl 50th anniversary dinner.

2. Two of the nation's top coaches, Vince Dooley of Georgia, left, and Texas' Fred Akers, right pose with CBAA VP Jim Brock prior to 1984 Classic.

3. Two Legends, Darrell Royal of Texas, at podium, and Ara Paraseghian of Notre Dame (now with CBS/TV) were featured at the 50th anniversary Cotton Bowl Dinner.

4. A proud symbol of the University of Texas at Austin.

5. Proud Texas A&M seniors display traditional Boots prior to 1986 Cotton Bowl Classic.

6. Cheerleaders play an important role in each Cotton Bowl Classic.

Cotton Bowl 1936
TCU 16 - Marquette 6

Blair Cherry
explains plan
to Longhorns
1947

J. Curtis Sanford
promoted first Cotton Bowl

Dick Todd
Texas A + M
37-38

Charles Moran
Texas A + M 1909

louis daniel

SHERRI MOEGLE . . . 1986 MAID OF COTTON

Top: The 1986 Maid of Cotton, Sherri Moegle, visits with Texas Governor Mark White at the New Year's Eve Ball.

Bottom: Sherri Moegle, the 1986 Maid of Cotton, waves to the overflow crowd on New Year's Day in the Cotton Bowl. Miss Moegle of Lubbock was selected earlier in the week to highlight the annual pageant in Dallas

DONNA BANFIELD,
1986 COTTON BOWL QUEEN, AND HER COURT

1. Donna Barfield, Texas A&M; 2. Pam Scott, Auburn; 3. Bettye Sturges, Arkansas; 4. Donna Reid, Baylor; 5. Kim Havard, Houston; 6. Patty Nghien, Rice; 7. Queens and escorts pose during New Year's Eve Ball; 8. Elizabeth Pool, SMU; 9. Teresa Alexander, Texas at Austin; 10. Jill Davis, TCU; 11. Holly Griffin, Texas Tech;

"AGGIE TRADITIONS"

"SALUTE TO THE CHAMPION"

1. (left to right), Lindsey Nelson, long-time voice of the Cotton Bowl, Mrs. Betty Sanford, wife of the late J. Curtis Sanford and Lamar Hunt of Dallas were featured at the 50th Anniversary Dinner.

2. Jim Brock chats with Darrell Royal, left, and Bob Lilly, right.

3. CBS Sports Lineup at 1985 Cotton Bowl, (left to right), Ara Parseghian, Pat Haden, Pat O'Brien and Lindsey Nelson.

4. Marquette's 1937 team pose at the 1986 Cotton Bowl 50th anniversary salute.

5. TCU's great 1937 Team gather for some fun at 50th anniversary dinner.

6. The family of the late J. Curtis Sanford is honored at the 1986 Cotton Bowl 50th Anniversary Dinner

By: Sherry Beadle

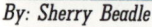

By: Darla Thornton Lyon

MASCOTS ADD COLOR TO AUTUMN AFTERNOONS

MARY PENNER - WILDLIFE ARTIST

1. Mallards; 2. Ring-necked Pheasant; 3. Green-winged Teal (pair); 4. Canada Goose (nesting);

1

2

3

4

1

2

3

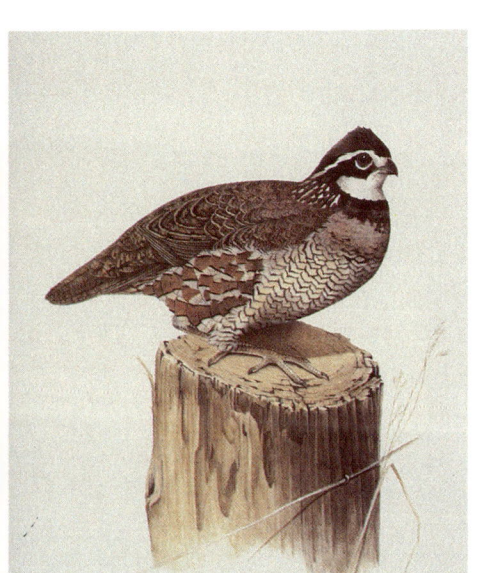

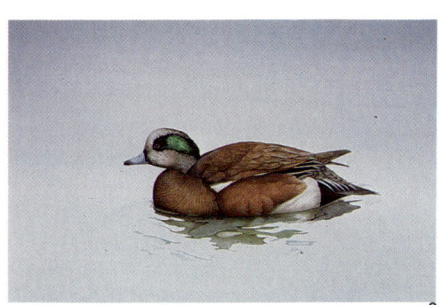

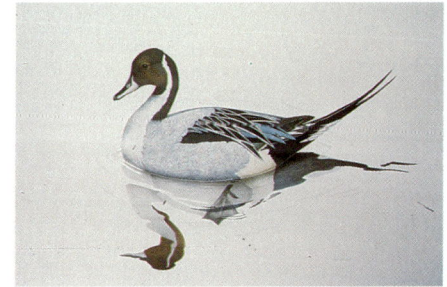

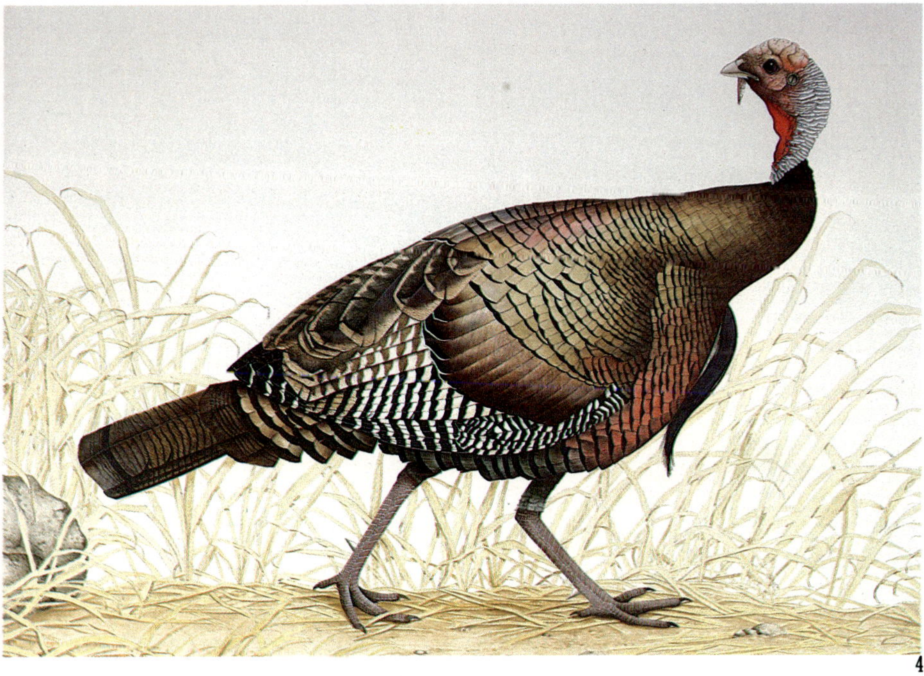

4

1. Bobwhite Quail; 2. American Widgeon; 3. Pintail; 4. Turkey;

"SCENES FROM THE 50TH ANNIVERSARY CLASSIC"

1. Mr. Cotton Bowl, Field Scovell and wife Mary pose with friend.

2. CBS Radio Team (left to right) Lindsey Nelson and Brad Sham.

3. Auburn Cheerleader cheers War Eagles on.

4. CBAA Prexy Jim Ray Smith presents handsome trophy to winning coach Jackie Sherrill with CBAA Chairman, J.L. Huffines, Jr. nearby.

5. Auburn's proud mascot, the famed War Eagle.

6. Texas A&M's proud coach Jackie Sherrill celebrates with his players during the 1986 Classic.

7. Scoreboard tells the story in 1986 Cotton Bowl.

The Fort Worth Club is the home of the nationally renown Davey O'Brien National Quarterback Award. Posing during ceremonies honoring the 1984 recipient, Doug Flutie of Boston College, are left to right, Mrs. Joan Flutie, Darren Flutie, Steve Young, Jim McMahon, Earl Campbell, Todd Blackledge, Mike Singletary and Tom Landry.

"SPOTLIGHTING THE COTTON BOWL TROPHY"

1. The handsome 50th Anniversary Cotton Bowl Trophy, sponsored by KODAK, was a highlight of the 1986 Classic.

Top to Bottom:

2. Cotton Bowl Officers and key quests pose with the new Cotton Bowl Trophy at City Hall.

3. Dallas Mayor A. Starke Taylor, Jr. and CBAA's Jim Brock, look over the new Cotton Bowl Trophy at City Hall.

4. A proud Jackie Sherrill, Texas A&M's Athletic Director and Head Football Coach, poses with Cotton Bowl trophy and CBAA brass following the 1986 Classic victory over Auburn.

Top: Sherry Beadle was influenced by a Southwestern ranch heritage and is distinguished as an international equine and western artist. She created her own techniques of using pastel on suede. Beadle recently met with President Reagan where he enthusiastically accepted the painting.

Bottom. Sherry Beadle shows her exceptional talent for accurate documentation of anatomy in this painting of Vice President George Bush. She has captured the special warmth of the man, while at the same time evoking his strength and pride in the United States Flag for which it stands. A Sense of movement in the flag conveys the spirit of freedom, value and responsibility for politicians, artists and Americans.

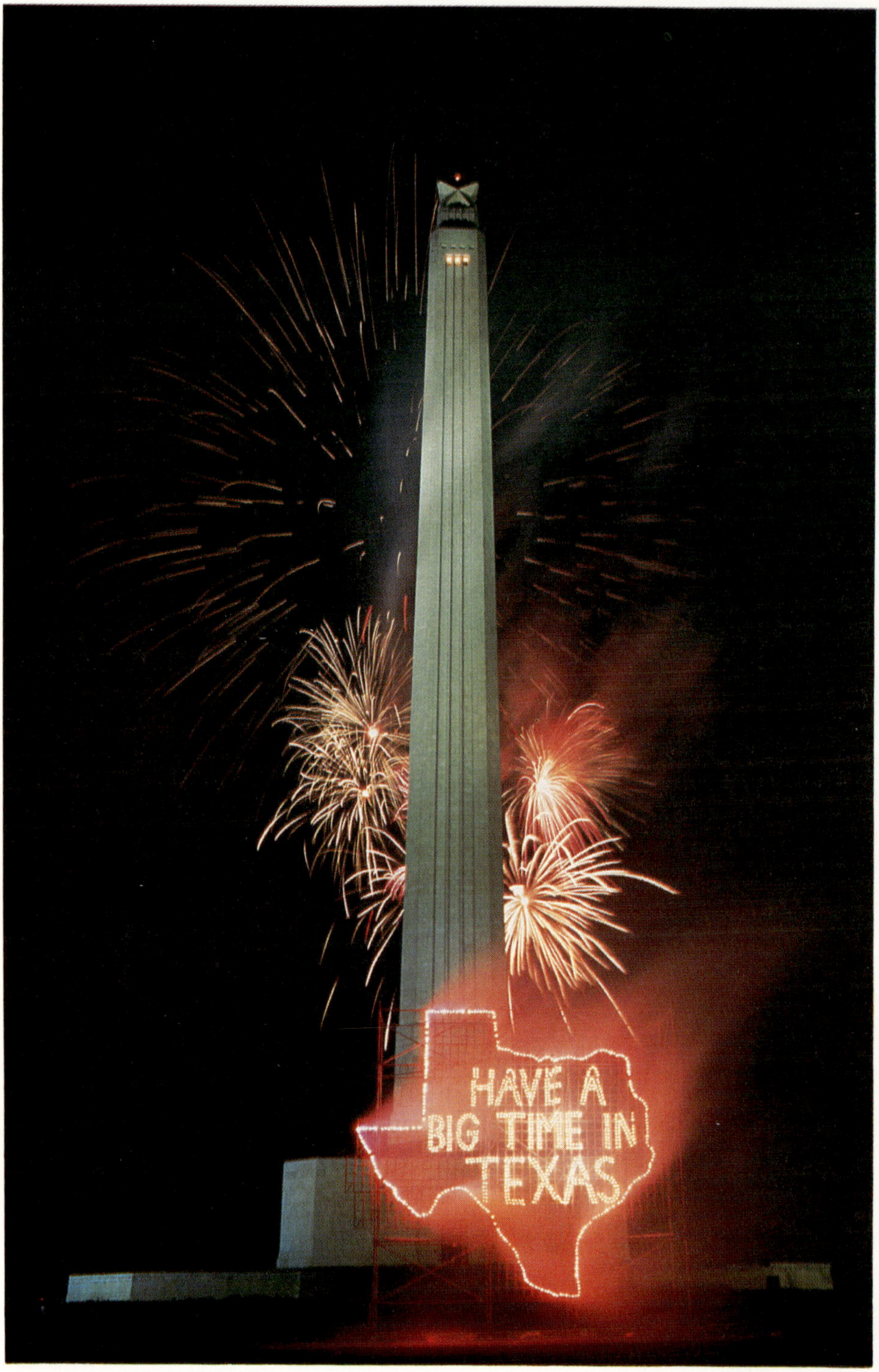
HAVE A
BIG TIME IN
TEXAS

POULET SAUTÉ AU CITRON

3 tablespoons butter
2 broiling chickens (2 to 2½ pounds each), split, backbone removed
Salt, to taste
Pepper, to taste

½ cup dry white wine
1 cup rich chicken stock (2 bouillon cubes mixed with 1 cup hot water)
Grated rind of 2 lemons

In a large skillet or saucepan, heat the butter and brown chicken on both sides over low heat. Season well with salt and pepper. Stir in wine and stock; cover and simmer for 20 to 25 minutes or until chicken is tender. Arrange chicken on a platter. Boil the cooking liquid with lemon rind until reduced by half. Adjust seasoning according to taste, then spoon sauce over chicken. Serve with parsley butter new potatoes and lemon fritters. Serves 4.

Paul R. Leonel, C.E.C.
The Fort Worth Club

BURGUNDY CHICKEN

6 whole chicken breasts, boned and halved
Flour
Salt
Pepper
Nutmeg

Cinnamon
Butter or margarine
1 large can pitted sweet cherries
2 small cans mandarin oranges
2½ cups Burgundy wine

Wash and dry chicken. Cover with flour which has been seasoned with salt, pepper, nutmeg and cinnamon. Brown in butter or margarine. Transfer to a baking dish. Cover with cherries and oranges. Make sauce of wine, cherry juice and orange juice. Cover and bake in a moderate oven until tender. Sauce may be thickened with a little flour or cornstarch, if desired.

Mrs. Frank W. Maddox (Lucille)

CLASSIC MILESTONE

1958 - Navy became the first eastern team to win the Cotton Bowl with a 28-7 victory over Rice.

FORDHAM NO-FUSS CHICKEN AND DUMPLINGS

2 whole chickens	1 teaspoon fresh or dried basil
1 large onion, chopped	4 quarts water (at least)
3 garlic cloves, chopped	½ teaspoon salt
¼ teaspoon white pepper	1 large package flour tortillas

Wash chickens and remove giblets from separate packaging. Combine onion, garlic, pepper, basil and water in a very large, heavy pan or soup pot. Add chickens and bring to a boil. Simmer for 1½ to 2½ hours. Remove chickens and giblets from the liquid; cool. Skin, bone and chop chicken. Giblets may be added, if desired. (For fat-free dumplings, refrigerate the pot of liquid for 3 hours or overnight. Skim off fat.) This portion of the recipe may be prepared well in advance of serving. When ready to assemble the complete dish, add salt and 2 cups water, and reheat the liquid to boiling. Add more water, if desired. Stir in the chopped chicken. Tear flour tortillas into small squares (about 2-inches) and drop into the boiling liquid. Reduce heat to simmer, stirring occasionally, for 30 to 40 minutes. Adjust seasoning as required. Serve with green salad. Serves 12.

Jay Wallace

FRIED CHICKEN STRIPS WITH LEMON SAUCE

4 chicken breast halves, skinned and boned	¾ cup water
1 large egg	1 cup flour
	2 cups vegetable oil for deep frying

Cut chicken breasts into ½-inch strips; set aside. Prepare batter by mixing egg, water and flour. Let mixture stand for 1 hour. Dip chicken in batter and deep fry a few strips at a time in oil that has been heated to 400°. Remove chicken when it reaches a light golden color; drain on paper towels. Place chicken on serving platter and cover with sauce. Serve at once.

LEMON SAUCE

1 cup chicken broth	1 tablespoon honey
¼ cup dry white wine	3 tablespoons lemon juice
1 tablespoon soy sauce	1 tablespoon cornstarch

Combine ingredients in a saucepan. Over medium heat, stir constantly until mixture comes to a boil. Simmer for 1 to 2 minutes.

Mrs. Tim Lindgren (Fran)
Wife, Cotton Bowl Committee

OXFORD OVEN FRIED CHICKEN

1 chicken fryer	1 tablespoon chopped fresh parsley
½ cup grated Parmesan cheese	Salt, to taste
¾ cup herbed bread crumbs	¾ stick margarine

Rinse fryer, cut into pieces then dry. Mix Parmesan cheese with bread crumbs, parsley and salt. Melt margarine. Dip chicken pieces in margarine, then shake in a brown bag containing the crumb mixture. Arrange chicken pieces at least 1 inch apart on a greased cookie sheet. Bake at 375° for 45 to 50 minutes.

Mary McVay

HOT CHICKEN CASSEROLE

1 (10-ounce) can chicken soup	½ cup slivered almonds
3 to 4 eggs, hard-cooked and sliced	3 tablespoons minced onion
4 chicken breasts, cooked and cubed	2 tablespoons lemon juice
2 cups finely chopped celery	¼ teaspoon pepper
1 cup sour cream	1 cup grated cheese
1 cup mayonnaise	1 (3-ounce) can French fried onion rings
1 (8-ounce) can water chestnuts, drained and sliced	

Spread undiluted chicken soup in bottom of a 2-quart casserole. Arrange eggs on top of soup. Mix chicken with celery, sour cream, mayonnaise, water chestnuts, almonds, minced onion, lemon juice, pepper and cheese. Layer over eggs in casserole. Bake at 350° for 20 to 25 minutes. Top with onion rings and bake an additional 10 minutes. Serves 8.

Mrs. Wilbur Evans (Lillian)
Wife, Cotton Bowl Director

RUSSIAN CHICKEN FOR BLITZING LINEBACKERS

8 chicken breasts, skinned and boned	8 ounces Russian salad dressing
Salt, to taste	1½ cups apricot/pineapple preserves
Pepper, to taste	1 envelope dry onion soup mix

Season chicken with salt and pepper. Mix Russian dressing, preserves and dry soup mix; pour over chicken in a greased casserole. Marinate overnight. Cover and bake at 350° for 1 hour.

Mrs. Charles Mayberry (Cathy)

STRAWBERRY-PINEAPPLE BAKED CHICKEN

1 cup buttery flavor Wesson oil
1 tablespoon pepper
1½ teaspoons salt
½ teaspoon seasoned salt
2 cups flour

Chicken legs
1 pint fresh or frozen strawberries
1 (8-ounce) can pineapple chunks
¾ cup dark rum

Preheat oven to 375°. Heat oil to medium temperature in frying pan. Add pepper, salt, seasoned salt and flour to a shaking container; shake well to mix. Add a few pieces of chicken at a time to the container and shake until well-coated. Cook the chicken in the oil until it is golden brown. Remove from frying pan and arrange in a casserole, skin-side up. Pour strawberries and pineapple chunks evenly over the chicken. Pour rum evenly over the fruited chicken. Cover and bake for 45 minutes or until chicken is tender. May be served on a bed of rice, garnished with parsley.

Lawrence Wm. Samuels

CHICKEN BARBECUE

Chicken
Paprika
½ cup water
⅓ cup vinegar
¾ stick butter (about 6 tablespoons)

4 teaspoons Worcestershire sauce
2 tablespoons catsup
2 tablespoons lemon juice
1 teaspoon Tabasco sauce
1 teaspoon salt

Cut up chicken and place in pan or skillet. Sprinkle with paprika. In a separate bowl, mix remaining ingredients. Pour over chicken. Cover and bake at 350° for 1½ hours or until tender. Turn chicken frequently.

Mary Ellen Durrett
Chairman, Department of Home Economics
The University of Texas at Austin

QUICKY CORNERBACK CHICKEN SUPPER

2 broilers or several pieces of frying
  chicken
1 can cream of chicken soup
1 can cream of mushroom soup

1 can cream of celery soup
¼ cup dry white wine (optional)
¾ cup slivered almonds
½ cup grated Parmesan cheese

Arrange chicken in greased casserole. Mix soups and wine and pour mixture over chicken. Sprinkle with almonds and top with cheese. Bake at 350° for 1½ hours or until done.

Mrs. Floyd Kinser (Dorothy)

CHICKEN BREAD BAKE

Boneless chicken breast, 4 to 6   5 eggs
2 cups milk   Salt
2 cups flour

Brown lightly-floured chicken breast in butter. Mix remaining ingredients very well on low speed. Pour batter in baking dish. Push chicken down into the batter. Bake in pre-heated oven 425° for 25 minutes. Reduce heat to 350° bake for an additional 15 to 20 minutes.

Double recipe to serve about 10.

Linda Cason
Convention Director
Kim Dawson Agency

CHICKEN CORDON BLEU PASS COVERAGE

4 chicken breasts, skinned and boned   2 tablespoons butter or margarine
4 cooked ham slices   3 tablespoons oil
4 Swiss cheese slices   ½ cup dry bread crumbs
Salt   ½ cup grated Parmesan cheese
Pepper   2 tablespoons flour
Garlic powder   ¾ cup chicken broth
1 egg   ¼ cup dry white wine
3 tablespoons water

Pound chicken breasts as thin as possible between 2 pieces of waxed paper. Place a slice of ham and cheese on top of chicken breast, fold over and secure with toothpick. Season to taste with salt, pepper and garlic powder. Whip eggs and water until thoroughly mixed. In a skillet, heat the butter and oil. Dip chicken first into egg mixture, then into mixture of bread crumbs and Parmesan cheese. Brown on all sides, then remove from skillet. To make sauce, add flour to skillet and brown slightly. Gradually add chicken broth until thickened. Stir in wine. Return breasts to skillet and simmer for 5 to 10 minutes.

Kenneth Stone

CLASSIC MILESTONE

1960 - National champion Syracuse ended its unbeaten season with a 23-14 victory over Texas. It also marked the first of ten Classic appearances by Texas coach Darrell Royal.

United States Senate

LLOYD BENTSEN

TEXAS

Dear Mr. Brock:

Thank you for your recent request. It is always a pleasure to share my favorite recipe.

BAKED CRAB IN SHELL

1 lb. lump crab meat
1 pint table cream
1 green pepper, diced
2 cups celery, diced
2 cup onion, diced
3-4 tablespoons butter
1 cup cracker crumbs
Tabasco Sauce
lemon for garnish
parsley
paprika
6-8 crab shells

Saute pepper, celery and onion in butter. In a bowl, mix cracker crumbs, cream, salt and pepper to taste. Add sauted vegetables and crab meat. Fill crab shells and top with paprika. Bake at 350 degrees for 40 minutes. Garnish with lemon and parsley.

I hope you enjoy it, and if you need further assistance, please do not hesitate to contact me.

Sincerely,

Lloyd Bentsen

TEXAS A&M UNIVERSITY

Department of Intercollegiate Athletics — Aggieland, Texas 77843-1228

HOT SHRIMP

2 lbs. large headless shrimp in shell
1 stick of butter or margarine
1 tsp. worcestershire sauce
1 tsp. tabasco sauce
1½ tsp. course ground black pepper
Salt to taste

In large skillet, melt butter and add seasonings. Saute shrimp until done, about 10-15 minutes. Pour remaining butter in skillet over shrimp and serve hot.

Lynn Amedee

UNIVERSITY OF COLORADO, BOULDER

Office of the Chancellor

Jonsson's Frestelse

onions
anchovies/brine
potatoes
butter
light cream
milk
boiling water

1. Butter baking dish

2. Pour 3½ cups boiling water over 2 (5.5oz) packages potatoes with onions (hash browns) and let stand 30 minutes (toss occasionally).

3. Have ready 4 cans (40) anchovies (smelts or sprats are Swedish anchovies) and additional sliced onions (2, perhaps).

4. Layer 1/3 potatoes first, 1/2 onion slices, and anchovy; 1/3 potatoes, 1/2 onion slices, and anchovy; then potatoes.

5. Sprinkle with 2 Tablespoons of anchovy brine and dot with butter.

6. Pour 2 Cups of light cream over layers.

7. Cover with foil and bake at 400° 45 minutes; remove foil (add up to 1 Cup milk if dish is dry), and bake 15 minutes more uncovered.

Serves 10-12.

Harrison Shull

SEAFOOD GUMBO

4 tablespoons vegetable oil	1 gallon water
5 garlic cloves, chopped	6 tablespoons Kitchen Bouquet
1 large onion, chopped	3 bay leaves
1 1/2 cups celery, chopped	1 (16 ounce) can tomatoes
1 bell pepper, chopped	1 tablespoon Worcestershire sauce
1/2 cup parsley, chopped	1 lemon, sliced
1 pound okra, sliced thick	2-3 pounds shrimp, raw, cleaned
1/2 pound bacon, cubed	1 (6 1/2-ounce) can crabmeat
1 thick slice ham cubed	2 tablespoons gumbo file
1/2 cup flour	Salt and pepper to taste
10 chicken bouillon cubes	Oysters (optional)

Using large Kettle, saute garlic, onion, celery, bell pepper, parsley,
okra, bacon and ham in oil. Sprinkle enough flour over above ingredients
to absorb all oil and liquid. Mix chicken bouillon cubes in 1 gallon
of water with Kitchen Bouquet, bay leaves, tomatoes, Worcestershire sauce
and lemon. Add to first mixture, cover and cook over low heat 2 hours.
Add shrimp and crab; cook 30 minutes longer. Add 2 tablespoons file.
Add salt and pepper to taste, If desired, oysters may be added before
serving.

Delicious served with a crisp green salad and hot French bread.

Mrs. Augie Erfurth (Ethel)
Wife of Former Athletic Director
Rice University

OFFICE OF THE GOVERNOR
STATE CAPITOL
SALEM, OREGON 97310

* OREGON SALMON SOUFFLÉ *

Grease a 6 cup mold with 1 tsp. butter and sprinkle with 2 Tbl. grated Parmesan cheese. Set oven for 350°.

2   Tbl. minced green onions or shallots
3   Tbl. butter
3   Tbl. flour
1   cup milk (or liquid from canned salmon plus milk to equal 1 cup).
1/2 tsp. salt
1/8 tsp. pepper
1   Tbl. tomato paste
1/2 tsp. oregano
4   egg yolks
3/4 cup (or more) shredded cooked or canned salmon
1/2 cup grated Swiss cheese

Lightly brown minced onions in melted butter. Add flour and cook over medium heat for two minutes. Remove from heat, beat in liquid all at once, and add seasonings and tomato paste. Bring to a boil, stirring constantly. Cook one minute and remove from heat.

With pan off heat, beat in egg yolks one at a time. Add salmon and all but 1 Tbl. cheese. Taste for seasoning and cover surface with plastic wrap while preparing the rest of the recipe.

5   egg whites
1/4 tsp. cream of tartar
pinch of salt

Beat egg whites slowly until they foam. Add cream of tartar and salt, increasing speed gradually. Beat until stiff but not dry. Stir one fourth of the beaten egg whites into the sauce mixture, then gently fold in the rest. Pour into the prepared mold and sprinkle with the remaining cheese.

Place the soufflé in the middle level of the oven and bake 30-35 minutes. Check it and bake 4-5 minutes after it is golden brown. (it is done when a skewer comes out clean). Serve immediately.

Note: Before baking, the soufflé may be placed on a doubled towel and covered with a large inverted pan for one hour.

The soufflé will keep for 5 minutes without collapsing in a turned off oven with the door open.

Vic Atiyeh
Governor

GEORGIA BULLDOGS
NATIONAL FOOTBALL CHAMPIONS
1980

Athletic Department
University of Georgia
Athens, Georgia 30613

Southeastern Conference
Champions

1942	1968
1946	1976
1948	1980
1959	1981
1966	1982

Rose Bowl
1943

Sugar Bowl
1947
1969
1977
1981
1982
1983

Orange Bowl
1942
1949
1960

Cotton Bowl
1966
1976
1984

Gator Bowl
1948
1971

Bluebonnet Bowl
1978

Tangerine Bowl
1974

Liberty Bowl
1967

Sun Bowl
1964
1970

Peach Bowl
1973

Oil Bowl
1946

Presidential Cup
1950

Stir Fry Shrimp with Fried Rice

3 tablespoons peanut oil (do not substitute)

I egg

4 green onions with tops, sliced

I clove garlic, minced

3/4 lb. shrimp, peeled and deveined

1/2 cup sliced water chestnuts

4 cups cooked rice – chilled in refrigerator

1/4 cup soy sauce

Add I tablesppon oil to skillet – Place on medium heat.   When
oil is hot, add egg and scramble.   Remove and set aside.   Increase heat – add remaining oil, onion and garlic.   Stir fry about
I minute.   Stir in shrimp and water chestnuts – cook until shrimp
turns pink – about 5 minutes.

Stir in cold rice and soy sauce until well mixed ....Stir 'till heated
through.

4-6 servings

Vince Dooley

The University of Mississippi

Department of Intercollegiate Athletics
University, MS 38677
(601) 232-7241

CAJUN SHRIMP CASSEROLE

½ lb. hot link sausage, or
  smoked sausage
3 TBS. bacon drippings
½ lb. ham, minced
1 cup chopped yellow onion
1 cup chopped green onion
1 cup chopped green pepper
3 garlic cloves, minced
1 bay leaf
½ tsp. thyme
2 cups long grain wild rice
  (uncooked)

1 TBS. tomato puree
2 cups chopped tomatoes
  (drain and keep liquid)
½ cup chopped celery
½ cup chopped parsley
2 tsp. salt
½ tsp. black pepper
  cayenne to taste
3 cups liquid from tomatoes
  and oysters
3 lbs. large raw shrimp (cleaned)
1 qt. oysters (reserve liquid)

In a 4 qt. heavy pan, sautee sausage until firm; remove with slotted spoon. Add bacon drippings to sausage drippings, and sautee ham for 3 minutes in drippings. Add onions, green pepper, garlic, bay leaf, thyme, and sautee 5 minutes. Add rice, sautee 3 minutes, stirring constantly. Add tomato paste and cook 3 minutes. Add sausage, tomatoes, celery, parsley, salt, pepper, and liquid. Bring to boil, reduce heat, and cook slowly covered, stirring occassionally, until rice is done... about 12-15 minutes. (Can freeze at this stage) Transfer to a shallow 4 qt. baking dish and stir in seafood. Place uncovered in a 350° preheated oven and cook until seafood is done...20-30 minutes. Stir twice while baking, using a large fork to fluff the rice and insure even baking. Serves 8-10.

Submitted by Warner Alford, Athletic Director, University of Mississippi (Ole Miss '61).

SHRIMP & CRABMEAT MADEIRA WALK-ON

3 tablespoons butter
2 tablespoons chopped shallots
¾ cup sliced mushrooms
½ pound uncooked shrimp
1 (6-ounce) can cooked crab, drained
½ cup Madeira wine
¼ teaspoon tarragon
1 tablespoon lemon juice

2 teaspoons tomato paste
2 egg yolks
¾ cup whipping cream
Salt, to taste
Pepper, to taste
Linguini
Chopped parsley

Melt butter in a saucepan. Sauté shallots, add mushrooms and continue cooking until liquid evaporates. Add shrimp and cook until they begin to turn pink. Add crab and Madeira and cook until almost reduced. Add tarragon, lemon juice and tomato paste, mixing well. Combine egg yolks with cream and add very slowly, stirring constantly. Season to taste with salt and pepper. Heat thoroughly. Serve over very thin linguini. Garnish with parsley. Serves 2.

Mrs. Charles Mayberry (Cathy)

TENNESSEE TIGER SHRIMP

Juice of 1 lemon
8 to 10 tiger shrimp (from South
    America, striped, about 6 inches long
    without the heads, available only
    from the finer fish markets, and boy,
    do they SMELL!)

1 bottle Italian dressing

Squeeze lemon juice over shrimp. Pour Italian dressing over shrimp and let stand for at least 2 hours. After you've eaten everything in the refrigerator waiting for the shrimp to soak in the dressing and the coals to glow in the grill, barbecue the shrimp! You may pour marinade over shrimp while they are cooking. Serve with melted butter. The shrimp are so rich they taste just like lobster - heaven!

Laura Bellomy

CLASSIC MILESTONE

1961 - Arkansas and Duke helped the Cotton Bowl celebrate its Silver Anniversary. With less than three minutes to play, the Blue Devils scored to upset the Razorbacks, 7-6.

GREEK ISLAND SCAMPI
Ancient Greek recipe.

Large shrimp (7 to 10 per pound count)　Small onions
Mushroom caps　Butter
Green pepper

Peel and devein shrimp, leaving tails. Add shrimp to marinade, tossing to mix well, and refrigerate for 4 to 5 hours. Skewer shrimp, mushroom caps, green pepper and small onions. Grill over hot coals and brush with butter when done.

MARINADE
Salad oil　Sherry
Oregano　Lemon juice
Salt　French dressing
Pepper　Barbecue sauce (small amount)
Dash Worcestershire sauce

Mix ingredients according to individual taste.

Bob Richards
TV Producer, Columnist, Radio Commentator

BAKED CLAMS WITH SNAIL BUTTER AND WALNUTS

2 large garlic cloves, peeled　Salt, to taste
2 shallots, peeled　Freshly ground pepper, to taste
8 walnut halves　36 or more littleneck clams on the half
½ cup loosely packed parsley leaves　　shell
¼ cup dry white wine　2 tablespoons or more freshly grated
½ pound butter　　Parmesan cheese
¼ cup fine bread crumbs

Preheat the oven to 500° or 550°. Place the garlic, shallots, walnut halves, parsley and wine in the container of an electric blender or food processor. Blend, stirring down as necessary, to make a fine puree. Knead the butter with the fingers and work in the contents of the blender, then knead in the bread crumbs and salt and pepper. Spoon about a teaspoon or less of the butter on top of each of the clams and arrange them on a baking pan (like a jelly roll pan) with edges. Sprinkle with cheese. Cover with foil. Place the pan in the oven for about 6 minutes. The clams must be thoroughly hot, but the less they cook the better. Cooking toughens them. Run the clams briefly under the broiler to brown lightly and serve piping hot. Serves 6.

Craig Claiborne
New York Times Food Editor

OREGON'S QUICK SALMON CASSEROLE

1 large can red salmon
6 bread slices, coarsely grated
1 small onion, finely grated

1 cup milk
Grated cheese

Mix salmon, bread, onion and milk; transfer to a buttered baking dish. Sprinkle with grated cheese. Bake at 350° for 20 to 35 minutes.

Mary McVay

SALMON CUCUMBER MOUSSE

1 (1-pound) can salmon, reserving juice
1 envelope (1 tablespoon) plain gelatin
3 tablespoons lemon juice
1 teaspoon prepared mustard

⅔ cup mayonnaise
Dash cayenne pepper
½ cup finely diced celery
¾ cup finely diced cucumber, peeled

Drain liquid from salmon into measuring cup and add water to make 1 cup liquid. Heat to simmering. Soften gelatin in lemon juice, add to the hot liquid and stir until gelatin is thoroughly dissolved. Cool until mixture is slightly thickened. Flake salmon into mixing bowl. Stir in mustard, mayonnaise and cayenne. Add the thickened gelatin and blend well. Fold in celery and cucumber. Turn mixture into a 1-quart mold and chill for several hours or until firm. I use a fish mold and when ready to serve I unmold on a bed of lettuce and garnish with cucumber slices and sprigs of mint or parsley. I use a radish slice for the eye. Serves 6 as a main course. Serves 10 to 12 as a salad or additional cold dish.

Mrs. R. Guy Carter (Phyllis)
Wife, Cotton Bowl Director

TIGER PRAWN SHRIMP

Split shrimp, devein and leave in shell. Put lemon vinegar and lowfat dressing of some kind (preferably homemade to control low oil content) on shrimp. Cook shell-side down on grill with lid of pot on top for 2 minutes. The lid allows it to cook through without turning and keeps moisture in. Serve with whole wheat rice pilaf or wild rice.

Mrs. C.E. Seal, II (Crickett)
Wife, Cotton Bowl Committee

FISH-N-BAKE BOOTLEG

3 to 4 pounds bass fillets
Salt, to taste
Pepper, to taste
Garlic, to taste

¾ cup chopped onion
3 jalapeños, chopped
½ pound butter
2 to 3 lemons, sliced

Season fish with salt, pepper and garlic. Crowd fish in baking pan. Sprinkle with onion and jalapeños. Top with butter and lemon slices. Bake, uncovered, at 350° for 30 to 35 minutes, or until fish is flaky.

Skeet George
Angelo's Bar-B-Q

BLACKENED REDFISH

Redfish or gulf red snapper fillet, skinned (allow ¼ to ⅓ pound per person)
½ stick margarine or butter

Paul Prudhomme Seafood Magic or Blackened Redfish Magic Seasoning
Lemon wedges

Let fish stand at room temperature for 30 minutes before cooking. Place cast iron skillet on high heat for 10 minutes. Skillet should be dry with no margarine in it. In another saucepan, melt margarine. Pour margarine in a shallow dish, reserving half of it for saucing the fish later, and run the fish through it to coat both sides. Generously sprinkle the Cajun Magic seasoning on both sides of fish. Immediately lay fish in super hot skillet, and immediately ladle about 1 tablespoon of melted margarine over fish. Try not to let any of the margarine spill over into the bottom of the skillet. Sear fish for 2 minutes only. Turn, ladle another tablespoon of margarine over the fish, and cook for 2 minutes. Serve promptly, pouring a little of the remaining melted margarine over the fish. Note: This will send up lots of smoke, so you will want to turn on your vent.

Harry C. Hoover, Jr.
Cotton Bowl Director

CLASSIC MILESTONE

1964 - It was the first time the Classic matched the nation's No. 1 and No. 2 teams. And the top-ranked Texas Longhorns left little doubt that they were the most deserving of the coveted ranking, handing the Midshipmen a decisive 28-6 defeat.

MY FAVORITE BAKED FISH

1½ pounds halibut steaks (can use ocean catfish, fresh or thawed)
Salt, to taste
Pepper, to taste
Oil
1 (1-pound) can small white potatoes, drained
½ cup minced onion

3 medium tomatoes, peeled and thinly sliced
1 cup sour cream
½ teaspoon dry mustard
1 tablespoon or more lemon juice
½ teaspoon salt
⅛ teaspoon pepper
Paprika

Sprinkle fish with salt and pepper. In skillet, heat oil and sauté fish, then potatoes and onion, until golden. Arrange in baking dish, topped with tomato slices. Sprinkle with additional salt. Combine sour cream, mustard, lemon juice, ½ teaspoon salt and ⅛ teaspoon pepper. Pour over tomato slices. Sprinkle with paprika. Bake at 350° for 15 to 20 minutes. Serves 4.

Ray Underwood

WHITE FISH PARISIAN IN STILLWATER

2 pounds white fish
1 cup French dressing
2 tablespoons lemon juice
¼ teaspoon salt

1 (3½-ounce) can French fried onion rings
¼ cup or more grated Parmesan cheese

Arrange fish in a shallow dish. Combine dressing, lemon juice and salt in a separate bowl. Pour mixture over fish. Let stand for 30 minutes, turning fish once. Transfer to a well-greased 12x8x2-inch baking dish. Crush onion rings and sprinkle over fish. Top with Parmesan cheese. Bake at 350° for 25 to 30 minutes, or until fish is flaky.

Joe Alan

CLASSIC MILESTONE

1964 - Navy's outstanding quarterback Roger Staubach is another Heisman Trophy winner to appear in the Cotton Bowl, but lost to No. 1 Texas, 28-6.

HOMARD AU WHISKEY
Lobster with whiskey cream sauce.

7 pounds lobster (4 to 6, depending on size)
¼ cup vegetable, peanut or corn oil
8 tablespoons butter
Salt, to taste
Freshly ground pepper, to taste
¼ cup finely chopped celery
½ cup finely chopped carrot
⅓ cup finely chopped onion
⅓ cup finely chopped shallots or green onions

1 bay leaf
2 fresh thyme sprigs or ½ teaspoon dried
1 teaspoon finely minced garlic
¾ cup bourbon whiskey
4 tablespoons tomato paste
1 cup fish stock or fresh or bottled clam juice
2 cups heavy cream
2 tablespoons flour
2 tablespoons chopped parsley

Plunge a knife into each lobster where the body and tail section meet to sever the spinal cord. This will kill the lobster instantly. Break off the tail and set aside in a large bowl. Break off the large claws and add to the large bowl. Cut off the small feeler claws and add to the bowl. Pull out and discard the interior of the chest portion of the lobster. But by all means reserve the coral and liver (the soft portions that are gray, black and sometimes red). Put this into a bowl by itself and set aside. In a large deep kettle heat the oil and add 2 tablespoons butter. When the oil and butter are quite hot but not brown, add the lobster tails, claws and so on. Do not add the coral and liver. Stir the lobster pieces around briefly and add salt and pepper, celery, carrot, onion, shallots, bay leaf, thyme and garlic. Cook about 5 minutes, stirring occasionally. Carefully pour off and discard any liquid that may have accumulated from the cooking (use the kettle lid to keep the lobster and other ingredients from falling out of the kettle as the liquid is poured off). Return the kettle to the stove and add ½ cup whiskey. Do not cover. Stir briefly and add the tomato paste. Cook, stirring, about 5 minutes and add the fish stock. Cover and simmer for 20 minutes. Uncover and transfer the claws and tails of the lobster to a platter to cool. Return the remaining pieces of lobster and sauce to the stove and cook over moderate heat about 5 minutes. Add the heavy cream and turn the heat to high. Stir briefly and cook, uncovered, about 10 minutes to reduce the cream. Add the flour and 4 tablespoons of butter to the coral and liver and stir to blend well with a whisk. Add this to the kettle and simmer for about 3 minutes, stirring. Pour the contents of the kettle into a food mill (this may have to be repeated several times if the food mill is small). Press to extract as much liquid as possible from the solid pieces of lobster shell. Discard lobster shells. Pour the sauce into a saucepan and let simmer. Remove the meat from the tail and claws. Cut each tail portion into 3 pieces. Discard shell. Heat 1 tablespoon of butter in a large skillet and when hot, add the lobster meat. Add remaining ¼ cup whiskey and cook briefly, shaking the skillet. Add half the sauce. Let the remaining sauce continue to simmer. Add the remaining 1 tablespoon of butter to the lobster and sauce mixture and swirl it in. Sprinkle with parsley. Serve in a rice ring or with rice on the side. Serve the remaining sauce on the side in a sauce boat. Serves 6.

Craig Claiborne
New York Times Food Editor

MARY PENNER

A Texas native, Mary Penner is an established name in wildlife art. She has won many awards, and her paintings are in several permanent museum and private collections.

Mary is a member of the Society of Animal Artists, the Cornell Laboratory of Ornithology, the American Ornithologists Union, and the Guild of Natural Science Illustrators.

Some important exhibits where she has shown her work are the Leigh Yawkey Woodson Art Museum, "Birds in Art" exhibition; the Wildlife Art Expo; the Smithsonian "Art in the Service of Science" exhibit; the "National Art Exhibition of Alaskan Wildlife" in Anchorage; and "Birds of New York" at Wave Hill Museum in New York, National Museum of Natural History, Smithsonian.

Mary has combined her artistic talent with her biology background, and over the past 10 years has spent much of her time studying, painting, and observing the wildlife in the rain and cloud forests of Northeastern Mexico. This effort will ultimately become an exhibit of 50 or more paintings of tropical wildlife scheduled to tour the U.S. within the next year.

Mary has been an active supporter of many Texas chapters of Ducks Unlimited. In addition to entering Federal duck stamp competition each year, for the past three years she has been nominated for National Ducks Unlimited "Artist of the Year."

PREPARATION OF DOVE AND QUAIL

The preparation of doves and quail is very similar with one exception: quail are generally best if skinned, and doves are best when plucked, like duck and geese, with the skin left intact.

Always clean doves and quail at the end of a day's hunt, or even once at the noon break. The simplest way is to make two shallow incisions at either side of the neck below the breast, and then peel the bird apart at that junction, leaving the breast whole, and everything attached at the rear end. Clean out all entrails, especially the glands in the backbone area. Then fold back together. You can stuff birds easily this way, or with a slight pull, separate the breast from the rest of the bird. Always pick all the pinfeathers from the cavity carefully.

PREPARATION OF DUCK, PHEASANT, AND GEESE

Try to bleed these birds immediately if you don't field clean them at once. It is best to dry pluck these birds in the field at the end of the hunt. Once you have done this, you will know why you don't want to try it at home. Remove all entrails and wash the cavity by cutting down the center of the back with a sharp, heavy knife. Remove as much shot as possible while cleaning. After plucking and cleaning, singe the fowl before you come home, if possible. Before cooking, salt the interior lightly then wash out with ½ cup of sherry or brandy. When cooking a very gamey tasting bird, sauerkraut is the best stuffing to reduce that flavor.

PREPARATION OF RABBIT & SQUIRREL

Young rabbits and squirrels are the best to eat and females are generally more tender yet. Bleed the animal immediately after shooting, and skin by making a shallow incision around the mid section and pulling toward each end. Sever the feet and head and discard with the skin. Slit the animal down the front and clean out entrails carefully, trying not to puncture the stomach or intestines. Wash the cavity and exterior completely with 20 percent vinegar/water solution. A good marinade generally improves flavor and tenderness if done for 24 hours in the refrigerator.

PREPARATION OF WILD TURKEY

Bleed, pluck and singe the turkey after killing. Leave the skin on. A turkey is best prepared by hollowing the cavity and carefully removing the entrails. There are many ways of doing this, but be especially careful when cleaning the bird. Always field dress the same day it is killed, preferably immediately.

When cooking, always roast a turkey with the breast side down to prevent drying of the white meat. Baste often, and turn the breast up to brown during the last hour of cooking.

PREPARATION OF FROG LEGS

Freshness is the key to good fish and good frog legs. Always skin the legs after removing, and strip the tendon. You may wish to make one or two incisions in the main muscle to reduce movement in the pan. Never freeze more than 30 days. Never go fishing, especially on Texas stock tanks, without bringing home a mess of frog legs. These are so good pan fried that you will forget about the fish.

PREPARATION TIPS FOR THE BEST VENISON

If you are interested in a trophy, by all means shoot the oldest buck with the biggest rack, but if you want delicious venison, bring home a young doe. Most counties in Texas will give you a doe permit. Most important, field dress and bleed your deer immediately. Take out all internal organs and glands, and skin the animal as soon as possible. Cover with muslin and let it hang to cool. Have it processed and wrapped as soon as practicable. This will ensure tender meat without too much gamey flavor. Marinated meat is more tender and takes less time to cook.

LOUISIANA FRIED GATOR

Alligator meat
Red wine vinegar
Lemon
Salt

Red pepper
Yellow cornmeal
Flour
Oil for frying

Slice alligator meat into thin strips, about the same size you would fry catfish. Remove all white fat. Cover the slices in a bowl with red wine vinegar, the juice of a lemon, salt to taste, and a dash of red pepper (2 dashes if you have Cajun blood). Marinate in this mixture for only 30 minutes, then roll in yellow cornmeal and flour mixed 2 to 1, seasoned with more red pepper. Deep fry these strips until golden brown, about 6 to 8 minutes. Serve with wild rice and mushrooms or as an hors d'oeuvre.

BOSQUE COUNTY RATTLESNAKE

Rattlesnake
Flour
Soda crackers
Salt

Pepper
Garlic
Sage
Oil for frying

Bosque County rattlesnakes aren't hard to find, just don't pick one too large, as it might be older and tougher. Skin the snake and remove the entrails. Wash the cavity with vinegar and water. Cut into edible chunks and roll in a batter of equal parts flour and crushed soda crackers seasoned with salt, pepper, garlic, and a hint of sage. Fry quickly in hot oil until golden brown. This goes well as a side tidbit to fried or baked rabbit.

WILD BIRD MARINADE

2 tablespoons apple vinegar
1 tablespoon honey
1 small can crushed pineapple
1 or 2 green onions, chopped

¼ cup soy sauce
¾ cup salad oil
1 teaspoon garlic salt

Blend these at high speed for 1 minute. Marinate birds in refrigerator for at least 12 hours. Charcoal birds and baste with the sauce. Quail take approximately 1½ hours to charcoal. Doves take about 45 minutes. Place fire to the side and cover to smoke.

QUICK MARINATED DOVE

Dove breasts
Good Seasons Italian Dressing

Bacon

Clean dove breasts and wash well. Mix dressing according to package directions. Marinate dove breasts in Italian dressing for about 6 to 8 hours. Remove from marinade and wrap each dove breast with ½ slice of bacon. Return to marinade for 2 more hours. Charcoal until done. Avoid direct flame. Allow 1 dove per person as an appetizer. As a main course, allow 2 to 3 per person.

BARBECUED DOVE

Bacon grease, heated
Doves

Barbecue sauce
¼ cup chopped onions

Using a glass syringe with a large needle, shoot hot bacon grease on each side of the breastbone of doves. Cook for 15 to 20 minutes on pit, breast side up. Do not turn. Baste with favorite barbecue sauce and onions. The doves will puff up like quail and will stay moist. (The bacon grease is the secret to keeping the birds moist. Do not omit this step.)

DOVES AND QUAIL

6 to 8 doves or quail
Onion, thinly sliced
Salt, to taste

Pepper, to taste
2 tablespoons ground sage
Water

Place doves, breast side up, in a casserole. Place onion slices, salt, pepper and sage over the birds. Layer a strip of bacon over each row of birds. Add about ¼ inch of water to casserole. Cover tightly with foil and bake at 350° for about 2 hours.

BAKED DOVE SPECIAL

Doves
Garlic salt
Salt, to taste
Pepper, to taste

Bacon
Worcestershire sauce
Lemon juice

Sprinkle doves inside and out with garlic salt, salt and pepper. Wrap with ½ slice bacon and secure with toothpick. Baste with 2 parts Worcestershire to 1 part lemon juice. Bake, covered, at 325° for 1 hour, or until tender, basting regularly. Remove cover and increase oven temperature to 350° to let meat brown the last 15 minutes.

MINGUS DOVE PIE

4 bacon slices, quartered
8 doves
3 tablespoons flour
1⅓ cups water
1 large onion, chopped

1 small can mushrooms (stems and
  pieces)
Salt, to taste
Pepper, to taste
Ground sage

In Dutch oven fry bacon until crisp. Remove bacon and brown birds in grease. Remove birds and add flour to drippings left in pan. Stir until smooth and light brown. Make gravy by adding water. Return birds and bacon. Add onions and mushrooms, and season to taste with salt, pepper and sage. Cover and simmer, adding water if necessary, for 1 to 1½ hours or until birds are tender. Arrange in a baking dish and cover with topping. Bake, uncovered, at 425° for about 20 minutes, or until topping browns. Serves 4.

TOPPING
1 cup flour
1 teaspoon baking powder
½ teaspoon salt

½ cup Crisco
⅓ cup milk

Stir ingredients together until smooth. Knead several times on floured board. Roll out to about ⅛ inch thickness and arrange to fit baking dish.

OPENING DAY DOVES
In memory of Charlie Stevens.

12 whitewing doves
Salt
Pepper
6 bacon slices, halved

Lemon juice
Butter
Garlic

Season birds inside and out. Wrap each bird with ½ slice of bacon; secure with toothpick. Grill slowly over charcoal for about 1 hour. Baste with a lemon, butter and garlic sauce. Serve with wild rice. Mesquite is a good substitute for charcoal, but be careful—it makes a very hot fire. Serves 6.

DOVE AND WINE

Salt
Pepper
Onion powder
Seasoned salt
6 doves
Garlic powder
Cayenne pepper
½ cup flour

2 tablespoons bacon drippings
1 bunch green onions, chopped
½ cup chopped celery
1 medium white onion, chopped
¼ green pepper, chopped
1 tablespoon chopped parsley
1¼ cups cooking sherry
1 cup water

Generously sprinkle salt, pepper, onion powder and seasoned salt on the inside and outside of the doves. Lightly sprinkle garlic powder and cayenne over doves. Roll in flour and brown in bacon drippings over medium heat in an iron pot. Remove doves. Stir in green onions, celery, white onion, bell pepper and parsley; sauté. Stir in 1 cup sherry and water. Replace doves; cook, covered, about 2 hours, or until tender. Turn periodically, adding more seasoning, if desired. Stir in additional ¼ cup sherry about 15 minutes before serving. Serves 2.

SMOTHERED DOVES

10 doves	½ medium onion, sliced
Salt	2 teaspoons Lea & Perrins
Pepper	Worcestershire sauce
Flour	½ teaspoon ground thyme
3 tablespoons oil	1½ cups water
2 bacon slices	½ teaspoon ground sage

Lightly season doves with salt and pepper; dredge in flour. In deep skillet, brown doves on all sides in oil. Add bacon, diced in ½-inch pieces, and all other ingredients. Cover and simmer over low heat until tender, about 1 hour. Serve over crisp toast points. Serves 5.

SMOTHERED DOVES II

12 doves	3 tablespoons flour
Butter	6 tablespoons Worcestershire sauce
Salt	6 bacon slices
Pepper	Water
1 teaspoon sage	White wine

Rub cleaned dove breasts with butter. Sprinkle inside and out with salt, pepper, sage and a little flour. Place breast side down in a shallow baking dish. Sprinkle with Worcestershire sauce and lay a half slice of bacon on each bird. Add enough equal parts water and white wine to half cover. Bake at 450° for 25 minutes. Reduce heat to 400° and continue to cook for about 45 minutes or until tender. If necessary to prevent dryness, add water during baking. Henry Penner learned this from his mother, Mary, without a recipe, only lots of practice. Serves 4.

BORDER WHITEWING DOVES

16 whitewing doves	1 pound butter or margarine
Salt	1 small bottle Worcestershire sauce
Pepper	1 cup cream sherry
Garlic Powder	1½ cups water
Flour	Sage

Season birds with salt, pepper and garlic powder. Dust heavily with flour. Melt butter in a large skillet, preferably iron. Cook birds quickly on both sides and place in ungreased baking dish. Pour remaining butter in skillet over birds. Mix Worcestershire sauce, sherry, water, more salt and pepper, and a dash of sage; pour over birds. Bake, uncovered, at 300° for 2 hours. Add equal parts of water and sherry as needed to keep moist. Serves 8.

SPICED DUCK OR GOOSE

2 ducks or 1 goose	1 apple, halved
2 tablespoons olive oil	1 cup water
1 tablespoon salt	1 cup cream sherry or port
½ teaspoon pepper	¼ cup water
½ teaspoon oregano	1 tablespoon flour
½ teaspoon garlic powder	½ teaspoon paprika
2 onions (1 halved, 1 chopped)	3 tablespoons chopped green onions
1 celery rib, chopped	3 tablespoons chopped parsley

Rub ducks, inside and out, with olive oil and a mixture of salt, pepper, oregano and garlic powder. In each duck cavity place an onion half, celery, and apple. In large Dutch oven, brown ducks, uncovered, in oven at 400° for about 1 hour, or until brown. Put chopped second onion around ducks. Add water and sherry. Reduce heat to 350°, cover, and cook until tender (goose, 3 to 3½ hours; ducks, 2½ hours). Baste and add more liquid if necessary. When ducks are done (tender when pricked with fork), make a paste with water, flour and paprika. Add this to drippings. Add green onions and parsley. Stir until blended and right consistency. Add more sherry if needed. Freezes. Serves 6.

OUR ALEDO DUCK

4 ducks, teal or younger large ducks	Pepper
Milk	Flour
1 egg, beaten	Oil for frying
Salt	

Remove breasts from ducks and slice into bite sized pieces. Marinate for 2 to 3 hours in enough milk to cover; drain. Measure 1 cup fresh milk. Add beaten egg, salt and pepper, stirring to mix well. Dip duck into mixture, place in large plastic bag containing flour, and shake until well coated. Preheat oil and fry duck at 350° until brown on both sides.

ORANGE GLAZED TEAL

Teal	Garlic powder
Salt	2 bread slices
Pepper	Red wine
Red pepper	Orange marmalade

Preheat oven to 350°. Generously season teal inside and out with salt, pepper, red pepper and garlic powder. Soak bread in wine, and stuff bread into cavity. Spread layer of marmalade on bird. Wrap tightly in heavy duty foil, avoiding puncture of foil with sharp bones. Place on cookie sheet in oven. Reduce heat to 275° and bake for 1½ hours. Check for tenderness. Spread more marmalade on and pour red wine over the bird. Reseal and bake until meat pulls away from breastbone.

BAKED DUCK

Salt
Wild duck, cleaned and slit with pocket
Onion, sliced
Celery, sliced
Apple, sliced

Bacon
Water
Wild rice
¼ lemon per duck

Salt duck inside and out. Stuff with onion, celery and apple slices. Place in roasting pan, breast side up. Place a strip of bacon on each bird. Bake at 450° for 30 minutes, covered. Lower temperature to 350° and continue baking for 1½ hours. Remove lid during last 30 minutes. Serve with wild rice or rice pilaf. (The juice of ¼ lemon squeezed over the duck halfway through baking will help reduce the gamey flavor.)

DUCKS WITH CHERRIES

2 (4 to 5-pound) ducks
Salt
Pepper
¼ cup sugar
3 tablespoons cornstarch
½ teaspoon dry mustard

½ teaspoon ginger
½ teaspoon salt
1 (1-pound) can dark red cherries
½ cup orange juice
1 tablespoon grated orange rind
¼ teaspoon red food coloring

Sprinkle cavity of ducks with salt and pepper. Place on rack in shallow roasting pan, skin side down. Roast at 350° for 2 to 2½ hours (30 minutes per pound). Combine sugar, cornstarch, mustard, ginger and salt in saucepan. Drain cherries, reserving syrup. Add cherry syrup, orange juice and orange rind to cornstarch mixture. Stir in food coloring. Cook, stirring constantly, until thick and clear. Add cherries. Heat thoroughly. Serve over ducklings. Serves 8.

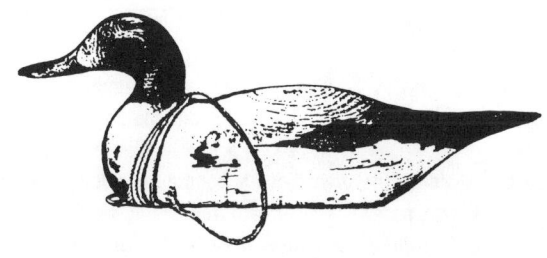

ROAST DUCK WITH PLUM SAUCE

½ cup packed brown sugar
1 tablespoon cornstarch
1 teaspoon dry mustard
⅛ teaspoon ground cloves
½ cup plum juice

⅓ cup orange juice
2 tablespoons brandy
2 cups pitted plums
Duck, roasted or baked

In a small saucepan, combine brown sugar, cornstarch, dry mustard and cloves. Stir in plum juice and orange juice until smooth. Cook, stirring constantly, until mixture thickens and comes to a boil. Add brandy, stir and simmer for 1 minute. Add plums and heat through. Serve over baked or roasted duck. Serves 4.

TEXARKANA TEAL

Teal
Salt
Pepper
¼ cup chopped onions
¼ cup chopped green pepper

¼ cup chopped celery
¼ cup chopped canned mushrooms
1 tablespoon French's mustard
½ teaspoon paprika
Margarine

Allow 1 teal per person. Season teal inside and out with salt and pepper. Mix onions, green pepper, celery and mushrooms; stuff teal with mixture. Blend mustard with paprika and rub mixture on teal. Spread a small amount of melted margarine in a baking dish. Arrange teal in dish and surround with remaining stuffing mixture. Cover and bake at 350° until tender, or pot roast on top of stove. Make gravy with drippings.

POT ROASTED STUFFED DUCK OR GOOSE

1 duck or goose
1½ medium onions, chopped
½ green pepper, chopped
½ cup chopped parsley
1 teaspoon pepper

1 teaspoon salt
Garlic (optional)
1 cup oil
1½ cups water
½ cup cooking sherry

Slit top of duck breast, following breastbone to bottom but not cutting through the bottom. Mix onions, green pepper, parsley, pepper, salt and garlic; stuff mixture into the opening. Heat cooking oil in a large pot and brown duck, turning several times. When well browned, pour in a mixture of water and cooking sherry. Cover and cook on medium heat for 1½ to 2 hours or until tender, adding more water if needed. (This yields a good gravy.)

QUICK BAKED DUCK OR GOOSE

Duck or goose
Salt
½ apple
Onion wedge

½ cup sauerkraut
Bacon slice
½ cup water
Flour

Season duck or goose inside and out with salt. Stuff cavity with apple, onion and sauerkraut. Lay bacon slice over breast. Bake in covered roaster at 500° for 20 minutes. Add water and cover. Lower heat to 325° and bake duck for 2 hours, goose for 3 hours. Thicken drippings with flour to prepare gravy.

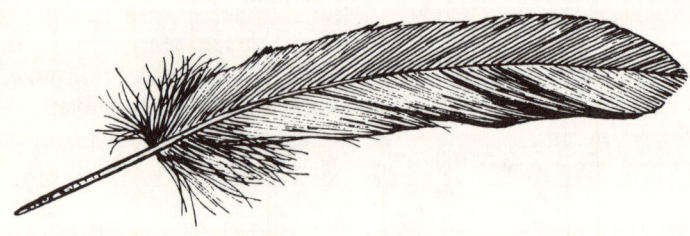

HOT POT DUCK

2 mallards or pintails
Salt
Pepper
Pinch of sage
1 large green pepper, chopped
2 large yellow onions, chopped
1 large apple or potato, chopped
3 tablespoons or more catsup

2 tablespoons Worcestershire sauce
1 teaspoon red pepper
1½ teaspoons salt
2 teaspoons pepper
Water
½ cup red wine
½ cup vegetable shortening

Season cleaned ducks with salt, pepper and sage. Prepare stuffing by mixing green pepper, onions, apple or potato, catsup, Worcestershire sauce, red pepper, salt and pepper. Stuff ducks and secure with toothpicks. Brown ducks in oil in a large iron pot over medium heat for about 40 minutes, or until brown on all sides. Add enough water to cover bottom third of duck. Cover and simmer until ducks are tender, 3 to 4 hours. Add water if necessary. Adjust seasonings. Add red wine during last 30 minutes of cooking. (The catsup helps remove the wild taste.)

PENNER SPECIAL

Breast of 1 (3½ to 4-pound) duck or
   goose
4 tablespoons sweet butter
3½ tablespoons chopped green pepper
4 medium mushroom caps
1 cup heavy cream

1 egg yolk
1 teaspoon salt
Few grains pepper
3 tablespoons sherry, warmed
6 truffle slices

Remove breasts from cooked duck and cut into large pieces. Melt butter in a shallow pan or chafing dish; add green pepper and cook for 2 minutes. Slice mushroom caps (about 1 cup sliced) and add to butter and green pepper; cook 2 minutes. Add meat and cream; cook for 2 minutes, stirring constantly. Remove from heat and blend in broken egg yolk. Season with salt and pepper and stir in sherry. Serve on hot toast with sliced truffles. Serves 4.

BARBECUED DUCK

2 large ducks
1 garlic clove, quartered
Vinegar
Salt
Pepper

1 green pepper, halved and cored
1 red onion, halved
1 celery rib, cut into chunks
1 small bottle barbecue sauce
6 ounces crushed pineapple

Slit both sides of duck breast and put ¼ garlic clove in each side. Rub duck with vinegar, salt and pepper. Stuff cavities with green pepper, onion and celery. Wrap tightly in foil and place in baking pan. Bake at 250° for 7 hours. Mix barbecue sauce with crushed pineapple. Open foil and add barbecue sauce mixture. Rewrap and bake 1 more hour. Serves 4.

CAJUN DUCK

3 wild ducks
Salt
Pepper
Pinch of oregano
Red pepper
Flour

2 cups chopped green onions
2 cups chopped parsley
Bread (optional)
Corn oil
1 tablespoon flour

Season ducks with salt, pepper, oregano and red pepper; roll in flour and stuff with onions and parsley. Close cavity with a slice of bread (optional). Place ducks in hot oil in Dutch oven. Brown and lower heat. Remove excess oil. Add flour and stir constantly to make a roux, using a small amount of water if necessary. Cover and steam until tender, about 40 to 50 minutes. Remove onions and parsley. Serve with steamed rice. Serves 3 to 6.

WILD DUCK WITH OLIVE SAUCE

6 small ducks
3 small onions, halved
Salt
Water
½ cup vinegar
12 peppercorns
¼ teaspoon thyme
¼ cup Worcestershire sauce
3 bay leaves

Salt
Pepper
6 bacon strips
2 tablespoons sugar
3 tablespoons cornstarch
1 (6-ounce) can frozen orange juice
   concentrate
2 cups water
½ cup chopped black olives

Stuff ducks with onion halves and season with salt inside and out. To tenderize, place ducks in a large pot half full of water, adding vinegar, peppercorns, thyme, Worcestershire sauce and bay leaves. Boil for 15 to 30 minutes, or until tender, but not falling apart. Remove ducks from vinegar solution and wash, removing onion. Arrange breast side down in deep roasting pan. Sprinkle with salt and pepper and lay a bacon strip on each duck. Mix sugar and cornstarch and blend in orange juice concentrate. Slowly add water, cooking over low heat until hot. Add olives. Pour over ducks. Bake, covered, at 350° for about 1 hour, basting often. Serves 4 to 6.

DUCK, SPANISH STYLE

Wild duck
Salt
Pepper
White onions, sliced
Olive oil
Boiling water
1 white onion, chopped

1 green pepper, chopped
1 garlic clove, chopped
½ cup chopped celery
½ cup chopped carrots
8 ounces mild picante sauce
Mushrooms, sliced
Stuffed olives, sliced

If duck is frozen and well cleaned, do not thaw. Season with salt and pepper, stuff with sliced onions and brown in a cast iron roaster. Add boiling water to the depth of ½-inch. Bake, covered, at 325° for 1 hour. Pour off liquid to remove the wild flavor. Remove onions. Sauté in a 3-quart Dutch oven the onion, green pepper and garlic. Add celery, carrots and picante sauce. Pour mixture over duck and bake, covered, at 350° for about 1½ to 2 hours, or until tender. About 5 minutes before serving, add mushrooms and olives. Serve sliced with gravy over steamed rice. Serves 4.

WILD DUCK

1 medium or large wild duck
8 garlic slivers (about size of grain of corn)
Salt
Red pepper
Pepper
1 large turnip, peeled and quartered
3 bacon slices
1 bay leaf

Pierce duck breast to the bone in 4 places. Insert garlic sliver into each hole. Season liberally with salt, red pepper and pepper. Insert turnip quarter into each duck cavity. Wrap each bacon strip completely around the duck, to almost completely cover it. Place duck on a bay leaf in a sheet of heavy foil. Wrap carefully to make as airtight as possible, raising ends to prevent drip. Avoid puncturing foil. Transfer to a pan and bake at 325° for 3 hours. Do not open foil. Serve in unopened foil, 1 duck per person. Best with wild rice mix and sautéed mushrooms.

FRICASSEED GOOSE

1 goose, cut in small pieces
Salt
Pepper
¼ cup bacon drippings
4 to 5 tablespoons flour
¾ cup chopped green onions
¼ cup chopped green pepper
¼ cup chopped celery

Parsley, chopped
3 cups water
½ cup red wine (Chianti)
¼ teaspoon hot sauce
Pinch garlic salt
Pinch Lawry's seasoned salt
Pinch Lawry's seasoned pepper

Season goose pieces with salt and pepper. Heat bacon drippings in a Dutch oven and brown goose pieces. Remove goose. Stir in flour to make a dark brown roux. Sauté onions, green pepper, celery and parsley. Add goose, water, red wine and hot sauce. Season to taste with garlic salt and Lawry's seasoned salt and seasoned pepper. Cover and slowly simmer for about 2 hours or until meat is tender. Better if prepared ahead. Serves 4.

APPLE-APRICOT GOOSE

1 (6 to 8-pound) young wild goose,
   thawed
Salt
Pepper
Juice of 1 lemon
¼ cup butter
¼ cup chopped onion

1 cup chopped tart apples
1 cup chopped apricots
2 cups soft bread crumbs
½ teaspoon salt, or to taste
⅛ teaspoon pepper
4 to 6 bacon slices

Rub goose inside and out with salt, pepper and lemon juice. Melt butter in large saucepan. Add onions and cook until tender. Stir in apple, apricots, bread crumbs, salt and pepper. Stuff mixture inside goose. Layer bacon strips over goose. Soak cheesecloth in melted butter; lay cheesecloth over goose. Roast at 325° for 20 to 25 minutes per pound, or until tender.

YOUNG PHEASANT OR CORNISH GAME HENS

4 pheasant or Cornish hens
2 teaspoons salt
2 teaspoons pepper

1 teaspoon sage or thyme
4 parsley sprigs
8 teaspoons butter

Preheat oven to 350°. Season each pheasant or hen with ½ teaspoon salt, ½ teaspoon pepper and ¼ teaspoon sage or thyme. Place in center of an 18-inch foil square. Top with a parsley sprig, and wrap securely with foil. Transfer to a baking sheet and bake for 1 hour. Remove pheasants or hens and increase oven temperature to 425°. Carefully open foil, then brush hens with butter. Return to oven to brown for 5 to 10 minutes. Serve with juices accumulated in foil. Serves 4.

BRANDIED PHEASANT

6 (1-pound) pheasants
Salt
Pepper
½ cup butter
2 carrots
2 bay leaves
2 celery ribs
2 garlic cloves

1 medium onion
6 peppercorns
12 parsley stalks
Pinch thyme
3 ounces brandy
1 pint chicken stock
½ cup flour
Mushrooms, sautéed

Preheat oven to 450°. Season birds with salt and pepper and brown with butter. Place in a pan over carrots, bay leaves, celery, garlic, onion, peppercorns, parsley and thyme. Add brandy and chicken stock, covering bottom third of birds. Bake, uncovered, until browned. Lower temperature to 350° and cover. This slow process may take about 1½ hours. Remove birds and thicken sauce with flour. Pour sauce over birds and garnish with sautéed mushrooms. Serves 6.

PHEASANT CASSEROLE

2 pheasants, split at breasts
1 pound fresh mushrooms, sliced

1 green pepper, sliced
3 celery stalks, sliced

Layer pheasant, mushrooms and green pepper in a deep casserole. Cover with sauce. Bake, uncovered, at 350° for 1 hour. Top with celery and bake 15 more minutes. Serve over rice. Serves 6.

SAUCE
1½ sticks butter
1 medium sized bottle Heinz 57 Savory
   Sauce

½ pint whipping cream

Combine sauce ingredients in saucepan. Heat on low.

EAST TEXAS QUAIL IN WINE SAUCE

8 quail
Salt
Pepper
Flour

Shortening
3 (10¾-ounce) cans cream of
   mushroom soup
1½ cups white wine

Season quail with salt, pepper and flour. Fry in shortening until golden brown. Transfer to a casserole dish. Mix soup with wine and pour mixture over quail. Cover and bake at 350° for 1½ hours. Remove cover and bake for 30 minutes. Serves 4.

QUAIL WITH BROWN RICE STUFFING

½ teaspoon coarse salt
Pinch pepper
¼ teaspoon curry powder

¼ teaspoon ginger
8 quail

Combine salt, pepper, curry and ginger. Rub mixture over birds.

STUFFING

1 tablespoon butter
1 small white onion, minced
1 garlic clove, minced
¼ pound fresh mushrooms, sliced
½ teaspoon curry powder

½ cup brown rice
2 tablespoons chopped green olives
1 cup plus 2 tablespoons chicken broth
2 teaspoons grated orange peel

Heat butter in a large skillet, stir in onions and garlic. Set aside 8 mushroom slices, and add remaining mushrooms to the skillet. Cook briefly, then stir in curry powder. Add rice and sauté over medium heat for 2 minutes. Stir in olives and broth. Cover skillet and bring mixture to a boil. Reduce heat and simmer for 30 minutes, or until rice is almost tender. Add grated orange peel. Fluff rice. Spoon stuffing into cavities, and pull a mushroom slice over the opening to seal. Secure legs with toothpicks.

TO FINISH

2 tablespoons butter
2 tablespoons oil
¼ cup dry white wine

Juice of ½ orange
1 egg yolk
Watercress

Heat butter and oil in a large skillet. Add the birds, 1 at a time, turning to coat and glaze all sides. Place birds on a rack in a roasting pan; baste with wine. Cover loosely with foil and roaast in a preheated oven at 375° for about 30 minutes. Uncover and baste with drippings and orange juice. Reduce temperature to 325° and bake for 20 more minutes, or until tender and golden. Reduce temperature to 150° and hold until ready to serve. Just before serving, strain the drippings into a small saucepan. Beat egg yolk with a little of the hot drippings, then return to pan and heat, stirring to thicken slightly. Do not boil. Place the birds on a large platter. Spoon some sauce over birds, and garnish with watercress. Serve remaining sauce separately. Serves 4.

QUAIL WITH CREAM SAUCE

12 quail	½ cup finely chopped green pepper
Salt	¼ cup minced parsley
Pepper	8 ounces mushrooms, lightly sautéed
1 stick butter, melted	1 cup table cream
1 tablespoon flour	¼ cup white wine
1 large onion, finely chopped	1 chicken bouillon cube

Season quail with salt and pepper. Brown in butter over medium heat in a Dutch oven. Remove birds. Stir in flour, onion and green pepper; cover and cook slowly over low heat until onion is transparent. Add parsley, mushrooms and cream. Stir in birds. Bake, uncovered, at 350° for 1 hour or until tender. Baste twice. Thin gravy if needed with equal parts white wine and water. Quail are cooked when fork easily enters breast. Serve on buttered noodles or rice. Serves 6.

TED'S WINTHORST BACON QUAIL

Quail	Butter
Salt	Bacon
Pepper	Water

Season quail with salt and pepper. Place a spoonful of butter into cavity of each bird. Wrap a bacon strip around bird and secure with toothpick. Transfer to a baking dish and top with a little butter. Add small amount of water to pan. Cover and bake at 350° for 2 hours or until tender. Birds prepared this way are often roasted on a green willow branch over a campfire. We've often had these as lunch during a hunt.

TOM CARVEY'S QUAIL BREASTS

4 to 6 quail breasts	¼ cup finely chopped onion
Salt	½ cup finely chopped mushrooms
Pepper	1 tablespoon finely chopped parsley
Flour	½ cup sauterne
Butter	½ cup heavy cream

Wash, dry and rub quail with salt and pepper. Dust with flour and sauté in butter. Remove birds and add onion, mushrooms and parsley. Return birds and add sauterne. Cook, covered, basting frequently for 30 minutes. At the last minute, stir in cream and heat thoroughly. Serve with wild rice. This recipe was given to Mary Talbot Penner by Tom Carvey, who managed the Fort Worth Club in the 1940s. Serves 4.

MESQUITE SMOKED TURKEY

Wild turkey	Onions
Garlic	Butter, melted
Ground sage	

Stuff turkey breast with garlic, sage and onions. Smoke on outdoor smoker, basting occasionally with melted butter. Cook approximately 45 minutes per pound with temperature not to exceed 250°. Wild turkey is tougher than domesticated and requires long, slow cooking. Use mesquite wood soaked in water to add a smoky flavor.

TURKEY IN WINE SAUCE

2 cups dry vermouth	2 garlic cloves, pressed
1 cup soy sauce	Juice of 1 lemon
1 cup Wesson oil	Wild turkey

Prepare sauce by mixing vermouth, soy sauce, oil, garlic and lemon. One day before serving, inject turkey with sauce, using a baster with an injector attachment. Inject and baste top of turkey hourly with sauce until ready to cook. Try not to make too many holes. The entire sauce recipe should be used by the time the turkey is ready to bake. Place turkey into a roasting bag and bake at 275° to 300° for 35 minutes per pound, or until done.

NORTH MAIN BARBECUED DEER

Deer ham
Meat tenderizer
Bacon

4 to 5 green onions
Homemade barbecue sauce

Cover deer ham with meat tenderizer; let stand for 30 minutes. Make at least 3 to 4 deep crosswise cuts in the ham. Be sure the cuts are as close to the bone as possible. Into each cut place a bacon slice. Cover the top of the ham with bacon slices and wrap with string. Wrap onions and ham in foil which has several slits in top. Smoke for 5 hours or longer, depending on size of ham. Baste with barbecue sauce each hour, and more often during the last hour.

MAC'S VENISON STEAK
My dad's recipe.

Flour
Salt
Red pepper
Pepper
2 to 3 pounds deer steak

Oil
1 large onion, chopped
2 tablespoons flour
¼ cup sherry

Mix flour, salt, red pepper and pepper. Roll steak in the mixture. Fry meat in oil until well done. While meat cooks, sauté onion in a small amount of oil in a covered, large iron pot. Set meat aside and pour off all but a small amount of grease. Brown flour in the grease, stirring constantly. Add enough water to make soupy and pour this into the sautéed onions. Add enough water to make a gravy and then add the meat. Cover and simmer for 45 to 60 minutes, or until meat is tender. Add sherry and more water as needed about halfway as gravy cooks down. Serve with jalapeños.

GRANDFATHER COFFMAN'S
RANGER TEXAS VENISON SAUSAGE

5 pounds venison
2½ pounds lean pork
2 pounds fatty pork
6 tablespoons salt
5 tablespoons pepper

3 teaspoons red pepper
3 tablespoons monosodium glutamate
2 tablespoons sage
Sausage casings

Grind venison and shape into large thin patties. Grind lean and fatty pork together, shape into patties and place on top of venison patties. Mix salt, pepper, red pepper, monosodium glutamate and sage in a jar; shake well. Sprinkle three-fourths of the seasoning as evenly as possible over the patties. Work seasoned patties with hands for several minutes to evenly distribute the ingredients. Fry small patty to test seasoning and adjust if desired. For sausage kept longer than 2 months, buy sausage casings. Rinse casings in water to remove salt, and make into link sausage. This usually takes 2 people—1 to turn the sausage press and 1 to guide the sausage into 1-foot links as it leaves the press. Freeze. Before cooking, puncture links several times with a fork.

JELLY GLAZED VENISON ROAST

8 pounds venison roast
Salt
2 teaspoons paprika
Garlic salt
2 tablespoons olive oil
1½ cups sherry

4 to 6 bacon slices
Bacon grease
1 tablespoon flour
¼ cup water
3 to 4 tablespoons currant jelly

The night before cooking, trim the meat well. Pierce meat and season with salt, paprika and garlic salt. Make crosswise slits in meat and rub with olive oil. Pour ½ cup sherry over roast. On day of cooking, cover meat with raw bacon slices and place on rack. Bake, uncovered, at 250° for 40 minutes per pound. Mix bacon grease and ½ cup sherry, and baste meat often with the mixture. One hour before serving (not included in baking time), remove meat from pan. Skim off as much fat as possible from the basting sauce. Mix the flour and water together and stir in with the sauce to form the gravy. Then add 2 tablespoons of the jelly to the gravy and mix well. Replace meat in pan with the gravy. Pour ½ cup sherry over roast and dot with remaining jelly. Continue baking at 275° for about 1 hour, basting with gravy. Let stand a few minutes before carving. (It is better to undercook than overcook.) Serves 8.

HONDO'S VENISON CHILI

My old camp counselor.

4 pounds ground venison
4 large white onions, chopped
2½ quarts water
5 (8-ounce) cans tomato sauce
3 ounces 2 Alarm Chili seasoning
   mixture

6 ounces chili powder
3 (15½-ounce) cans pinto beans
Salt, to taste
Red pepper, to taste

In large pot cook meat and onion in water until tender. Add tomato sauce, chili seasoning and chili powder. Cook 2 hours on medium to low heat, allowing chili to softly bubble. Add beans 30 minutes before serving. Season to taste. Serving suggestions: place Doritos in a large bowl, top with chili, chopped onions and grated cheese. In South Texas, they use Mexican black beans instead of pintos. Hondo Crouch loved to talk about this chili.

DUDE RANCH VENISON

2 pounds venison backstrap
1 stick butter
2 teaspoons garlic powder
1 teaspoon cumin
2 teaspoons celery salt
2 tablespoons Maggi or Worcestershire
   sauce

1 (16-ounce) package Philadelphia
   cream cheese
¼ cup dry sherry
1 jigger brandy (optional)

Preheat oven to 350°. Remove all fat from venison. Melt butter, reserving 2 tablespoons. Add garlic powder, cumin and celery salt. Place venison in oblong pan and pour melted seasoned butter and Maggi sauce over meat. Bake, uncovered, for 35 minutes. Turn while cooking. While venison is baking, place the reserved butter in a large skillet. Add cream cheese and mash with a spatula over medium heat for 20 minutes, or until mixture becomes a thick gravy. Add sherry and cook for 10 more minutes. (Carefully watch gravy to prevent burning.) Remove backstrap from oven and cut into ½-inch steaks. Pour juices from venison into gravy and mix. Add venison and cook for 5 more minutes. Add brandy, ignite and serve flaming at the table. Serve over noodles tossed in butter and parsley. Serves 4.

BROILED VENISON ROAST

1 (3 to 4-pound) venison roast
Seasoned salt
Bacon (¼-inch slices)
Garlic, thinly sliced
1 cup wine vinegar
3 cups water

1 medium onion, chopped
1 tablespoon peppercorns
1 tablespoon hot sauce
1 teaspoon cloves
2 celery stalks, chopped

Make slits in the roast. Sprinkle seasoned salt over bacon and garlic; mix well. Stuff mixture inside slits in roast. Mix remaining ingredients over low heat. Pour over roast in an enamel or glass baking dish and marinate for 8 to 12 hours, turning every hour. Remove from the marinade and drain. Brown well over a charcoal fire, insert a meat thermometer, cover and cook slowly until desired doneness. If fire goes out, finish in oven at 325°. For a jucier roast, place bacon slices over meat as it cooks. Serve with wild rice and hot pepper jelly.

PENNER'S DRUNK SQUIRREL

Salt
Pepper
Flour
3 squirrels, cut into pieces

Oil
2 cans beer
Comino

Mix salt, pepper and flour; coat squirrel pieces in the mixture. Fry in deep hot oil until brown; drain on paper towels. Place in casserole, pour beer over, and sprinkle with comino. Bake, covered, at 300° for at least 2 hours, or until tender. Freezes well. You'll never have a tough squirrel with this recipe, and the beer gravy is terrific. This method may also be used on doves if you're not sure they are young and tender.

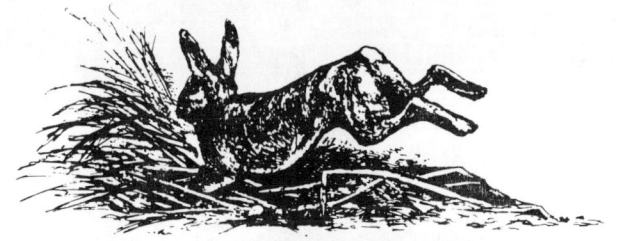

GRANDMA MC'S RABBIT AND SAUCE

1 rabbit, cut into pieces
¼ cup wine
¼ cup cider vinegar
½ teaspoon celery salt
¼ cup oil
2 cups chopped onion
½ can tomatoes

½ can Ro-Tel tomatoes
2 garlic cloves, minced
1 cup water
1 teaspoon salt
½ bunch green onion tops, chopped
¼ cup minced parsley

Soak rabbit overnight in mixture of wine, cider vinegar and celery salt. Remove from marinade and drain. Save marinade. Brown rabbit in hot oil in a 4-quart heavy Dutch oven. Remove each piece as it is browned. In same oil brown onions until dark. Add tomatoes and Ro-Tel tomatoes. Continue stirring until dark. Add marinade, garlic and water. Let cook over low heat until oil rises to top. Add rabbit pieces and salt. Cover and cook slowly until rabbit is tender, usually 2 hours. Just before serving, add green onion tops and parsley. Serve over hot, fluffy rice. Serves 4 to 6.

SAUTÉED RABBIT AND ONIONS

Rabbit
Salt
Pepper
Flour

3 tablespoons butter
Onion, chopped
1 cup sour cream

Cut rabbit into pieces. Mix salt, pepper and flour; roll rabbit pieces in the mixture. In skillet, heat butter and sauté rabbit until golden brown. Cover with thick layer of chopped onions. Pour sour cream over rabbit and onions. Transfer to greased baking dish, cover and bake at 300° for 1 hour or until rabbit is tender.

JACKSBORO FROG LEGS

Frog legs (4 per person)
Buttermilk
Flour

Salt
Pepper
Oil

Soak frog legs in buttermilk for 1 hour. Mix flour, salt and pepper in a paper bag. Shake 4 to 6 frog legs at a time in the bag. Fry in hot oil in a heavy iron pot until golden brown.

SAUCE
1 stick butter, melted
½ teaspoon Tabasco
2 tablespoons lemon juice

1 teaspoon Worcestershire sauce
1 garlic clove, pressed

Combine ingredients in a saucepan; heat. Serve frog legs on a large platter with the sauce drizzled liberally over them.

FROG LEGS PROVENCAL

12 frog legs
¼ pound butter
1 small onion, thinly sliced
8 fresh mushrooms, sliced
1 carrot, finely chopped

4 ripe tomatoes, chopped
1 garlic clove
1 teaspoon basil
Salt
Pepper

Sauté frog legs lightly with butter, onion and mushrooms. Remove frog legs. Add carrots, tomatoes, garlic and basil. Simmer until mixture thickens, about 10 minutes. Season to taste with salt and pepper. Pour over frog legs in buttered baking dish and bake at 350° for 15 to 20 minutes. Serves 4.

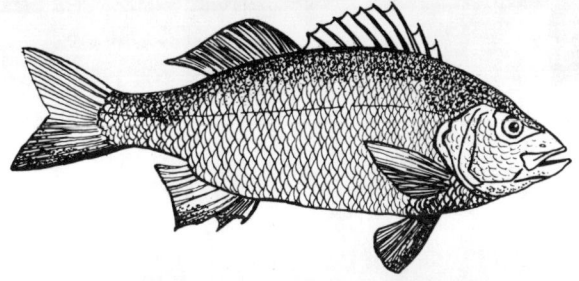

MY DAD'S PERCH FILLETS

4 perch fillets, boned
Pepper
3 tablespoons chopped chives
1½ tablespoons butter, melted

Salt
¼ pint lump crabmeat
2 ounces water

Pat fillets dry. Sprinkle with pepper. In a heavy skillet, sauté chives in butter. Add fillets and cook until outer rim turns white. Turn over, salt, and place half the crab meat around outer edge of skillet. Cook on high heat until fillets turn slightly white all over; turn fillets and crab meat; season with salt. Add water, cover tightly, and cook for 1 minute. The entire cooking time should be only 3 to 3½ minutes. Serve immediately on hot dinner plates, spooning chives and crab meat over fillets. Serves 2.

MARY PENNER'S BAKED BASS

1 (3½ to 5-pound) bass, dressed
Butter
Salt
3 bay leaves
4 onion slices

½ cup white wine
2 cups tomato puree
2 tablespoons Worcestershire sauce
1 thick bacon slice

Dry fish thoroughly. Rub inside and out with butter and salt. Stuff cavity with bay leaves and onion slices. Mix wine, tomato puree and Worcestershire sauce. Baste fish with this sauce and top with bacon. Cover and bake at 350° for 1 hour.

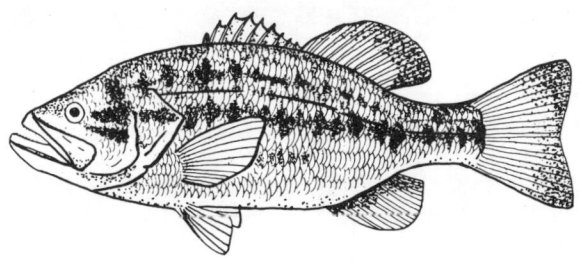

FRIED CATFISH

Fresh caught Brazos Catfish Fillets
Corn Meal
Lemon Pepper
Pepper
Flour
Salt
Milk

Mix Lemon Pepper, Pepper, Flour and Salt in Cornmeal. Dip Catfish in Milk and place in a paper sack with Cornmeal Mix.

Deep fry in an iron skillet. Serve with French Fries, White Gravy, Lemon, and Ice Tea.

David L. McWilliams

QUAIL

8 quail	1½ sticks butter or margarine
Milk	Water or white wine
Flour	1 tablespoon Worcestershire sauce
Salt	Garlic salt
Pepper	Juice of 2 lemons

Put quail in a deep bowl and cover with milk; soak for 2 hours. Drain and pat dry. Lightly flour and salt and pepper the quail. Brown in butter in a skillet. Transfer to a baking dish, breast side up. Pour water in skillet and scrape bottom; pour over quail in baking dish. Sprinkle each quail with ½ teaspoon Worcestershire sauce, dash of garlic salt and lemon juice. Cover with foil and bake at 350° for 1 hour or until tender. Serve over toast points with pan juices.

Louis Ramsay
Cotton Bowl Director

WILD DUCK

2 ducks, wild or domestic	1 cup water
Salt, to taste	1½ cups sherry
Pepper, to taste	1 tablespoon flour
2 onions	¼ cup water
1 celery rib	3 tablespoons chopped parsley
¼ cup oil	

Season the ducks inside and out with salt and pepper. In the cavity of the ducks place 1 onion and ½ celery rib. Brown ducks in an open, heavy roasting pan at 400° in the oil. Wilt the chopped second onion in the fat around the ducks. Add 1 cup water and the sherry. Reduce heat to 350°, cover and roast until done. Baste and add more liquid if needed. Toward the end of the cooking time, make a paste of flour and water; add to drippings, stirring constantly. Add chopped parsley. If desired, add more sherry. Serves 6.

Morgan "Major" Ogilvie, Jr.
Joe Piper Inc.

CHARLEY'S DEER LEASE CHILI

2 pounds ground chuck
2 ounces chili powder
1 teaspoon cumin
1½ teaspoons salt

½ teaspoon pepper
1 teaspoon garlic powder
Cracker crumbs
Kidney or pinto beans (optional)

In a large pot place enough water to cover the meat. Add chili powder, cumin, salt, pepper and garlic powder; bring to a boil. Reduce heat and simmer for 2 hours or until meat is tender. Thicken with cracker meal and simmer over low heat for another 30 minutes. Kidney or pinto beans may be added before serving. Serves 8.

Ann Shira
Administrative Assistant
Cotton Bowl Athletic Association

ANGELO'S QUAIL GOURMET

8 to 10 quail
Salt
Pepper
Flour

Vegetable oil
3 whole garlic
1 can Bing cherries
1 cup rosé wine

Season quail with salt and pepper. Dredge in flour. In large skillet, heat vegetable oil and brown quail on all sides. Drain oil but leave flour crust in skillet. Dice garlic and add cherries, juice and all, and wine. Cover. Simmer on low heat for 30 minutes or until tender. Serve with white, brown or wild rice.

Angelo George
Angelo's Bar-B-Que

COLORADO MOUNTAIN TROUT

Poach trout filets in a small amount of champagne, not more than 5 minutes, over a low heat. If you are poaching **4 medium sized trout filets**, you should use approximately ½ **cup of champagne.**

Remove the filets to a plate gently and set aside. Reserve ¼ **cup of the champagne** and **fish broth** from the pan. If you do not have enough liquid, add more champagne to make ¼ cup.

Add 1 **cup of heavy cream** and simmer slowly till the liquid is reduced by half.

Add 1 **cup shredded sorrel** and ¼ **cup of green peppercorns** to the liquid and simmer to desired thickness. Pour sauce over filets and serve immediately.

Serve with rice, a green vegetable and vegetable fruit wedges.
Recipe used at the Governor's Mansion in Denver, Colorado.

Mrs. Richard D. Lamm
Governor's Mansion
Denver, Colorado

Vegetables

SOUTHERN METHODIST
UNIVERSITY

An independent coeducational institution located in Dallas, Southern Methodist
University was founded in 1911 by what is today The United Methodist Church. Classes
began in 1915 in two buildings with 706 students.

With an undergraduate enrollment of 6,117 and a faculty of 603, SMU offers an in-
timate learning environment. The programs available to students include 670 undergraduate majors in Dedman College and three undergraduate professional schools.

Leading figures in the administration of SMU athletics are university president Dr. L.
Donald Shields, SWC faculty representative Lonnie Kliever, athletic director Bob Hitch,
and head football coach Bobby Collins.

dallas cowboys football club

ZUCCHINI – SQUASH CASSEROLE
(Serves 6)

1-1/2 cups sliced zucchini

1-1/2 cups sliced yellow squash

1/2 cup sour cream

3/4 cup grated cheddar cheese

1/2 teaspoon oregano

3 Tablespoons butter

1/2 cup chopped onion

Simmer squash until tender. Saute onion in butter and add oregano. Heat sour cream stirring in cheddar cheese and onion to make sauce. (Do not boil.) Drain squash and place in buttered casserole and cover with cheese sauce. Bake at 350° for 20 minutes.

Tom Landry

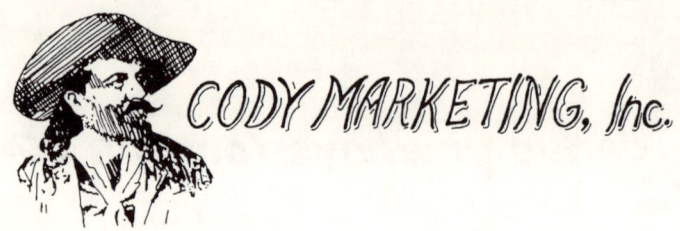

CODY MARKETING, Inc.

Dallas, Texas, July 8, 1986

Gentlemen:

The following recipe for SWEET & SOUR BLACK-EYED PEAS is a
favorite of both of our families.

```
3     (15-ounce) cans black-eyed peas, drained
2     cups cooked carrots, diced
1     medium onion, chopped
1     medium green pepper, chopped
1     (4-ounce) can diced pimento, drained
1     clove garlic, minced
3/4   cup sugar
3/4   cup vinegar, white
2/3   cup cooking oil, (Wesson)
5     tablespoons Worcestershire sauce
1     (10-ounce) can condensed tomato soup
```

Mix all ingredients together. Chill and serve. Keeps for days
in refrigerator and improves with age. Great served hot in
winter.

Good luck with your new book!

Betty Lee Stringer

Jackie Day

BAKED HASH BROWNS

Two - 1 lb. packages of defrosted frozen hash brown potatoes
1/2 cup melted margarine
1 teas. salt
1/4 teas pepper
1 1/2 cup chopped onion
1 can cream of chicken soup (undiluted)
1 - 12 oz. carton sour cream

1/2 cup melted margarine
2 cups crushed corn flakes

Mix first seven ingredients together and place in an ungreased 11 x-

13 x 2 inch baking dish.

Top with corn flakes mixed with melted margarine.

Bake at 350 degrees for 45 minutes.

HANK STRAM

State of Louisiana

EXECUTIVE DEPARTMENT

Baton Rouge

70804-9004

GOVERNOR EDWARDS' FAVORITE RECIPE

LAS VEGAS RICE

1 Stick Margarine	1 Teaspoon Salt
2 Cups of Rice	4 Cups of Water
1 Medium Onion Chopped	1 Can Ripe Olives Choppe

Melt margarine; add rice and cook over medium heat until rice is dark brown. Add onions, continue to cook until rice is very brown, about 20 minutes. Add water and salt, boil until water is almost evaporated and is just bubbling on top of rice. Cover and reduce heat to simmer for about one hour or until rice is thoroughly cooked. When ready to serve, add olives and serve immediately.

Serves: 6 to 8

CORN PUDDING

2 cups white corn (canned whole kernel or fresh, cut off cob)	4 Tablespoons melted butter
	4 eggs
8 Tablespoons flour	4 teaspoons sugar
4 cups milk	1 teaspoon salt

Beat eggs well; add milk; and stir into a mixture of the corn, flour, salt, sugar, and butter. Bake in a 450 degree oven in a round, 2-quart or an 8-inch square pyrex. Bake for 40-45 minutes. Stir vigorously with a long-handled fork at 10-minute intervals while baking, disturbing the top as little as possible.

This traditional southern vegetable pudding is a wonderful accompaniment for fried chicken or country ham.

Folklore says that eating Black-eyed Peas on New Year's Day brings good luck!

Aunt Rublelene's Black-eyed Peas with Rice

2 slices bacon
1 medium onion, chopped
1 (15-ounce) can black-eyed peas, drained
1 (14-1/2-ounce) can stewed tomatoes, undrained
1 cup cooked regular rice
1/4 teaspoon salt
1/4 teaspoon pepper

Cook bacon in a large skillet until crisp; remove bacon, reserving 2 tablespoons drippings in skillet. Crumble bacon, and set aside. Saute onion in drippings until tender. Add remaining ingredients, stirring well. Spoon mixture into a 1-1/2 quart casserole. Bake at 350 degrees for 30 minutes. Garnish with reserved bacon. Yield: 6 servings.

Gene Street

Representing: Balboa Cafe; Black-eyed Pea Restaurants; Blue's Lakefront Bar and Grille; Dixie House Restaurants; SRO Bar and Bistro; Tamales; Metropol; The Wine Press.

BLACK BEANS CARIBBEAN STYLE

1 pound black beans
2 large onions, chopped
2 garlic cloves, finely chopped
3 large green peppers, chopped
8 ounces olive oil

2 tablespoons salt
8 ounces ham, diced
6 bay leaves
8 ounces red wine vinegar

Soak beans overnight. Sauté onions, garlic and green pepper in half the olive oil. Add to beans with salt, ham and bay leaves. Cook in the same water the beans were soaked in, until the beans are tender and the liquid thickens. Stir in vinegar and remaining olive oil. Serve over yellow rice. Delicious with crisp French bread and salad!

Mr. and Mrs. Burt Shryock (Judy)
Cotton Bowl Director

WAX BEANS CREOLE

2 cans wax beans
2 tablespoons chopped onion
2 celery stalks, chopped

1 small can tomato sauce
Margarine (optional)

Mix beans with onion and celery; boil gently until onions and celery are fork-tender. Pour off liquid. Stir in tomato sauce. Simmer for a few minutes. Season with margarine, if desired.

Mrs. Otto H. Eisenlohr (Nell)
Wife, Cotton Bowl President 1952-1954

BROCCOLI & RICE OWL CASSEROLE

½ cup chopped onions
¾ stick butter
20 ounces fresh broccoli, chopped

2 cups cooked rice
1 can cream of mushroom soup
1 cup grated Cheddar cheese

Preheat oven to 350°. Sauté onions in butter. Pour onions into bowl, mix in the chopped broccoli. Stir in remaining ingredients. Transfer to a greased casserole dish and bake for 1 hour. Serves 6.

Harlan Streater
Mama's Pizza

CHEESE BROCCOLI CASSEROLE

1½ pounds fresh broccoli
2 eggs, lightly beaten
¾ cup cottage cheese
½ cup grated Cheddar cheese (2 ounces)
2 tablespoons finely chopped onion

1 teaspoon Worcestershire sauce
½ teaspoon salt
⅛ teaspoon pepper
¼ cup fine dry bread crumbs
1 tablespoon butter, melted

Wash and trim broccoli; cut stalks into spears. Cover and cook in a small amount of boiling unsalted water for 10 minutes or until crisp-tender; drain. In a bowl, mix eggs, cottage cheese, Cheddar cheese, onion, Worcestershire sauce, salt and pepper. Arrange broccoli spears in a shallow 1½-quart baking dish; spoon cheese mixture on top. Stir together bread crumbs and melted butter; sprinkle mixture over casserole. Bake, uncovered, at 350° for 15 to 20 minutes or until heated through and egg mixture is set. Serves immediately. Serves 4 to 6.

Clif Overcash, Jr.
Overcash Goodman Enterprises

CAMPUS POLICE EGGPLANT PARMIGIANA

1 medium eggplant
2 eggs, beaten
1 cup Italian-style bread crumbs
¾ cup olive oil
2 cups cottage cheese

1 (14-ounce) jar spaghetti sauce
12 ounces mozzarella cheese, grated
1 teaspoon Italian herb seasoning
½ cup grated Parmesan cheese

Cut eggplant into ½-inch slices. Dip slices in beaten eggs, then in bread crumbs. Slowly heat oil in a large skillet. Sauté eggplant until browned, about 2 minutes each side; drain. Arrange eggplant in a greased 12x8-inch glass baking dish. Cover with layers of cottage cheese, sauce, mozzarella cheese, herb seasoning and Parmesan cheese. Bake, uncovered, at 350° for 20 to 30 minutes.

Mrs. Angelo George (June)

CLASSIC MILESTONE

1965 - Arkansas gained the Football Writer's Association of America national championship by springing a 10-7 victory over Nebraska. (Wire service champion Alabama was upset by Texas later that evening.)

GALUPSI-STUFFED CABBAGE

This is a 200-year-old family recipe from my late mother-in-law, Mrs. Sally Sterns Wells.

1 large head cabbage
2 onions, sliced
½ stick margarine
1 (29-ounce) can whole tomatoes
3 teaspoons salt
½ teaspoon pepper
1 pound beef bones
5 pounds ground chuck

4 tablespoons grated onion
3 tablespoons uncooked rice
3 tablespoons cold water
1 egg
¼ cup seedless raisins
¼ cup lemon juice
3 tablespoons honey

Put cabbage in pot of boiling water and set aside for 10 minutes. Sauté onions in margarine; add tomatoes, half the salt and pepper, and the beef bones. Cook, uncovered, over low heat for 30 minutes. Mix beef, onion, rice, water, egg, remaining salt and pepper. Roll mixture in cabbage leaves and secure with toothpicks. Place in pan with bones cover and cook slowly for 1½ hours. Add raisins, lemon juice and honey. Cook, uncovered, for 30 minutes. Makes 12 to 14 cabbage rolls.

Bob Richards
TV Producer, Columnist, Radio Commentator

VILLA MONTANA CABBAGE

1 head cabbage
2 tablespoons butter
1 teaspoon sugar
1 onion, sliced
1 green pepper, sliced

2 cups canned tomatoes, drained, or 4
  fresh tomatoes, sliced
Salt, to taste
Pepper, to taste
¾ cup grated Cheddar cheese

Cut cabbage in 6 wedges and cook about 10 minutes. Transfer to buttered 2-quart casserole. Sauté butter, sugar, onion and green pepper. Add tomatoes, salt and pepper. Pour mixture over cabbage and sprinkle with cheese. Bake at 350° until heated all the way through. Serves 8.

Mrs. Darrell Royal (Edith)

CLASSIC MILESTONE

1966 - LSU snapped Arkansas' 22-game winning streak before the Classic's largest crowd to date of 76,200 with a 14-7 upset. The loss prevented the Razorbacks from claiming their second consecutive national title.

EGGPLANT SOUFFLÉ SENIORITIS

1 large or 2 small eggplants
¼ cup butter or margarine
¼ cup flour
2 cups milk, scalded
2 cups grated Cheddar cheese

4 eggs, well-beaten
½ teaspoon salt
½ teaspoon white pepper
1 cup cracker crumbs

Peel and dice eggplant. Cook in salted water until tender; drain and mash. Melt butter or margarine over low temperature. Stir in flour. Stir in scalded milk and cook until mixture thickens. Remove from heat and stir in 1½ cups of the Cheddar cheese. Cool mixture. Add eggs, salt and pepper. Combine mashed eggplant, cheese sauce and cracker crumbs; pour into a greased 2-quart casserole. Sprinkle with remaining ½ cup cheese. Bake at 350° for 30 minutes or until firm. For variation, substitute fresh squash for the eggplant, but do not peel the squash. Serves 8.

Bob Horan
Colonial Supply Company

OKLAHOMA OKRA GUMBO

1 cup chopped dry salt pork
1 cup chopped onions
1 pound fresh okra, cut into ¼-inch
    slices

5 to 6 medium tomatoes, peeled and
    chopped
½ teaspoon fresh ground black pepper

In black iron skillet, sauté salt pork to render fat. Remove pork pieces and reserve. Sauté onions and okra. Add tomatoes and cook until okra is done. Stir only enough to mix ingredients. Cover and cook on medium heat. Stir in reserved pork pieces, if desired, before serving. Note: Sautéeing the okra keeps it crisp. This recipe is good in combination with shrimp and other seafoods or eaten as a vegetable.

Mrs. George W. Bailey (Novella)

CLASSIC MILESTONE

1967 - Actually, this was the second Cotton Bowl Classic played in 1966. Georgia outdueled SMU 24-9 on December 31, 1966. This was the only Classic played prior to New Year's Day.

ITALIAN MUSHROOMS

My grandmother's recipe, Mrs. Lisante Pucciariello.

Vegetable oil
2 garlic cloves, chopped
2 onions, sliced
2 pounds fresh mushrooms

2 (29-ounce) cans whole tomatoes
Salt, to taste
Pepper, to taste

Cover bottom of pan with vegetable oil. Add garlic, onion and mushrooms to fill pan. Cover and cook until mushrooms are reduced. Add tomatoes, salt and pepper, and cook until thick, stirring often. Best served hot.

Bob Richards
TV Producer, Columnist, Radio Commentator

HOPPING JOHN CRACK BACK BLOCK

1 can onion soup
1 can water
¼ teaspoon salt
½ to ¾ teaspoon Tabasco sauce
2 cans black-eyed peas
1½ cups diced ham or leftover
   Christmas turkey

2 tablespoons oil
1½ cups water
1½ cups packed pre-cooked rice
   (Minute Rice)

Boil soup, water, salt and Tabasco sauce. Add peas. Cover and simmer for 15 minutes. Sauté ham or turkey in oil. Add 1½ cups water and the rice to the pea mixture. Stir in meat. Simmer until the rice absorbs most of the water. Adjust Tabasco to taste ... we like lots! This is an annual event in our home—Hopping John and the Cotton Bowl game on New Year's Day. Be sure to count how many black-eyed peas you eat because that's how many days of good luck you will have in the coming year! This recipe makes enough for a side dish. For a main course, double or triple the recipe.

Mr. and Mrs. Norm Bulaich (Susie)

CLASSIC MILESTONE

1968 - It was a Classic rematch: Texas A&M vs. Alabama. The two teams met 26 years earlier in the sixth Cotton Bowl game when the Crimson Tide turned seven Aggie interceptions and five fumbles into a 29-21 victory. This time around, however, A&M coach Gene Stallings turned the tables on his former mentor—Paul "Bear" Bryant—to deal the Tide a 20-16 defeat.

PROFESSOR OF ENGLISH PEA CASSEROLE

2 (10-ounce) packages frozen peas
½ cup chopped onion
1 cup chopped celery
½ cup butter, melted
1 cup water chestnuts, drained

1 small jar pimentos
1 can cream of mushroom soup
2 cups bread crumbs
¾ cup butter

Cook peas and onions according to directions on frozen pea package. Combine celery, ½ cup melted butter, water chestnuts, pimentos and mushroom soup. Transfer to buttered casserole. Mix bread crumbs and ¾ cup butter and spread over pea mixture. Bake at 350° for 30 minutes.

Mrs. Lee Jackson (Jean)

BUFFET POTATOES PITTSBURGH

2 pounds frozen hash brown potatoes
½ cup butter, melted
¼ cup chopped onion
1 (10¾-ounce) can cream of chicken
    soup

1 cup sour cream
1½ cups grated cheese

Thaw potatoes about 45 minutes. Thoroughly mix potatoes with remaining ingredients. Bake at 350° for 1 hour. Note: This can be made ahead and frozen.

Mr. and Mrs. Buddy Dike (Sara)
Cotton Bowl President 1976-1978

FIX AHEAD MASHED POTATOES

8 potatoes, peeled and boiled
2 sticks butter or margarine
8 ounces sour cream
8 green onions, chopped

2 teaspoons seasoned salt
¼ teaspoon white pepper
Half and half

Mash potatoes; mix in butter, sour cream, onion, seasoned salt and white pepper. Add enough half and half to give potatoes the right consistency. Mix until smooth. Transfer to a greased casserole dish. Just before serving, bake for 20 minutes.

Jim Erwin (Sarah)
Cotton Bowl Director

JALAPEÑO SPINACH

Just the right amount of "heat" gives this recipe the Texas touch.

2 packages frozen leaf spinach
¼ cup water
4 tablespoons butter
2 tablespoons flour
½ cup evaporated milk
½ cup liquid from cooked spinach
2 tablespoons minced onion

½ teaspoon black pepper
¾ teaspoon celery salt
¾ teaspoon garlic salt
1 (6-ounce) roll jalapeño cheese, cubed
6 tablespoons butter
3 bread slices

Cook spinach in water just until spinach has separated. Drain, reserving juice. Melt 4 tablespoons butter in skillet; stir in flour. Mix in evaporated milk and ½ cup spinach liquid. (May have to add water to equal ½ cup.) Cook over medium heat until mixture thickens. Remove from heat and stir in onion, pepper, celery salt, garlic salt and cheese. Stir until cheese melts. Stir in spinach. Transfer to a greased baking dish. Melt 6 tablespoons butter in skillet. Trim crusts from bread and cut slices into large croutons. Add to skillet and stir to coat croutons with butter. Sprinkle over spinach in baking dish. Bake at 375° for 25 to 30 minutes or until casserole is hot and bubbly.

Karen Haram
San Antonio Express and News

SWEET (DIMITRIA) TEXAS YAMS

4 pounds Texas yams
½ cup honey and maple syrup
¼ pound butter

¼ teaspoon vanilla
¼ teaspoon cinnamon
Marshmallows

Peel and cut yams in small pieces. Cook in unseasoned water until soft; mash. Add honey and maple syrup, butter, vanilla and cinnamon, mixing well. Transfer to a greased casserole dish and bake at 350° for 30 minutes. Add a handful of marshmallows and mix together. Top with a small amount of marshmallows and brown under broiler.

Coke Gage

Coke Gage, whose family pioneered Wise County, is the former mayor of Decatur. He is an oilman/rancher and a true gourmet and gourmand of world renown.

CLASSIC MILESTONE

1969 - In the first of six consecutive Cotton Bowl appearances, Texas steamrolled Tennessee 36-13 in the first Classic display of the wishbone "T" formation.

SPINACH CASSEROLE

3 (10-ounce) packages frozen chopped
   spinach
4 ounces cream cheese, softened
1 medium onion, chopped

¼ cup margarine
½ pint sour cream
1 (7-ounce) can artichoke hearts
Paprika, to garnish

Cook spinach as directed; drain well. Add cream cheese to hot spinach, blending well. Sauté onion in margarine until transparent then stir in sour cream. Combine with spinach mixture. Pour into a greased medium casserole dish. Drain artichoke hearts and arrange on top of casserole, pushing artichokes down until only the tops show. Sprinkle with paprika and bake in a moderate oven for 25 to 30 minutes.

T.R. (Bob) Frymire (Mary Alice)
Cotton Bowl Director

BAKED SQUASH MISSED BLOCK

5 pounds fresh yellow squash (can use
   frozen, but not as good)
1 cup diced green pepper
1 cup diced onion
1 cup diced celery

½ cup margarine
1½ teaspoons salt
½ teaspoon pepper
2 tablespoons sugar
½ cup bread crumbs

Slice squash, and cook in salted water for 10 to 15 minutes until tender. Drain well and mash. Sauté peppers, onions and celery in margarine until tender. Add to mashed squash with salt, pepper and sugar. Add bread crumbs. Place in buttered casserole and cover with topping. Bake at 375° until crumbs are brown. For variation, substitute eggplant for the squash, but reduce green pepper to ½ cup.

TOPPING
2 cups bread crumbs
2 tablespoons melted margarine

½ teaspoon paprika

Mix ingredients.

Bob Horan
Colonial Supply Company

LIB KOOSA BOM BAH

1 large onion, chopped
1 garlic clove or garlic powder
4 or 5 large yellow squash, washed and
   sliced

Salt, to taste
Pepper, to taste

Sauté onion and garlic. Stir in squash, salt and pepper. Cook over low heat until done.

Al Sankary
Al's Formal Wear

SQUASH CASSEROLE I

2 to 3 pounds yellow squash
Salt, to taste
Pepper, to taste
1 can chopped green chilies

1 small jar stuffed olives, cut
2 to 3 eggs, beaten
Grated American sharp cheese

Cook and mash the squash. Add salt, pepper, green chilies, olives and eggs, mixing well. In a greased casserole dish layer the mixture with the cheese, topping with cheese. Bake at 350° for 25 minutes.

Mrs. John P. Thompson (Debra)
Wife, Cotton Bowl President 1978-1980

SQUASH CASSEROLE II

3 pounds yellow squash
Salt, to taste
Pepper, to taste
1 large onion, chopped

Butter
⅛ pound Velveeta cheese, cubed
1 egg, beaten
Bread crumbs

Cook squash and season with salt and pepper; set aside. Sauté onion in butter. Add to squash. Add half the cheese, stirring to mix. Transfer to a greased casserole dish. Cover with bread crumbs and remaining cheese. Bake at 350° for 20 minutes.

Mrs. John P. Thompson (Debra)
Wife, Cotton Bowl President 1978-1980

TRAP PLAY SQUASH CASSEROLE

5 pounds squash
1 medium onion, chopped
1 teaspoon sugar
1 package corn bread mix

1 can mushroom soup
10 ounces Cheddar cheese, grated
¾ stick margarine, softened

Cook squash with onion and sugar. Mix with remaining ingredients. Transfer to greased casserole and bake at 300° for 30 minutes.

Mrs. Charles Mayberry (Cathy)

GRANNY'S PICKLED GREEN TOMATOES

5 pounds sliced green tomatoes
1½ cups pickling lime
3 gallons water
2 tablespoons whole cloves
2 tablespooons allspice
½ package stick cinnamon

½ tablespoon white mustard seed
1 tablespoon celery seed
½ gallon white vinegar
4 pounds sugar
1 heaping teaspoon alum
2 heaping tablespoons salt

Combine sliced tomatoes, lime and water in a large pot; let stand overnight. Rinse tomatoes in the morning; let stand until early afternoon to completely drain water. Wrap cloves, allspice, cinnamon, mustard seed and celery seed in cheesecloth. Place in a large (10 to 12-quart) boiler the vinegar, sugar, alum, salt and cheesecloth-wrapped spices. Bring to a boil. Add tomatoes and let boil for 30 minutes. Transfer tomatoes to quart jars. Fill each jar with enough liquid to cover the tomatoes. Be sure that the jars are hot so the liquid does not crack the glass. Before sealing, wipe top of jar with a damp cloth to ensure a good seal. Seal jars, then turn them upside down. This also encourages a good seal. Serve chilled or at room temperature. Yields approximately 8 quarts.

Jim O'Donnell
InterFirst Venture Corporation

CLASSIC MILESTONE

1970 - No. 1 Texas spoiled Notre Dame's first bowl trip in 45 years. The Fighting Irish' last bowl appearance was the 1952 Rose Bowl, and the three surviving members of the famed Four Horsemen rode into Dallas for the 34th Classic. But, Texas fought off the Notre Dame challenge for a hard earned 21-17 triumph and the Longhorns' second national championship.

MISSOURI MARINATED TOMATOES
Must make ahead of time.

4 large tomatoes, peeled	2 tablespoons cider vinegar
⅓ cup chopped parsley	1 teaspoon salt
1 garlic clove, pressed	½ teaspoon leaf basil
⅓ cup olive oil	¼ teaspoon Tabasco

Cut tomatoes into ½-inch slices. Arrage in shallow serving dish; set aside. Combine other ingredients, mixing well. Pour over tomatoes. Refrigerate for 4 hours or overnight. Serve over lettuce.

Mrs. Richard E. Miles (Karen)

STUFFED TOMATO

5 slices bacon	5 drops Tabasco sauce
1 small onion, finely chopped	½ teaspoon salt
1 small green pepper, finely chopped	¼ teaspoon pepper
5 large tomatoes	½ cup grated Parmesan cheese
7 thin bread slices, broken into small pieces	

Fry bacon crisp and crumble. Sauté onion and green pepper in 3 or 4 tablespoons bacon grease until onions are transparent. Slice stem end of each tomato, remove pulp and seeds, leaving tomato shells intact. To tomato pulp, add bread, Tabasco sauce, salt and pepper. If mixture is too moist, add more bread. Stuff mixture into tomato shells and sprinkle with cheese. Bake at 400° for 30 minutes. Serves 5.

Mrs. Jane Ray Dietrich
Cotton Bowl Director

HOW TO COOK RICE

Wash 1 cup rice in cold water several times until water poured off is clear. Add 1½ cups cold water. Place in pot and cover. Boil over a hot fire until the water is evaporated. Do not stir while rice is boiling; otherwise rice will not stand out as separate grains. Keep warm until ready to serve, leaving the cover on. If an electric stove is used, heat may be turned off and the covered pot kept on the burner. If it is cooked on a gas stove, turn the flame very low after the water has evaporated. One cup of uncooked rice makes 2 cups of cooked rice.

Anabel Humberd
Realtor
A&E Real Estate

RICE CASSEROLE

2 cups cooked rice (¾ cup uncooked)	1 tablespoon chopped onion
1 cup grated sharp cheese	¼ cup chopped parsley
¼ cup butter, melted	3 egg yolks, beaten
Salt, to taste	3 egg whites, stiffly beaten
Pepper, to taste	

Thoroughly mix all ingredients except egg whites. Fold in beaten egg whites. Transfer to a greased baking dish and bake at 350° for 25 minutes. May be served with creamed crab or shrimp. Serves 6 to 8.

Mrs. Otto H. Eisenlohr (Nell)
Wife, Cotton Bowl President 1952-1954

SOUR CREAM AND RICE
Deliciously different.

Rice	Seasoned salt
Chicken bouillon	Monterey Jack cheese
Butter	Jalapeño peppers
Salt	Sour cream

Cook rice according to instructions. When cooking, add chicken bouillon to water with butter and salt. When rice is ready, pour a layer into a buttered casserole dish. Sprinkle seasoned salt on top. Put several pats of butter on top of rice. Add a layer of Monterey Jack cheese, then a layer of jalapeño peppers, then another layer of rice. Top with cheese. Bake at 350° until cheese melts. Remove from oven, and while very hot, just before serving, spread sour cream on top. Serve immediately. Use jalapeño peppers according to taste. If you like lots of peppers, then use them; but if not, use a few thin strips. Or you can use green chilies for a milder flavor if you want. We like jalapeños, but it may be too hot for non-Texan taste. To serve 10 to 12 people, use 8 cups water and 3 cups Uncle Ben's rice. This is the best rice recipe for a special dish to serve with either beef or chicken.

Mary C. Crowley
Dallas

CLASSIC MILESTONE

1971 - One year later, it was Notre Dame's turn to play the spoiler's role, ruining the Longhorn's national championship dreams with a 24-11 surprise. The Irish victory snapped Texas' 30-game winning streak. Ironically, 14 years earlier the Irish also were the ones responsible for breaking Oklahoma's record 47-game win streak.

Cakes
Pies
Cookies
General Desserts

UNIVERSITY OF TEXAS, AUSTIN

UNIVERSITY OF TEXAS

Having started life in 1883 with one building, eight faculty members and 221 students, the University of Texas at Austin has grown into a bustling community of more than 60,000 which includes about 48,000 students, 2,100 faculty, and 11,000 support personnel.

About 6,300 courses are taught in UT's eight colleges, eight schools and 54 departments. More than 110 buildings are located on the main campus of more than 300 acres.

The university leads the South in number of doctoral degrees awarded. UT's professional graduate programs in botany, linguistics, Spanish, civil engineering, Germanic languages, classics, zoology, and computer sciences rank among the best in the nation.

Serving as president is Dr. William Cunningham. Dr. L. O. Morgan is the SWC athletic representative. Administering the athletic program is DeLoss Dodds. The football fortunes are guided by head coach Fred Akers.

ONE HUNDRED DOLLAR CHOCOLATE CAKE

1/2 cup butter
4 oz. melted chocolate
2 cups flour
2 teaspoons baking powder
2 tablespoons vanilla
2 cups sugar
2 unbeaten eggs
1 1/2 cups milk

Preheat oven to 375 degrees. Cream butter, sugar and vanilla. Add chocolate and eggs. Add baking powder and flour, gradually add flour alternately with milk. Spread into greased 13" x 9" baking pan. Bake at 375 degrees for 25 - 30 minutes.

ICING

1 stick butter
2 oz. melted chocolate
1 teaspoon vanilla
1 lb. (box) powdered sugar
1 egg, beaten
1 cup nuts

Mix all ingredients. Spread over cake.

Sherry Beadle, J.

This $100 cake comes from a cowboy connection in Southeast New Mexico. Seems a couple of cowboys were dining at a restaurant and praised the chocolate cake. One cowboy said that the cake was so good, he'd pay $100 for the recipe and the chef received $100. The recipe was passed on to my mother by another ranch lady.

SHERRY BEADLE PRODUCTIONS

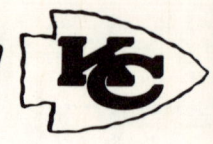

CHEESE CAKE

3 8oz. cream cheese
4 Eggs
1 Cup Sugar
1 Tsp. vanilla

1 Graham cracker crust

Mix top 4 ingredients together till smooth.
Put mixture on top of graham cracker crust.

Bake 45 min. at 275. Let stand 15 min.

Topping:

1 Cup sour cream
4 T sugar
1 tsp. vanilla

Mix and spread on top of cheese cake.
Bake 5 min. at 400.
Use an oblong glass baking dish.

Todd Blacsledge

CITY OF DALLAS

A. Starke Taylor Jr.
Mayor

Being a chocolate lover, this is one of my favorite recipes:

TEXAS CAKE

1 tsp baking soda
2 eggs
2 cups flour
2 cups sugar
1/2 tsp. salt
1/2 cup sour cream
2 sticks butter
2 bars unsweetened baking chocolate
1 cup water

Melt butter, chocolate and water in saucepan. Mix flour, baking soda, eggs, sugar, salt & sour cream together. Mix hot mixture with remaining ingredients. Bake 20 minutes in 13x9x2 inch greased & floured pan.

ICING:

1 box powdered sugar
1 tsp. vanilla
1 stick butter
1/3 cup milk
2 bars Bakers unsweetened chocolate

Boil butter, milk & chocolate. Add vanilla, then sugar, and pour icing over cooled cake. Serve and enjoy - it's delicious!

Best regards,

A. Starke Taylor Jr.
Mayor, City of Dallas

U A Razorbacks

Head Football Coach

CHOCOLATE CHIP CHOCOLATE POUND CAKE

1 Package (12 oz.) mini-chocolate chips
1 Package (2-layer size) chocolate fudge cake mix
1 Package (4-serving) chocolate fudge instant
  pudding and pie filling
4 Eggs
1 Cup sour cream
½ Cup water
¼ Cup oil
½ teaspoon vanilla extract
½ teaspoon almond extract

Grease Bundt pan. Blend all the ingredients, except the mini-chocolate chips, and then beat for 4 minutes at medium speed with mixer. Stir in chips. Pour into Bundt pan and bake at 350 degrees for 60-70 minutes or until cake begins to pull away from the sides of pan. Remove from pan and top with powdered sugar.

Submitted by: *Sandy Hatfield*

Sandy Hatfield

STATE OF GEORGIA

OFFICE OF THE GOVERNOR

ATLANTA 30334

Joe Frank Harris
GOVERNOR

SOUTHERN APPLE CAKE

1 cup corn oil	1 teaspoon baking soda
2 cups sugar	1 teaspoon salt
3 eggs, beaten	1 cup chopped pecans
3 cups flour	3 cups fresh apples, peeled
1 teaspoon vanilla	and chopped

Combine well the corn oil and sugar. Add beaten eggs. Sift together flour, baking soda and salt. Combine with egg mixture. Stir in the chopped pecans and apples, and add vanilla. Pour into well greased baking pan. Start in cold oven, turn to 325 degrees and bake for 45 minutes or until done. In the meantime, make topping.

TOPPING

1/2 cup margarine	1/4 cup evaporated milk
1/2 cup light brown sugar	1 teaspoon vanilla
1/2 cup white sugar	

Combine butter, sugars and milk in saucepan, heat over low heat and boil 2 minutes. Stir in vanilla and beat until smooth. Pour over cooked cake in pan. Cut in squares to serve. Top with whipped cream, if desired.

Joe Frank Harris

COCONUT CAKE

1 - box Duncan Hine's Yellow Cake Mix

2 - 6oz. pkgs. frozen coconut (tnawed)

1 - 8oz. Cool Whip

1 3/4 C. milk   (
             (Heat
  1/2 C. sugar (

Make cake according to instructions #
adding 1 pkg. of frozen coconut.

While still hot, poke holes in the cake
and spoon over the milk and sugar mixture -
let stand until cold.

TOPPING

Reserve 2 TB. frozen coconut from the
second pkg. Mix the rest of the coconut
with the Cool Whip and spread over the
cake. Sprinkle reserved coconut over the top.

This cake should be made in a 3qt. glass
Pyrex casserole, greased and floured, and
made the day before. KEEP REFRIGERATED.

All the best,

Don Whitenie

Rear Admiral US Navy (RET)

COTTON BOWL ATHLETIC ASSOCIATION

JIM BROCK
EXECUTIVE VICE PRESIDENT

MOTHER-IN-LAW'S
CHOCOLATE CAKE

2 c. sugar
1 c. butter
3 eggs
2 c. flour
dash salt
1 t. baking powder
½ c. buttermilk
1 t. soda (dissolve in buttermilk)
½ c. cocoa
1 t. vanilla
1 c. hot water (add last)

Cream sugar & butter. Add eggs and beat well. Add flour, baking powder, and salt.
Mix buttermilk (with added soda) and cocoa together and add to mixture. Add vanilla
and hot water. Bake at 350 degrees for about 20 to 25 minutes. Makes three layers.
(Mixture will be thin)

Pineapple Filling:
⅓ c. sugar
1 T. flour (heaping)

    MIX

1 small can crushed pineapple
1 T. butter

Cook until thick and spread between layers. Be sure that cake is very cool before
stacking and filling.

Icing:
1 stick butter
4 T. cocoa
6 T. buttermilk
Bring above ingredients to a boil. Then add, 1 box powdered sugar and 1 t. vanilla.
Beat until smooth.

Mrs. Jim Brock (Shirley)

COMMONWEALTH OF PENNSYLVANIA
OFFICE OF THE GOVERNOR
HARRISBURG

RECIPE SUBMITTED BY GINNY THORNBURGH

GINNY'S APPLE CAKE

1-1/2	cups oil
2	cups sugar
3	eggs
3	cups flour
1	teaspoon salt
1	teaspoon cinnamon
1	teaspoon baking soda
1	teaspoon vanilla
3	cups peeled, cored and thickly sliced Delicious apples
1	cup chopped walnuts
1	cup raisins, optional
	Vanilla ice cream, optional

1. Preheat oven to 350 degrees F.

2. Beat the oil and sugar together with an electric mixer while assembling the remaining ingredients.

3. Add the eggs and beat until the mixture is creamy.

4. Sift together the flour, salt, cinnamon and baking soda. Stir into the batter. Add all the remaining ingredients, except ice cream, and stir to blend.

5. Turn the mixture into a buttered and floured nine-inch angel-food tube pan. Bake one hour and 15 minutes or until done. Cool in the pan before turning out. Serve at room temperature with ice cream, if desired.

Yield: 12 servings

The University of Mississippi

Department of Intercollegiate Athletics
University, MS 38677

OLD FASHION POUND CAKE

2½ sticks butter (room temp.)
3   cups sugar
4   eggs (room temp.)
3½ cups plain flour
¼ tsp. Soda
1¼ cups buttermilk
1½ tsp. vanilla
1½ tsp. lemon flavoring

Mix dry ingredients, add liquids and mix thoroughly. Use
large tube pan or two loaf pans and bake 1½ hours at 275°.
Leave in pan about 10 minutes before turning out. Freezes
well but must be opened up so it will not get soggy while
thawing.

Submitted by Reed Davis, Associate Athletic Director for
Finance, University of Mississippi (Ole Miss "64)...Played
in the 1962 Cotton Bowl, scoring Rebs' lone touchdown in
12-7 loss to Texas.

Oklahoma State University

DEPARTMENT OF ATHLETICS

STILLWATER, OKLAHOMA 74078-0300
GALLAGHER HALL

June 2, 1986

Dear Russell:

Responding to your recent request, I am sending you the recipe for a favorite coffeecake of mine. It is called "Holiday Coffeecake" and it is great!

1/2 cup shortening
3/4 cup sugar
2 eggs
1 1/2 cups sifted all-purpose flour
3/4 teaspoon salt
2 teaspoons baking powder
2/3 cup milk
****
4 Tablespoons regular dry cocoa
1/2 cup sugar
1/3 cup chopped pecans
4 Tablespoons butter

Cream together shortening, sugar and eggs till light and fluffy. Sift together flour, salt and baking powder. Add to creamed mixture alternately with milk, beating well after each addition. Spoon 1/3 of batter into well-greased bundt pan.

Mix cocoa, sugar and nuts; sprinkle half over batter in pan; dot with half the butter. Repeat layers, ending with batter. Bake at 350 degrees for 35 minutes or till done. Let stand 5 minutes; turn out of pan. Serve warm.

If I can be of any further assistance, please let me know.

Sincerely yours,

Myron Roderick
Athletic Director

MR:mld

CENTENNIAL
DECADE
1980·1990

APPLE KUCHEN ALL OUT RUSH

½ cup butter, softened
1 package yellow cake mix
½ cup flaked coconut
1 (20-ounce) can apple pie filling or 2½
    cups peeled, sliced baking apples

½ cup sugar
1 teaspoon cinnamon
1 cup sour cream
2 egg yolks or 1 egg
Chopped nuts (optional)

Heat oven to 350°. Cut butter into dry cake mix until crumbly. Stir in coconut. Pat mixture lightly into ungreased oblong pan (13x9x2 inches), building up slight edges. Bake 10 minutes. Arrange apple slices over warm crust. Mix sugar and cinnamon, then sprinkle over apples. Blend sour cream and egg yolks; drizzle over apples. (Topping will not completely cover apples.) Bake 25 minutes or until edges are light brown. Serve warm. Serves 12.

Vernon Uecker

DALE'S APPLE CAKE

1 cup whole wheat flour
1½ cups all-purpose flour
1 teaspoon salt
1 teaspoon soda
2 teaspoons baking powder
1 to 2 teaspoons cinnamon

1½ cups sugar
¾ to 1 cup oil (not melted shortening)
2 eggs, beaten
4 cups peeled, cored and chopped Red
    Delicious apples
1 cup chopped pecans

Combine flour, salt, soda, baking powder and cinnamon; set aside. In a large bowl, mix sugar, oil and eggs. Stir in the dry ingredients. Batter will be very stiff. Add apples slowly and mix for 1 to 2 minutes. Stir in nuts. Pour into a greased and floured tube or bundt pan. Bake at 350° for 1 hour. This is Dale Raymond's famous apple cake.

Lynn Hohertz
Lubbock Avalanche-Journal

CLASSIC MILESTONE

1975 - Baylor claimed its first Southwest Conference championship in 50 years and earned its first ever Cotton Bowl appearance, but fell to Penn State as the Nittany Lions established a Classic scoring record, 41-20.

AUBURN APPLE CAKE

2 cups flour	½ cup oil
2 teaspoons soda	2 cups sugar
½ teaspoon salt	2 teaspoons vanilla
2 teaspoons cinnamon	4 cups diced apples
2 eggs, lightly beaten	1 cup chopped nuts

Sift flour with soda, salt and cinnamon; set aside. In a large mixing bowl, mix by hand the eggs, oil, sugar and vanilla. Mix in dry ingredients. Stir in apples and nuts. Pour batter into a greased and floured 13x9-inch pan and bake at 350° for 45 minutes.

ICING

6 ounces cream cheese	1½ cups confectioners' sugar
⅛ teaspoon salt	2 teaspoons vanilla
3 tablespoons butter	

Blend ingredients. Spread on cooled cake.

Mrs. George W. Bailey (Novella)

A Friend from Memphis—TEXAS, that is!

APPLE-RAISIN SPICE CAKE

3 cups unsifted flour	½ teaspoon nutmeg
2 cups sugar	½ teaspoon salt
1 cup Hellmann's real mayonnaise	¼ teaspoon cloves
⅓ cup milk	3 cups peeled, chopped apples
2 eggs	1 cup seedless raisins
2 teaspoons soda	½ cup chopped walnuts
1½ teaspoons cinnamon	

Grease and flour 2 (9-inch) round cake pans. In large bowl, with mixer at low speed, beat first 10 ingredients for 2 minutes, scraping bowl frequently. (The batter will be very thick.) You may beat vigorously 300 strokes by hand. With spoon, stir in apples, raisins and walnuts. Spoon batter into prepared pans. Bake at 350° for 45 minutes or until toothpick inserted in center comes out clean. Cool in pans for 10 minutes. Remove. Frost cake with cream cheese icing.

Mrs. Juanita Nelms

CHIFFON SHIFT BANANA CAKE

2 eggs, separated
1⅓ cups sugar
2 cups sifted cake flour
1 teaspoon baking powder
1 teaspoon soda
1 teaspoon salt

⅓ cup Wesson oil
1 cup mashed bananas
⅔ cup buttermilk
1 teaspoon vanilla
½ cup chopped nuts (optional)

Heat oven to 350°. Grease and flour 2 (8-inch) cake pans. Beat egg whites until fluffy. Gradually beat in ⅓ cup sugar. Continue beating until very stiff and glossy. In a separate bowl, sift remaining sugar, flour, baking powder, soda and salt. Add oil, mashed bananas and half the buttermilk. Beat 1 minute at medium speed. Scrape sides and bottom of bowl constantly. Add remaining buttermilk, egg yolks and vanilla. Beat 1 more minute. Fold in meringue. Pour batter into prepared pans. Bake for 30 to 35 minutes.

ICING
½ cup Crisco shortening, softened
½ cup butter, softened
2 cups confectioners' sugar

1 teaspoon vanilla
2 tablespoons milk
Chopped nuts

Blend Crisco with butter, then mix in sugar, vanilla and milk. Beat until smooth. Stir in nuts.

Vernon Uecker

HONEY BANANA CAKE

1 cup packed brown sugar
½ cup butter or margarine, softened
2 large, ripe bananas
¾ cup sour cream
2 medium eggs
½ cup honey
1 teaspoon vanilla

2¼ cups flour
1 teaspoon soda
1 teaspoon baking powder
1 teaspoon ginger
½ teaspoon salt
½ teaspoon cinnamon
1 cup chopped pecans

Cream ½ cup of the brown sugar with butter. Puree one of the bananas in a blender, and beat it in with the sugar-butter mixture, sour cream, eggs, honey and vanilla. Combine the flour, soda, baking powder, ginger, salt and cinnamon. Beat this into the banana mixture. Grease 2 (8½x4½-inch) loaf pans, and sprinkle ¼ cup pecans in the bottom of each. Spread half the batter in each pan, and sprinkle each with ¼ cup brown sugar and ¼ cup pecans. Slice the second banana evenly over the top of the mixture in each pan. Spread the remaining batter over the tops. Bake in a preheated 350° oven for 45 to 50 minutes. Cool slightly and invert onto a wire rack to cool.

Mrs. Kenneth P. Dowell (Jo)
Wife, Cotton Bowl President 1970-1972

BLACKBERRY WINE CAKE

½ cup chopped pecans
1 package Duncan Hines Butter Fudge
  Cake Mix
1 package instant vanilla pudding mix
½ cup water
½ cup buttery Wesson oil

½ cup Mogen David Blackberry Wine
4 eggs
1 cup sugar
1 stick margarine
½ cup water

Sprinkle chopped pecans in bottom of greased Bundt pan. Mix cake mix with pudding mix, water, oil, wine and eggs. Pour batter into prepared pan and bake at 350° for 50 to 60 minutes. Remove from oven. In saucepan, mix sugar, margarine and ½ cup water. Boil for 5 minutes. Pour mixture over cake in Bundt pan. Let cool in pan for 1 to 2 hours. For best flavor, keep 2 to 3 days before serving. Serve with whipped cream.

Mrs. Rodger Meier (Joyce)
Wife, Cotton Bowl Director

LONGHORN CARROT CAKE

2 cups flour
1 teaspoon soda
1 teaspoon baking powder
1 teaspoon cinnamon

2 cups sugar
1½ cups Wesson oil
4 eggs
3 cups grated carrots

Mix flour, soda, baking powder, cinnamon and sugar. Blend in oil. Add eggs, one at a time, beating well after each addition. Stir in carrots. Pour into 3 greased and floured cake pans and bake at 350° until lightly browned. Cool, then ice with burnt orange icing.

BURNT ORANGE ICING
1 (8-ounce) package cream cheese
1 stick margarine
1 box confectioners' sugar

2 teaspoons vanilla
1 can shredded coconut
½ cup chopped pecans

Blend cream cheese and margarine. Mix in sugar, vanilla, coconut and pecans

Susan H. Hasslocher
Frontier Enterprises
President, Texas Restaurant Association

SPONGE CAKE RANGERETTE

For people who cannot eat cake made with flour.

8 eggs
1 cup sugar
Juice and rind of 1 lemon

¾ cup potato starch
Pinch of salt

Separate eggs; set aside the whites. Beat yolks and ½ cup sugar until light and sugar is dissolved. Measure 3 teaspoons lemon rind and set aside. Add the remaining juice and rind to the yolk mixture. Blend in the potato starch; set aside. Beat whites, adding a pinch of salt, until soft peaks form. Gradually add the remaining ½ cup sugar. Beat until all sugar is dissolved. Add the 3 teaspoons lemon juice and rind. Fold in the yolk mixture. Bake in a 10-inch pan at 350° for 50 minutes to 1 hour. Invert pan. Let cake cool completely in pan. Can be iced when cool.

Lillie Siegel

YUMMY CHOCOLATE SHEET CAKE

2 cups flour
2 cups sugar
1 teaspoon soda
Pinch of cinnamon
½ teaspoon salt
1 cup margarine

¼ cup cocoa
1 cup water
½ cup buttermilk
2 eggs
1 teaspoon vanilla

Mix flour, sugar, soda, cinnamon and salt; set aside. In saucepan, mix margarine, cocoa and water. Boil about 1 minute, then pour over dry ingredients. Stir in buttermilk, eggs and vanilla. Pour batter into prepared 10x15-inch jelly roll pan. Bake at 400° for 18 to 20 minutes. While cake bakes, prepare the following icing.

ICING
½ cup margarine
¼ cup cocoa
5 tablespoons milk

1 (1-pound) box confectioners' sugar
1 teaspoon vanilla

In saucepan, boil margarine and cocoa until blended. Beat in milk, sugar and vanilla. Spread over hot cake.

Ara Parseghian

PIÑA COLADA CAKE

CAKE

1 (5¼-ounce) box vanilla instant
   pudding mix
1 box super deluxe white cake mix

1 cup vegetable oil
4 eggs
1 cup water

Mix ingredients and beat on medium speed for 2 minutes. Pour in a prepared 13x9x2-inch cake pan. Bake at 350° for 35 to 40 minutes or until wooden pick inserted in center of cake comes out clean. Cool completely. Punch holes into cake with plastic straw.

ICING

1 can Piña Colada thick creamy mix
1 can Eagle Brand sweetened condensed
   milk

Blend together and pour over entire cake.

TOPPING

1 large carton Cool Whip, thawed   1 can flaked coconut

Spread Cool Whip over cake. Sprinkle with flaked coconut.

Darla Simpson McKey

RUM CAKE

1 Duncan Hines yellow deluxe cake mix
1 small box butter pecan *instant* pudding
   mix
4 eggs
½ cup oil

¾ cup rum
¼ cup water
1 cup chopped pecans (reserve ½ cup
   for bottom of greased bundt pan, ½
   for mix)

Combine all ingredients above. Preheat oven to 325°. Bake for 50 to 60 minutes.

ICING

1 stick butter
1 cup brown sugar

1 cup rum

Bring to boil and pour over bottom and down sides of done cake. Cut cake out of pan and pour rest of mix on top of cake. Add brown sugar crumbles and eat until all gone.

Joe Dealey, Sr.
Cotton Bowl President, 1968-1970

PERUNA'S PRUNE LAYER CAKE

¾ cup butter
1 cup sugar
3 tablespoons sour cream
3 eggs
1 teaspoon soda

2 cups flour
2 teaspoons cinnamon
1 teaspoon allspice
Few grains salt
1 cup chopped, cooked prunes

Cream butter, sugar and sour cream. Add eggs, one at a time, beating well after each addition. Add dry ingredients and beat well. Stir in prunes. Pour batter into prepared pans and bake at 350° for 1 hour and 15 minutes.

FILLING
2 eggs
1 cup sugar
½ cup sour cream
1 cup chopped, cooked prunes

2 tablespoons butter
Few grains salt
1 teaspoon vanilla

Mix eggs, sugar, sour cream, prunes, butter and salt in a saucepan. Cook until mixture thickens. Remove from heat and stir in vanilla. Spread between cake layers.

Melba Tompkins

ROYAL RUM CAKE

1 cup chopped pecans
1 yellow cake mix
1 small package instant vanilla pudding
   mix
4 eggs

½ cup cold water
½ cup Wesson oil
½ cup rum

Preheat oven to 325°. Grease and flour Bundt pan. Sprinkle nuts over bottom of pan. Using electric mixer, mix all ingredients. Pour batter into pan. Bake for 1 hour. Cool. Invert on serving plate. Prick top with fork and drizzle glaze over cake. Repeat until all glaze is used.

GLAZE
¼ pound butter
¼ cup water

1 cup sugar
½ cup rum

Melt butter in saucepan. Stir in water and sugar; boil 5 minutes, stirring constantly. Remove from heat; stir in rum.

Doris Null

CRIMSON TIDE COCONUT POUND CAKE

1 box Duncan Hines Butter Recipe
   Golden Cake Mix
5 eggs
¾ cup Crisco vegetable oil
1 teaspoon coconut flavoring

1 teaspoon butter flavoring
8 ounces sour cream
½ cup milk
1 can Angel Flake coconut

Mix ingredients. Set electric oven at 325° or gas oven at 350°. Pour batter into greased and floured Bundt pan and bake for one hour. Test. Cool 10 minutes in pan. Pour glaze over cake and leave in pan until cool.

GLAZE
1 cup sugar
½ cup water

½ cup butter
1 teaspoon coconut flavoring

Combine all ingredients and mix well.

Mrs. Ted Roe (Maudi Walsh)

SPORTSWRITERS' 7-UP POUND CAKE

3 sticks margarine
3 cups sugar
5 eggs

3 cups flour, sifted
¾ cup 7-Up
2 tablespoons lemon extract

Cream margarine and sugar at high speed for about 10 minutes or until smooth and fluffy. Add eggs, one at a time, and beat well. Add flour and mix in at low speed. Add 7-Up and lemon extract. Pour into a greased and floured Bundt or tube pan. Bake at 325° for about 1 hour.

Nell B. Robinson

CLASSIC MILESTONE

1976 - An overflow crowd of 77,500—the largest in Classic history—looked on as Arkansas stormed back from a ten-point deficit to defeat the Junkyard Dawgs of Georgia, 31-10.

SIN-NAMON COFFEE CAKE
So named because it's sinfully good!

2¼ cups flour
½ teaspoon salt
1 tablespoon cinnamon
¼ teaspoon ginger
1 cup packed brown sugar
¾ cup sugar

¾ cup vegetable oil
1 cup chopped walnuts
1 teaspoon soda
1 teaspoon baking powder
1 egg, well beaten
1 cup buttermilk

Combine flour, salt, 1½ teaspoons cinnamon, ginger, brown sugar, sugar and oil in a large bowl. Mix well. Measure and remove ¾ cup of the mixture to a separate bowl; add walnuts and remaining cinnamon. Mix well and set aside. To the remaining batter, add soda, baking powder, egg and buttermilk. Mix just to combine ingredients, being careful not to overmix. (Small lumps in batter are okay.) Pour batter into well-greased 13x9-inch pan. Sprinkle reserved nut mixture evenly over the top of the batter. Bake in a preheated 350° oven for 40 to 45 minutes or until toothpick inserted in center of cake comes out clean.

Karen Haram
San Antonio Express and News

CREAM CAKE FUMBLE
Quick! Easy! Elegant! Yummy!

1 German chocolate cake mix
2 packages coconut-pecan frosting mix

2 (12-ounce) containers Cool Whip
5 crunchy Heath candy bars

Mix cake and bake as directed in 2 (9-inch) pans or a tube pan. Cool and slice into 4 layers. Mix coconut-pecan frosting mix with Cool Whip. Frost all layers, sides and top. Chop candy bars into bits and sprinkle on top and sides of cake. Freeze or refrigerate until time to serve.

For Chocolate Lovers
Follow directions above for cake. Frost as follows: mix 1 package of coconut-pecan frosting mix with 1 (12-ounce) container Cool Whip. Frost all layers and top of cake with mixture. Frost sides of cake with pre-mixed container of milk chocolate frosting. Chop 3 Heath bars into bits and sprinkle on top of cake. Freeze or refrigerate until time to serve.

Trudy Rains Richards
Party and Event Planner
Combined Concepts Unlimited

SCORE KEEPER FRUIT CAKE

16 ounces flour
2 teaspoons allspice
½ scant teaspoon salt
½ teaspoon nutmeg
4 ounces glace cherries
12 ounces brown raisins
16 ounces currants

16 ounces sultanas
4 ounces mixed peel
8 eggs
12 ounces castor sugar
12 ounces butter
2 tablespoons treacle
2 scant tablespoons vinegar

One secret of successful cake making is to prepare everything in advance so that no time is lost after the cake is mixed in getting it into the oven. Line the cake tin with a double thickness of greaseproof paper; no grease is required. Mix the flour, allspice, salt and nutmeg. Cut cherries in half, reserving a few to sprinkle on top of unbaked cake. Mix cherries, raisins, currants, sultanas and peel. Mix 2 teaspoons flour with the fruit to prevent the fruit from sinking to the bottom of the cake. Break the eggs separately in a cup, then transfer into a bowl. With a fork, break the yolks so that they mingle with the whites, but do not beat. In a separate bowl, cream sugar with butter, beating until the mixture is not only creamy, but light and fluffy. Add the treacle and continue beating. Add the vinegar and beat until absorbed. Pour in about a third of the eggs, beating well. Pour in another third, beat again, then beat in the remainder. Now mix in flour the same way. When smooth, mix in the prepared fruit. Turn mixture into the prepared tin. Smooth the top with the back of a mixing spoon dipped frequently in cold water. Arrange some cherry halves on top. Place cake in the middle of the oven. The oven should be moderately hot, or about 350°. After an hour's baking, when the cake should have risen, reduce the heat to 250°. Do not open oven door for at least 2 hours. When baked, the cake should be a lovely even brown on top. Leave cake in tin to cool before removing it. Remove greaseproof paper. Wrap cake in fresh paper and store in tin. Leave at least a week before cutting. A small apple or part of one placed in the tin with the cake will help to keep it moist without in any way affecting the flavor.

Mrs. John Galvin (Jean)

CARD SECTION CHEESECAKE

Graham cracker crust
2 large packages cream cheese, softened
1 cup sugar

3 eggs
2 teaspoons vanilla

TOPPING

1 cup sour cream
4½ teaspoons sugar

1 teaspoon vanilla

Prepare graham cracker crust; bake at 450° for 3 to 4 minutes. Mix cream cheese, sugar, eggs and vanilla until smooth. Pour filling into crust. Bake at 350° for 18 minutes. Cool. Spread topping over cake and bake at 350° for 7 minutes.

Mrs. John S. Howell

HORNED FROG CHEERLEADER PINEAPPLE CHEESECAKE

CRUST

1 tablespoon butter
2 cups graham cracker crumbs
¼ cup confectioners' sugar

6 tablespoons melted butter
1 tablespoon grated orange peel
½ teaspoon cinnamon

Grease sides and bottom of a 9x2-inch deep springform baking pan with 1 tablespoon butter. Mix graham cracker crumbs, confectioners' sugar, melted butter, orange peel and cinnamon. Press against sides and bottom of pan. Refrigerate.

CHEESECAKE

3 (8-ounce) packages cream cheese
5 eggs
1½ cups sugar
¼ teaspoon salt

1½ teaspoons lemon juice
1½ teaspoons vanilla
1 tablespoon grated lemon peel

Preheat oven to 350°. Mix cream cheese, eggs, sugar, salt, lemon juice, vanilla and lemon peel. Pour into pan and bake for approximately 55 minutes. Cool and chill.

TOPPING

3 tablespoons sugar
1 tablespoon cornstarch
1 cup unsweetened pineapple juice

¼ teaspoon grated lemon peel
1 can pineapple rings

Mix sugar and cornstarch in a saucepan. Combine pineapple juice and lemon peel. Heat, stirring constantly, until mixture comes to a boil. Cook and stir until thick and clear. Cool to room temperature. Cover cheesecake with canned pineapple rings cut in half. Spoon glaze over pineapple slices. Chill for 1½ to 2 hours. Garnish with whipped cream, if desired.

Ralph Carr

CLASSIC MILESTONE

1977 - In Houston's first year of eligibility in the Southwest Conference, the Cougars tied Texas Tech for the championship and went on to post a 30-21 victory over previously unbeaten Maryland.

TEXAS PRALINE CHEESECAKE
State Fair winner.

NUT CRUMB CRUST
¾ cup graham cracker crumbs
¾ cup pecans

6 tablespoons butter, melted
¼ cup sugar

Preheat oven to 350°. In a mixing bowl, mix crumbs, pecans, butter and sugar. Blend well. Press mixture onto the bottom and halfway up the sides of a greased 9-inch springform mold. Smooth crumb mixture along the bottom to an even thickness. Bake for 10 minutes. Cool before filling.

CHEESECAKE
1½ pounds cream cheese, room
  temperature
1 cup dark brown sugar
2 tablespoons flour

3 large eggs
1 teaspoon vanilla
⅓ cup chopped pecans

Preheat oven to 350°. Beat cream cheese with the sugar and flour until smooth. Add eggs, one at a time, beating well after each addition. Add vanilla and pecans; blend well. Pour mixture into prepared crust. Bake for 50 minutes. Open oven door and allow cake to cool to room temperature.

TOPPING
Maple syrup

Pecan halves or chopped pecans

Brush cooled cheesecake with maple syrup. Place pecans in desired shape over cake or sprinkle cake with chopped pecans.

Marcella Leeper

MINCEMEAT CAKE

1 jar (1 pound, 2 ounces) mincemeat
  with brandy and rum
1 cup broken pecans
1 cup white raisins
½ cup melted margarine
1 cup sugar

3 eggs
3 egg whites
1 teaspoon baking soda
1 tablespoon boiling water
2 cups flour (sifted)
1 teaspoon vanilla

Put first 5 ingredients in a bowl. Add beaten egg yolks and baking soda dissolved in boiling water. Add flour. Fold in stiffly beaten egg whites and vanilla. Pour into greased and floured Bundt pan and bake at 300° for 1½ hours.

Note: 8 ounces of candied fruit may be added if desired.

Frances Dollar
Bob Dollar Antiques

David Wade

KRLD RADIO
NEWS - SPORTS
INFORMATION
1080 AM

DAVID WADE'S LEMON PIE

1/4 cup cornstarch
3 tablespoons flour
1 3/4 cup sugar
1/4 teaspoon salt
1/2 package unflavored gelatin
4 egg yolks, slightly beaten
1/2 cup lemon juice
1 tablespoon grated lemon peel
1 tablespoon butter

In medium-sized saucepan, combine cornstarch, flour, sugar,
salt and gelatin. Mix well. Gradually add 2 cups water
and stir until mixture is smooth. Bring to a boil over
medium heat. Boil 1 minute then remove from heat and
quickly stir some hot mixture into slightly beaten egg
yolks. Return to hot mixture. Cook over low heat 5 minutes,
stirring constantly. Remove again from heat and stir in
lemon juice, lemon peel and butter. Pour mixture into
baked pie shell. Top with meringue and brown meringue.
Cool completely before serving.

MERINGUE

4 egg whites, room temperature
1/4 teaspoon cream of tartar
1/2 cup sugar

Add cream of tartar to egg whites and beat mixture until
stiff but not dry. Add sugar slowly.

 University of
Nebraska
Lincoln

CHEESECAKE PIE

Crust:
  1 cup fine graham cracker crumbs
  1/4 cup sugar
  1/4 cup melted butter or margarine

Filling:
  2 8- ounce packages white cream cheese
  2 unbeaten eggs
  1/3 cup sugar
  1/2 cup Pet Evaporated Milk
  1 teaspoon vanilla

Cherry, peach or pineapple preserves

To make crust, mix together graham cracker crumbs, sugar and melted butter or margarine. Press on bottom and sides of 9 inch pan. Build up edge of crust about 1/4 inch above rim. Set aside until needed.

To make filling, let cream cheese stand in a 1 1/2 quart bowl until softened. Beat cheese until fluffy, either by hand or with an electric beater at medium speed. Add eggs and sugar and beat until smooth. Add evaporated milk and vanilla, a little at a time, beating until smooth each time. Pour into crumb crust. Bake 300 near center of oven 45 minutes. Take from oven and cool at room temperature. Pie will settle as it cools. Spread with your choice of preserves. Serve chilled.

Best regards,

M. A. Massengale

M. A. Massengale
Chancellor

SCHOLARSHIP PAGEANT

THREE LAYER RAISIN PIE

1 cup seedless raisins
1 cup dairy sour cream
1 cup sugar
2 eggs
½ teaspoon cinnamon
¼ teaspoon cloves

¼ teaspoon salt
1 tablespoon butter
1 3-oz. package cream cheese softened
½ cup sifted powdered sugar
1 cup whipping cream

Chop raisins, add sour cream, sugar, eggs, spices, and salt.
Bring to a boil, then cook over reduced heat until thickened,
stirring constantly.
Add butter; cool completely.
Blend cream cheese and powdered sugar together.
Whip cream and fold into cheese mixture.
Spread half of the cheese mixture into a baked 9" pie shell.
Add the raisin mixture and then top with remaining cheese combination.

B. Don Magness
Chairman of the board
Miss Texas Scholarship Pageant

The University of Alabama
Department of Athletics
P. O. Box K
University, Alabama 35486

National Football Champions
1961, 1964, 1965, 1973, 1978, and 1979

The Crimson Tide

Rose Bowl	Sugar Bowl	Orange Bowl	Cotton Bowl	Bluebonnet Bowl	Liberty Bowl	Gator Bowl	Sun Bowl
1926-1927	1945-1948	1943-1953	1942-1954	1960-1970	1959-1969	1968	1983
1931-1935	1961-1963	1962-1964	1967-1972		1976		
1938-1946	1966-1973	1965-1971	1981-1982		1982		
	1975-1978	1975					
	1979-1980						

STATE OF ALABAMA

GOVERNOR'S OFFICE

MONTGOMERY 36130

GEORGE C. WALLACE
GOVERNOR

CHOCOLATE PIE

2 squares chocolate (unsweetened)
2 Tablespoons butter
1/3 cup flour or cornstarch
1 cup sugar
1/4 teaspoon salt
2 1/2 cups milk (scalded)
3 eggs separated
3/4 teaspoon vanilla
Baked 8 inch pastry shell

Meringue:

1/3 cup sugar
3 egg whites

Melt chocolate and butter. Mix flour or cornstarch, sugar, and salt - stir into chocolate. Mix until blended. Add 1 cup of hot milk and stir until smooth. Add remaining milk and cook until thickened. Add some of the chocolate mixture to 3 well-beaten egg yolks and then put back in the rest of the chocolate mixture. Cook for 2 minutes.

Pour into baked pastry shell and top with the meringue. Bake 12-15 minutes at 350 degrees.

Sincerely yours,

George C. Wallace

ROBERT D. ORR
GOVERNOR

The Governor likes Mrs. Orr's Crumb Apple Pie recipe. Here it is . . .

CRUMB APPLE PIE

8 tart apples (about 4 pounds)	CRUST
2/3 cup sugar	
1/2 teaspoon cinnamon	1/2 cup firmly packed brown sugar
1/4 teaspoon nutmeg	1/2 cup butter
2 tablespoons lemon juice	1 cup flour
2 tablespoons water	
2 tablespoons butter	

Pare and slice the apples thin to get about 12 cups sliced apples. Put into a deep 9-inch pie pan. Stir together the sugar, cinnamon and nutmeg. Mix together lemon juice and water and sprinkle over apples. Sprinkle sugar mixture on top and mix to coat all slices, dot with butter.
For the crust, cream together the brown sugar and butter, add flour. Sprinkle on top of apples. Bake in a 350-degree oven 45 to 50 minutes. Serve slightly warm with ice cream, whipped cream or slices of cheddar cheese.

NOTE: If too warm, the pie will be hard to cut.

STRAWBERRY PIE

(Serves 6)

1 1/3 cups granulated sugar
1 1/4 cups cold water
1/4 cup cornstarch
1/8 teaspoon salt
1 tablespoon lemon juice
Few drops red food coloring
1 quart fresh strawberries, sliced
    or whole
1 baked pie shell
1 small carton whipping cream, whipped

Mix sugar and 1/2 cup water. Dissolve
cornstarch in remaining water. Add
salt and lemon juice and food coloring.
Cook mixture until thick and clear.
Pour over strawberries. Cool. Pour
into baked shell. Chill several hours,
top with whipped cream, and serve.

Bobby Collins

CORNERSTONE
INVESTMENT CORPORATION

Jim Williams, Jr. *President*

BLUEBERRY DREAM PIE
(Makes 2 pies)

2 pkg Dream Whip
8 oz cream cheese
1 cup powdered sugar
2 pie shells
1 cup chopped pecans
2 - 3 1/2 cups washed, drained blueberries
1 carton Cool Whip

Prepare Dream Whip and mix with cream cheese and powdered sugar

Bake 2 pie shells with half chopped pecans in bottom of each and cool

Spread cheese mixture on bottom and then fill with blueberries

Cover with cool whip before serving

From the desk of —

LEE TREVINO

Lee's Favorite Pumpkin Pie

1 3/4 cup canned pumpkin
1 cup sugar
4 eggs
1 cup milk
1 teas. cinnamon
1/2 teas. ginger
1/2 teas. allspice
pinch of salt

Preheat oven to 475.

1. Add pumpkin, sugar and spices.
2. Beat eggs with a little sugar.
3. Add milk.
4. Bake in a deep dish pie crust -
15 minutes at 475, then 45 minutes at 350.
When knife comes out clean - it's done.

KEN TRACEY'S LEMON CHIFFON PIE

1 (9-inch) pie shell
1 envelope unflavored gelatin
¼ cup cold water
4 eggs

½ cup lemon juice
1 cup sugar
¼ teaspoon salt
1 tablespoon grated lemon peel

Bake the pie shell. Let cool completely before filling. Sprinkle gelatin over water in a measuring cup or small bowl; set aside to soften. Separate eggs, placing whites in large bowl of electric mixer, yolks in double boiler top. Set whites aside to warm to room temperature until ready to use in about 30 minutes. Beat yolks slightly with wooden spoon. Stir in lemon juice, ½ cup sugar and the salt. Cook over hot—not boiling—water (water should not touch bottom of double boiler top), stirring constantly until mixture thickens and coats metal spoon—about 10 minutes. Add gelatin mixture and lemon peel, stirring until gelatin is dissolved. Remove pan from hot water. Refrigerate, stirring occasionally, until cool and the consistency of unbeaten egg whites—about 35 minutes. At high speed, beat egg whites until foamy throughout and soft peaks form when the beater is slowly raised. Gradually beat in remaining ½ cup sugar, 2 tablespoons at a time, beating well after each addition. Continue to beat until stiff peaks form when beater is raised. With rubber scraper or wire whisk, gently fold gelatin mixture into egg white mixture, just until combined (using an under and over motion). Gently turn into cooled pie shell, mounding high. Refrigerate for 3 to 6 hours or until firm.

Kenneth D. Tracey
Executive Director
Sigma Alpha Epsilon

BAVARIAN CREAM PIE

2 small cans crushed pineapple, drained, reserving juice
1 small jar maraschino cherries, drained and chopped, reserving juice
1 small package lemon gelatin
1 (1-pound) package vanilla wafer crumbs

2 sticks margarine or butter
3 medium ripe bananas, mashed
¾ cup chopped pecans
12 miniature marshmallows, cut in small pieces
½ pint cream, whipped
3 tablespoons sugar

Measure 1 cup juice from pineapple and cherries, adding water if necessary to yield 1 cup. Heat in a saucepan until just warmed. Mix with gelatin, stirring until dissolved. Transfer to large bowl and refrigerate until mixture becomes syrupy. Meanwhile, make 2 pie crusts by mixing vanilla wafers with margarine; refrigerate the prepared crusts. Mix pineapple, cherries, bananas, pecans, marshmallows. Combine with the gelatin mixture. Fold in the whipped cream which has been mixed with the sugar. Pour into pie crusts. Sprinkle any leftover crumbs on top. Refrigerate for 12 hours before serving.

Mrs. Jimmie E. Franklin

KEY LIME PIE DELTA GAMMA

4 eggs
1 can sweetened condensed milk
1 cup lime juice
1 tablespoon grated lime rind
¼ teaspoon salt

⅓ cup sugar
¼ teaspoon salt
2 to 3 drops green food coloring
1 graham cracker pie crust

In a medium bowl, beat eggs well and add condensed milk. Mix in lime juice and grated rind a little at a time. Beat until stiff. Stir in sugar, salt and food coloring. Pour into crust and bake at 350° for 15 minutes. Cool, chill and serve. For a decorative touch, slice a lime as thinly as possible. Make a cut from the center of the slice to the outside surface. Twist each slice until it forms a spiral shape. Garnish individual pie servings with the spiral lime slice.

Kathy Nelms

STRAWBERRY BANANA PIE

1 (10-ounce) package frozen sweetened
  strawberries
Water
½ cup sugar
2 tablespoons cornstarch
Juice of 1 large lemon
1 tablespoon unflavored gelatin

2 tablespoons cold water
1 (9-inch) pie crust, baked
2 or 3 bananas
½ pint whipping cream
1 tablespoon sugar
Few drops vanilla

Thaw strawberries and drain off juice. Measure juice and add enough water to make 1 cup. Blend ½ cup sugar with the cornstarch and add strawberry juice. Bring to a boil over medium heat, stirring constantly, and cook for about 3 minutes. Remove from heat and add lemon juice and gelatin which has been softened in the 2 tablespoons cold water. Let cool. Add strawberries and chill in refrigerator until slightly thickened. Spread half the strawberry mixture in the baked pie crust. Add sliced bananas. Top with remaining strawberry mixture. Chill until firm. Whip the whipping cream and fold in 1 tablespoon sugar and the vanilla. Pile lightly on pie.

PIE CRUST
1½ cups flour
½ teaspoon salt

½ cup Crisco
3 to 4 tablespoons ice water

Sift together the flour and salt. Cut in Crisco. Mix in water, a little at a time. Roll out on dough board and fit in pie pan. Bake at 375° for about 15 to 20 minutes or until lightly browned.

Mrs. Frank Rowland (Lorene)

KAPPA KEY AMARETTO PIE

1 pound Hershey's milk chocolate with almonds
1½ to 3 ounces amaretto
2½ cups heavy cream, whipped

1 (8-inch) graham cracker or chocolate cookie crust
Chocolate sprinkles, to garnish

Melt chocolate in a double boiler. Remove from heat. Add amaretto to whipped cream, then mix with chocolate and pour into crust. Chill at least 1 hour. Garnish with additional whipped cream and chocolate sprinkles. Serves 8 to 9.

Sue Isbell

PECAN PIE ALPHA PHI

1¼ cups sugar
4 eggs, well beaten
¾ cup Log Cabin syrup
¾ cup evaporated milk

½ teaspoon salt
1 teaspoon vanilla
1½ cups coarsely chopped pecans
2 (8-inch) unbaked pie shells

In large bowl mix sugar, eggs, syrup, milk, salt and vanilla. Add pecans and mix well. Pour into unbaked pie shells and bake at 350° for about 10 minutes; reduce heat to 325° and continue baking for about 35 to 40 minutes, or until a knife inserted into center of pie comes out clean.

Madeline Russell

PECAN PIE POINTS AFTER

4 eggs
1 cup sugar
⅛ teaspoon salt
1½ cups Karo corn syrup
2 tablespoons plus 1 teaspoon butter, melted and cooled

1 teaspoon vanilla
1 cup pecan halves
1 (10-inch) unbaked pie shell

Preheat oven to 350°. Beat eggs until just blended, but not frothy. Add sugar, salt and corn syrup. Add butter and vanilla, mixing just enough to blend. Spread nuts in bottom of pie shell. Pour in filling. Place pie in oven. Immediately reduce heat to 325°, and bake for 50 to 60 minutes. I make this pie in great numbers and give as gifts to friends and neighbors at Christmas. One pie serves 8 to 10.

Mrs. John Stuart (Barbara)
Wife, 2nd Vice President
Cotton Bowl Athletic Association

PECAN ALPHA DELTA PIE

¼ teaspoon salt
1 cup sugar
1 cup white Karo syrup
3 eggs, beaten
1 tablespoon vanilla

3 tablespoons milk
1½ cups chopped pecans
1 (9-inch) unbaked pie shell
Butter

Mix together salt and sugar. Add Karo and mix well. Combine beaten eggs, vanilla and milk and stir into syrup mixture. Add pecans and stir until coated. Pour into pie shell, dot with butter on top and bake at 350° for about 1 hour. Note: Butter or margarine is the secret to a good pecan pie. You will not have the sticky, chewy part around your crust if you use thin ¼-inch to ½-inch round butter dots placed 1-inch apart over the top of the pie.

Donna Cook
Artist

FLUFFY PEANUT BUTTER PIE BETA PHI

1 (8-ounce) package cream cheese,
   softened
1 (14-ounce) can Eagle Brand milk
¾ to 1 cup creamy peanut butter
3 tablespoons lemon juice

1 teaspoon vanilla
1 cup Cool Whip
Chocolate syrup

Beat cream cheese until fluffy. Add Eagle Brand milk and peanut butter, beating until smooth. Stir in lemon juice and vanilla. Fold in Cool Whip. Turn into crust and drizzle chocolate syrup over pie. Using a knife, gently swirl chocolate syrup into pie filling to produce a marbled effect. Chill 4 hours.

CRUST
1 cup flour
1 cup chopped pecans

½ cup butter, softened

Mix ingredients and pat into the bottom of a lightly greased pie plate. Bake at 350° for 20 minutes.

Mr. and Mrs. Norm Bulaich (Susie)

CLASSIC MILESTONE

1978 - Notre Dame became the first Cotton Bowl team to receive a million dollar check for its New Year's Day appearance against Texas. In the process, the Fighting Irish spoiled the Longhorns' national championship hopes with a 38-10 upset. The victory vaulted Notre Dame into the No. 1 spot. It was the seventh time the national title was either won or lost in the Cotton Bowl.

CHOCOLATE CREAM PIE POWER SWEEP

¾ cup sugar
⅓ cup cornstarch
2 squares unsweetened chocolate
½ teaspoon salt
2½ cups milk

3 egg yolks
½ teaspoon vanilla
1 pie shell, baked
1 carton Cool Whip

Mix sugar, cornstarch, chocolate, salt, milk, egg yolks and vanilla in saucepan or double boiler; cook until thick. Pour into baked pie shell; cool. Garnish with Cool Whip to serve.

Mrs. Donny Anderson (Karen)
Wife, Cotton Bowl Director

ICE CREAM DOUBLE TEAM DELIGHT PIE

2 cups sifted flour
½ cup Minute Oats
½ cup brown sugar
2 sticks butter, softened

1 cup pecans
½ jar caramel topping
½ gallon butter pecan ice cream

Combine flour, oats and sugar in a mixing bowl. Cut in butter. Stir in pecans. Pat mixture into cookie sheet. Bake at 400° for 15 minutes. Remove from oven and stir to crumble the mixture. Cool. Spread about half the crumbs into the bottom of a pie plate. Drizzle caramel topping over crumbs. Top with ice cream. Sprinkle remaining crumbs over ice cream.

Doris Null

CHOCO-TEX SMOOTHIE PIE

1 cup mayonnaise
1 pound cream cheese, softened
1 cup sugar
4 eggs

12 ounces chocolate chips
Water
½ teaspoon vanilla
1 chocolate cookie pie crust

Blend the mayonnaise with the cream cheese and sugar. Add eggs, one at a time. Melt chocolate chips in a little water and add to cream cheese mixture. Stir in the vanilla. Pour into a chocolate cookie pie crust and bake at 350° for about 20 minutes.

Donald R. Lear
Director of Food and Beverage
Neiman-Marcus

GEORGIA BULLDOGS

These are as good as they sound!

KILLER BROWNIES

1 small bag caramels
2/3 cup evaporated milk
1 pkg German Chocolate cake mix
3/4 c. soft margarine
1 c. chopped nuts
6 oz pkg of chocolate chips

Melt 1 small bag caramels with 1/3 c. evaporated milk. Let cool.

Mix: Chocolate cake mix, margarine, 1/3 c. evaporated milk, 1 c. nuts (opt).
Press 1/2 of the cake mixture in a greased and floured pan (large oblong).
Mixture may stick to spoon, use flour and pat down. Bake 350° for 6 minutes.

Remove from oven and sprinkle chocolate chips over baked layer.
Pour caramel mixture over the chocolate chips then put the rest of the batter
over that mixture. This is easier to do if you pat down some batter in your
hands and lay it over caramel mixture.

Bake at 350° for 15 minutes.

This recipe is really good and is easy when you are on the run.

NO PEEK STEW

1½ lb. beef stew meat
carrots
celery
potatoes
onions

1 Tbsp. cornstarch
1 can beef bouillon soup
1½ Tbsp. sugar
3 Tbsp wine or wine vinegar
1 bay leaf
1 can tomatoe paste or 2 cans tomatoes

Combine all ingredients. Bake, covered, at 325° and don't peek for 6 hours.

Best regards,

Kent Lawrence

Kent Lawrence

LOUIS DANIEL Illustration and Design

Lemon Bars

1 C butter (unsalted)
1/4 tsp. salt
1/2 C Powdered sugar
2 C flour

Blend together until dough forms.
Press into 13 x 15 jelly roll pan.
bake @ 350° for 25-30 minutes.

4 eggs slightly beaten
4 T. lemon juice
2 C sugar
4 T. flour
grated rind of 1 lemon

Mix flour in sugar, add to eggs
and stir well. Add lemon juice
and rind and pour over first
mixture. Bake @ 325° for 25-30
minutes (until firm).
Cut when cool. Dust with powered sugar.
Keep in refrigerator.

shirley & Louis daniel

Executive Director: Randy Matson '67

THE ASSOCIATION OF FORMER STUDENTS

WHOLE WHEAT CHOCOLATE CHIP COOKIES

1	Cup Crisco	1	teaspoon baking soda
1½	Cups packed brown sugar	½	teaspoon salt
2	Eggs	2	Cups chopped pecans
1	teaspoon vanilla	1	Cup (6 ounces) Hershey's
2¼	Cups whole wheat flour		semisweet chocolate chips
	(sift 3 times, then measure)		

Cream Crisco, brown sugar, eggs and vanilla. Sift flour several times; then sift together with baking soda and salt. Add to creamed mixture. Stir in pecans and chocolate chips. Drop by large rounded teaspoonsful onto ungreased cookie sheet. Bake at 375° approximately 8 to 10 minutes, until light brown.

EXECUTIVE OFFICE
STATE OF MISSOURI
JEFFERSON CITY

JOHN ASHCROFT
GOVERNOR

JANET'S CHOCOLATE CHIP COOKIES

4½ cups flour
2 teaspoons baking soda
1 teaspoon salt
1½ cups sugar
1½ cups brown sugar
2 cups shortening (not butter)

2 teaspoons vanilla
1 teaspoon water
4 eggs
12 oz. chocolate chips
2 cups chopped pecans

Combine flour, baking soda and salt. Set aside. In a
separate bowl combine sugar, brown sugar, shortening,
vanilla and water. Beat until mixture is creamy. Beat
in eggs. Add flour mixture a half cup at a time and mix
well. Stir in chocolate chips and nuts. Refrigerate
dough several hours or overnight. Shape teaspoonfuls of
dough into balls and place on greased cookie sheets. Bake
at 325 degrees for 10 minutes. Allow to cool for at least
1 minute before removing from pans.

GOVERNOR

DEPARTMENT OF INTERCOLLEGIATE ATHLETICS FOR MEN

THE UNIVERSITY OF TEXAS AT AUSTIN

Austin, Texas 78713-7399

GRANDMA PATTIE'S CHOCOLATE COOKIES

2 cups brown sugar
1 cup shortening (Crisco)
2 eggs
3/4 cup cocoa--dissolved in small amount of hot water
3 cups flour
1/2 tsp. salt
2 tsp. soda--dissolved in 1 tbsp. hot water
1 cup sour milk (buttermilk)
1 cup raisins (optional)
1 cup chopped nuts (optional)
1 tsp. vanilla

Cream sugar and shortening. Add eggs and beat well. Use just enough hot water to dissolve cocoa and cool. Add cocoa and dissolved soda. Alternate adding flour and sour milk. Last, add raisins and nuts, if desired, and vanilla.

Drop by spoonful onto cookie sheet. Bake about 15 minutes or until finger dent will not remain on cookies in 350° oven. Makes about 7 dozen. May or may not be frosted. Make frosting with butter, cocoa, buttermilk and powdered sugar.

DeLoss Dodds

APPLE CRUNCH

1 can apple pie filling
1 small package Jiffy white cake mix
¾ cup finely chopped nuts

¼ cup shredded coconut (optional)
1 stick butter, melted

Spread pie filling on ungreased 10x10-inch pan. Spread dry cake mix over pie filling. Spread chopped nuts mixed with coconut over cake mix. Spoon melted butter on top and bake at 350° for 30 to 35 minutes. Serve hot, warm or cold. Note: You may vary this with another fruit pie filling such as cherry, peach, etc. I like the almonds with apple, and pecans with cherry.

Mrs. Floyd Kinser (Dorothy)

CAMPUS BOOKSTORE BABY BLINTZES
Very easy and very yummy!

Thin bread slices
Whipped cream cheese
Butter, melted

Cinnamon
Sugar

Remove crusts from bread. Spread bread slices lightly with cream cheese. Roll each slice jelly roll style. Cut each roll into fourths. Dip in melted butter, roll in mixture of cinnamon and sugar, and broil for 2 to 3 minutes.

Mr. and Mrs. Mike Gore (Linda)

ALABAMA CHEWS

¼ pound butter
2 cups sugar
4 eggs
2½ cups flour

2 teaspoons baking powder
2 cups brown sugar
1 teaspoon vanilla
1 cup or less pecans

Cream butter with sugar. Separate 2 of the eggs. Add the 2 egg yolks and the remaining 2 whole eggs to the creamed mixture. Mix in flour and baking powder. Spread mixture into 2 greased 8x8-inch pans. Beat the 2 egg whites with the brown sugar until stiff. Stir in vanilla. Spread over first mixture in pans. Sprinkle with pecans. Bake at 350° for 30 minutes. Cut into squares while hot.

Mr. and Mrs. Theodore Pibil (Lenora)

RANGER COOKIES

1 cup flour	1 egg, well beaten
¼ teaspoon baking powder	1 teaspoon vanilla
½ teaspoon soda	¾ cup quick-cooking rolled oats
½ teaspoon salt	½ cup chopped walnuts or pecans
⅔ cup shortening	¼ cup pitted, chopped dates
1 cup brown sugar	1 cup corn flakes

Sift flour with baking powder, soda and salt; set aside. Cream shortening, gradually add sugar, and cream until light. Add egg and vanilla; mix thoroughly. Add flour mixture; mix well. Stir in oats, nuts and dates. Gently stir in corn flakes. Drop by teaspoon onto lightly greased cookie sheet. Bake at 375° for 10 to 12 minutes. Note: If dates are dried out, cut into small pieces, add a little water and simmer for a few minutes. Cover and let stand for a few minutes.

Mrs. Otto H. Eisenlohr (Nell)
Wife, Cotton Bowl President 1952-1954

PEP RALLY PECAN CHEWS

¼ pound plus 1 teaspoon butter	2 teaspoons baking powder
2 cups sugar	2 cups brown sugar
4 eggs	1 teaspoon vanilla
2½ cups flour	1 cup shelled pecans

Cream butter with sugar; stir in 2 eggs. Separate remaining 2 eggs and set aside the egg whites. Add yolks to butter mixture. Mix flour and baking powder and mix into butter-egg mixture. Pour into 2 greased 8x8-inch pans. Beat egg whites with brown sugar until stiff. Stir in vanilla. Pour or spread over batter in pans. Sprinkle with pecans. Bake at 350° for 30 minutes. Cut into squares while hot.

Mrs. William R. Gardner (Mary Ann)

CLASSIC MILESTONE

1978 - The 42nd Classic featured six individual national awards as well as the nation's top ranked Texas Longhorns and No. 5 Notre Dame. The Longhorns featured Earl Campbell, the winner of the Heisman Trophy, and Outland Trophy recipient Brad Shearer. Notre Dame was led by the Lombardi and Maxwell Award winner Ross Browner, who also won the previous year's Outland, and that season's Walter Camp honoree, Ken MacAfee.

KAREN'S PECAN CHEWIES

1 box light brown sugar
1 (35-cent) package biscuit mix

4 eggs
1½ cups pecans

Mix ingredients well. Spread mixture in a lightly greased 9x9-inch pan and bake at 350° for 45 minutes. Let cool. Slice into squares. Yields 12 squares.

Karen Hopkins

SOUR CREAM COOKIES

3 cups flour, sifted
1 teaspoon baking powder
½ teaspoon soda
½ teaspoon salt
1 cup margarine
1½ cups sugar

2 eggs
1 cup sour cream
1 teaspoon vanilla
¼ cup sugar
1 teaspoon cinnamon

Sift flour with baking powder, soda and salt; set aside. In large bowl of electric mixer, on medium speed, beat margarine, 1½ cups sugar and eggs until light. At low speed, in small bowl, beat sour cream and vanilla until smooth. Add to egg mixture in large mixing bowl. Gradually blend flour mixture and cream mixture until well blended. Refrigerate batter for several hours or overnight. Drop by teaspoon onto greased cookie sheet. Sprinkle sugar and cinnamon mixture over cookies before baking. Bake at 375° for 10 to 12 minutes or until brown. Makes 10 dozen cookies.

Mrs. Otto H. Eisenlohr (Nell)
Wife, Cotton Bowl President 1952-1954

PECAN KISSES A LA MAID OF COTTON
This was my grandmother's recipe.

2 egg whites, stiffly beaten
½ cup sugar

1 cup pecans

Fold the egg whites with two-thirds of the sugar. Mix in remaining sugar and pecans. Bake in a very low oven for 40 minutes.

Mrs. Robert F. Jones (Annetta)

ECONOMICAL OATMEAL COOKIES

1 cup butter
1 cup sugar
1 cup brown sugar
½ teaspoon vanilla
2 eggs
1¼ cups flour

1 teaspoon soda
½ teaspoon salt
½ teaspoon cinnamon
3 cups oatmeal
½ cup nuts

Cream butter, sugar and brown sugar. Stir in vanilla and eggs. Mix flour, soda, salt and cinnamon and stir into creamed mixture. Add oatmeal and nuts. Roll and slice or drop by spoonfuls onto baking sheet. Bake at 350° for 10 to 15 minutes.

Mrs. Phil Gramm (Wendy)
Wife of U.S. Congressman

OATMEAL 'LASSES NUGGETS
Tasty fortified morsels.

1 cup brown sugar, packed
1 stick margarine
2 eggs, well beaten
⅓ cup dark molasses
2 cups flour

2 teaspoons baking powder
2 cups quick-cooking oats
½ cup chopped nuts
1 cup raisins, dates or other dried fruit

Cream brown sugar and margarine. Stir in eggs and molasses, beating to blend ingredients. Mix flour with baking powder and add to the creamed mixture, stirring until batter is stiff. Stir in oats, nuts and raisins. The dough should be very stiff and firm. Add more oats, if necessary. Drop by large spoonfuls onto a cookie sheet and bake at 375° for 10 to 12 minutes or until light golden brown.

Mina W. Lamb
Professor Emeritus
Texas Tech University

BOILED COOKIES

2 cups sugar
½ cup milk
1 stick butter
4 tablespoons cocoa

2½ cups quick cooking oats
¼ cup chopped nuts
½ cup peanut butter
2 teaspoons vanilla

Cook sugar, milk, butter and cocoa in a saucepan for 30 seconds. Remove from heat and add oats, nuts, peanut butter and vanilla. Beat until blended. Spoon onto waxed paper. Chill for 20 to 30 minutes.

Angel Hightower
Miss Dallas USA 1986

LEMON BARS

CRUST
1 cup butter   ½ cup confectioners' sugar
2 cups flour

Combine ingredients using dough blender until mixture resembles small crumbs. Press into a 16x8-inch pan and bake at 350° for 15 minutes.

FILLING
4 eggs, lightly beaten   2 teaspoons grated lemon rind
2 cups sugar   4 tablespoons flour
4 tablespoons lemon juice   1 teaspoon baking powder

Mix ingredients and pour over baked crust. Bake at 350° for 20 to 25 minutes. Sift small amount of confectioners' sugar over filling when partially cool. Cut and remove from pan when cool.

Mrs. R. Guy Carter (Phyllis)
Wife, Cotton Bowl Director

CHOCOLATE NO-BAKE SQUARES

2 cups sugar   3 cups oatmeal
½ cup cocoa   1 cup peanut butter
½ cup milk   1 teaspoon vanilla
½ cup butter

In a saucepan mix sugar, cocoa, milk and butter; heat and boil for 1 minute. Stir in oatmeal, peanut butter and vanilla, mixing quickly. Pour into pan and let set for 1 hour. Cut into 2-inch squares to serve.

Cindy Losoya
Miss Fort Worth

CLASSIC MILESTONE

1979 - Notre Dame quarterback Joe Montana rallied his team from a 22-point fourth quarter deficit to tie the game at 34 on the final play of the contest. Then Dallas native Joe Unis came on to add the extra point to down the Houston Cougars, 35-34. It truly was a miracle finish.

"This is a dish my mother-in-law made for me the
first time I visited Sweden. It is one of my
favorite desserts."

PLATTAR

To serve 6 to 8
3 eggs
2 cups milk or 1 cup of milk and one
                    cup of light cream
1 cup flour
6 tablespoons unsalted butter, melted
½ teaspoon salt

Beat the eggs together with ½ cup of milk for 2
or 3 minutes with a rotary beater or whisk. Add
the flour all at once and beat to a heavy, smooth
consistency. Beat in the remaining milk and then
the melted butter and salt. Because of the large
amount of butter in the batter, the skillet will
require little additional buttering.

A heavy cast-iron skillet can be used, but first
grease it lightly with a pastry brush or paper
towel dipped into a little melted butter (this
step need not be repeated). When the skillet is
very hot, drop 1 tablespoon of batter into the
pan for each pancake; each should form a 3-inch
circle. When the edges brown lightly after about
1 minute, turn the pancakes with a spatula and
cook another minute or two. In Swedish families,
the plattar are served "from pan to plate" but if
necessary, set each batch of pancakes aside on a
platter and keep them warm in a 200 degree oven
while you complete the rest.

Serve with a filling of fresh strawberries crushed
with a little sugar. Put a spoonful in between
each little pancake. Stack 4 or 5 high and finish
off with a generous spoonful of whipped cream.

COTTON BOWL ATHLETIC ASSOCIATION
POST OFFICE BOX 47420 ● DALLAS, TEXAS 75247-0420
214/634-7525

MIKE JUSTICE
BUSINESS MANAGER

HOMEMADE ICE CREAM

5 eggs
1 can Eagle Brand milk
2 pints half & half
1 teaspoon vanilla
3/4 cup sugar
Fill with milk
Rock salt & ice

To the above recipe, add any of the following ingredients. Process for approximately 30 minutes in electric or hand-crank ice cream freezer. For an extra creamy mixture, place additives in a blender with a small portion of liquid mixture and then return to the remainder of ingredients.

Additives:

    Bananas
    Chocolate chips
    Peppermint (round candy)
    Peaches
    Nestle's Crunch Bars
    Strawberries
    Cherries

Mike Justice

ICE CREAM

FIVE THREE SHERBERT

3 CUPS WATER

3 CUPS SUGAR

3 ORANGES (OR 1 CAN CONCENTRATE)

3 LEMONS

3 BANANAS

MIX JUICE, MASHED BANANAS, SUGAR AND WATER.
CHILL THOROUGHLY.   ADD 1 CAN (LARGE) PET MILK
AND FINISH FILLING GALLON FREEZER WITH FRESH
MILK.   FREEZE IN ICE CREAM FREEZER--DELICIOUS!

Bob Hitch

Texas House of Representatives

Gibson D. (Gib) Lewis
SPEAKER

CHOCOLATE MOUSSE

1 pound sweet chocolate
6 eggs
1 cup butter
whipping cream
vanilla or rum
pinch of salt
sugar
1/3 cup chopped nuts or grated chocolate

Melt the chocolate in a double boiler. Add the egg yolks one at a time,
beating each one in thoroughly. Keep heat very low. Next add butter
which should be very soft, not melted. Beat vigorously. Remove from
heat. Beat the egg whites stiff, but not dry, with a pinch of salt and
fold into the chocolate mixture thoroughly so that no egg whites show.
Put in a greased 6 cup mold, bowl, or individual cups. Let stand in
refrigerator overnight. About an hour before serving, turn out dessert.
Dip into hot water once or twice to facilitate turning it out unto a
plate. Frost with whipped cream flavored with a little sugar and
vanilla or rum. Sprinkle with nuts or grated chocolate. Chill before
serving. Serves 8 to 10.

Gib Lewis

Office of the
Head Football Coach

HOMEMADE VANILLA ICE CREAM

4 eggs
2¼ cups sugar
Dash of salt
Pint of half & half
10 cups whole milk
2 Tablespoons Adams Best vanilla (key to recipe)

Beat eggs, add sugar, salt, cream, milk and vanilla. (For a
creamier texture use 1 16 oz. can evaporated milk instead of
pint of half & half. Freeze according to the directions of
ice cream freezer. Makes one large freezer container.

HOT FUDGE SAUCE

4 squares unsweetened chocolate
3 cups sugar
¼ lb. butter
1 large can evaporated milk

Melt butter and chocolate. Stir in sugar, adding milk a little
at a time. Boil until smooth. (This may be done in the
microwave instead).

Serve over ice cream or fresh strawberries.

BLACKBERRY COBBLER

1 cup shortening
2 cups flour
    water
5 cups blackberries
4 thin slices butter
3/4 cup granulated sugar
2 teaspoons cornstarch

Cut shortening into flour until course like cornmeal. Add water, a little at a time, to make dough
stay together. Roll as thin as possible and place
in deep baking pan. Fill with berries. Mix cornstarch and sugar together. Sprinkle mixture evenly
over the berries. Dab the butter on top of the
sugar mixture. Cover with crust, folding together
at the edges. Slit dough and bake at 350 degrees
in oven until brown.

Mrs. Lamar Alexander

Sandy Hatfield

SCALLOPED PINEAPPLE

4 Cups bread cubes
2 (15½ oz.) cans crushed pineapple, undrained
½ Cup butter
1½ Cup sugar
3 Eggs
½ Cup milk

Cream sugar and butter. Add eggs, mix well. Add milk and then the remaining ingredients. Spread into a 9" x 13" pan. Sprinkle brown sugar and nutmeg over the top. Bake one hour at 350 degrees, uncovered.

Sandy Hatfield

Fairy Floss (Cotton Candy) Dessert

If you live in a low humidity area and can buy cotton candy wrapped air-tight on a stick or paper cone you have a memorable dessert.

Try this for a children's party, ladies' luncheon, or an important dinner party. Place cotton candy on plate in nest. Add ice cream ball in center. Pistachio ice cream is pretty, or if you have several assorted colors and flavors, make small balls ahead of time and place in freezer. When ready to serve, add assorted ice cream or sherbet balls to cotton candy and serve. May be topped with fresh berries.

TIP:
Purchase cotton candy not more than 24 hours in advance. Store in a cool, dry place in a plastic bag.

From PARTIES, PARTIES © *1984 Fran Chiles. Gulf Publishing Company, Houston, Texas.*

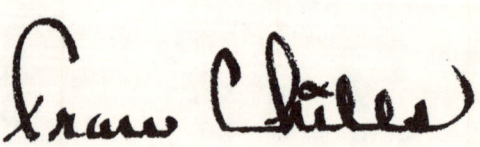

APPLE-GO-ROUND-PIZZA

Plain pastry recipe that calls for 2 cups
  of flour
7 to 8 medium apples
1½ tablespoons lemon juice
⅓ cup sugar

1 teaspoon cinnamon
¼ teaspoon nutmeg
¾ cup flour
½ cup sugar
½ cup butter

Roll pastry out to fit a large pizza pan (15-inch for example). Trim edges of pastry with pastry wheel; place pastry on pan. Core and slice apples. Beginning ¾-inch from edge of pastry, make circles, one inside the other, of overlapping apple slices. Sprinkle apples with lemon juice. Combine the ⅓ cup sugar with the spices; sprinkle over apples. Combine flour and the ½ cup sugar; cut in butter till crumbly. Sprinkle over top. Turn up the ¾-inch rim of pastry and flute. Bake in very hot oven (450°) 20 to 25 minutes or till crust is brown and apples are tender. Serve warm. Garnish center with wedges of gouda cheese. Makes 10 servings.

Ann Shira
Administrative Assistant
Cotton Bowl Athletic Association

PEACH CRISP REVEILLE

1 can peach pie filling
1 (5-ounce) stick pastry mix
¼ teaspoon cinnamon

½ cup brown sugar
¼ teaspoon nutmeg
Ice cream or whipped topping

Spread pie filling in buttered 8-inch layer cake pan. Mix pastry mix, cinnamon, sugar and nutmeg until crumbly. Sprinkle evenly over pie filling. Bake at 375° for 25 to 30 minutes, or until topping is golden. Serve warm or cool with ice cream or whipped topping.

Mrs. Bob Bolen
Wife, Mayor
Fort Worth, Texas

BANANA PUDDING

Quick, easy and no one can tell you use instant pudding!

1 (3-ounce) package instant vanilla
  pudding mix
2 cups milk
1 cup sweetened condensed milk
1 (8-ounce) carton sour cream

1 teaspoon vanilla
1 (4½-ounce) carton whipped topping
1 (12-ounce) box vanilla wafers
2 pounds bananas, sliced

Beat pudding mix and milk until smooth. Add condensed milk, sour cream, vanilla and whipped topping; mix until smooth. In serving dish, layer wafers, bananas and pudding mixture. Top with crushed wafers. Better after refrigeration overnight. Adjust amount of wafers and bananas to suit your own taste.

Mrs. Darrell Royal (Edith)

GRANDMA'S OUT OF BOUNDS BREAD PUDDING

4 generous cups stale biscuit crumbs
3 stale white bread slices, crumbled
3 eggs, lightly beaten
2 cups milk

2 cups sugar
½ teaspoon cinnamon
½ teaspoon allspice

Combine biscuit crumbs, bread crumbs, eggs, milk and sugar; mash together to mix well. Stir in cinnamon and allspice; let mixture stand until mushy. Pour into lightly greased loaf pan. Sprinkle top lightly with cinnamon and sugar. Bake at 300° for 1½ hours.

Debbie Crites
Portrait Artist

HAUPIA

Hawaiian coconut pudding.

6 cups fresh grated coconut
3 cups hot milk

6 tablespoons cornstarch
6 tablespoons sugar

Soak coconut in hot milk; let stand for 15 minutes. Strain liquid and measure 3 cups. Mix the cornstarch and sugar, adding enough coconut milk to make a smooth paste. Heat the remaining milk to boiling and slowly stir in the cornstarch paste. Boil until the mixture thickens, stirring frequently. Pour into a square cake pan, making a layer 2-inches thick. Allow the pudding to cool. Cut into 2-inch squares and serve on Ti leaf strips Hawaiian style!

Paul E. Bowman

PERSIMMON, DATE AND NUT PUDDING

2½ cups flour
2 cups sugar
2 teaspoons soda
3 teaspoons baking powder
1 teaspoon salt
1 cup fine bread crumbs

3 tablespoons melted butter or margarine
1 cup milk
1 teaspoon vanilla
2 cups persimmon pulp
2 cups chopped dates
2 cups chopped nuts

Sift flour, measure, then sift again with sugar, soda, baking powder and salt. Stir in the bread crumbs. Combine the melted butter with milk and vanilla; add to dry ingredients and mix until blended. Stir in the persimmon pulp, dates and nuts. Turn into greased pans. You may use 2 (8-inch) square pans, a 13x9-inch pan, or about 2 dozen large muffin cups. Bake at 350° for 1 hour for a loaf cake, or about 30 minutes for cupcakes. Serve with lemon sauce, whipped cream or ice cream.

LEMON SAUCE
½ cup butter
1 cup sugar
¼ cup water

1 egg, well-beaten
3 tablespoons lemon juice (1 lemon)
Grated rind of 1 lemon

Combine ingredients in a saucepan. Cook over medium heat, stirring constantly, until mixture comes to a boil. Yields 1⅓ cups.

Mary Ellen Durrett
Chairman, Department of Home Economics
The University of Texas at Austin

COURTYARD CHOCOLATE NUT PUDDING

8 eggs
4 cups sugar
1 cup flour
1 pound butter

6 ounces semisweet chocolate chips or 6 (1-ounce) squares Baker's semisweet chocolate
2 cups chopped pecans

In a medium mixing bowl, combine eggs, sugar and flour and beat until smooth and creamy. In 2 separate saucepans, melt the butter and chocolate. (Chocolate can be melted in double boiler or in a regular saucepan with a little water added to keep it from sticking.) When butter melts, beat in the egg mixture. Pour into an 11x9-inch pan that has been sprayed with Pam. Sprinkle the pecans evenly over the top and drizzle the chocolate over the pecans. With a spoon, marble the chocolate and pecans through the batter. DO NOT MIX. It should be MARBLED. Place the pan in a preheated 350° oven for 20 to 30 minutes. The pudding will be slightly firm around the edges of the pan and gooey in the center. Serve warm or cooled with whipped cream. Top with more pecans. Makes 6 to 8 servings.

Mrs. James C. Wright, Jr. (Betty)
Wife of U.S. Congressman

HERSHEY BAR DESSERT

6 Hershey almond bars
2 eggs, separated
2 tablespoons sugar
1 cup whipping cream

2 dozen crushed vanilla wafers
9 coconut macaroons, broken
½ cup chopped pecans

Melt chocolate bars in double boiler. Add egg yolks, cook a little. Stir in sugar. Remove from heat; cool. Beat egg whites; set aside. Whip cream, then mix with egg whites. Mix in chocolate mixture. Sprinkle crushed wafers, broken macaroons and chopped pecans into a buttered Pyrex dish. Pour mixture over wafers. Refrigerate for 48 hours. (I prefer to make this in 2 layers and serve garnished with whipped cream.)

Jim Williams, Jr.
1st Vice President
Cotton Bowl Athletic Association

4 LAYER LINEBACKER DELIGHT

1 cup flour, sifted
1 stick margarine, melted
½ cup chopped nuts
1 (8-ounce) package cream cheese,
  softened

1 cup confectioners' sugar
1 container Cool Whip
1 large package instant chocolate
  pudding mix
Chocolate shavings

Mix flour, margarine and nuts and spread in bottom of baking pan. (Will be very thin.) With a mixer, beat cream cheese with confectioners' sugar. After blended, mix in 1 cup Cool Whip. Pour into crust. Prepare pudding according to package directions; spread over mixture in pan. Cover with remaining Cool Whip. Top with chocolate shavings. Refrigerate for 24 hours.

Mrs. Al Worn (Carol Ann)

TEACHER'S PET PEANUT CLUSTERS

1 package Wilton chocolates

24 ounces dry-roasted unsalted peanuts

Melt chocolate over boiling water in double boiler. When completely melted, add nuts and stir until nuts are covered. Dip clusters onto waxed paper by small spoonfuls. Let cool.

Mrs. Al Worn (Carol Ann)

BUTTER SCOTCH CARAMELS

First place at San Angelo Stock Show and Rodeo.

3 cups sugar
1¾ cups white Karo syrup
2 cups heavy cream

1 cup butter
3 to 4 cups chopped pecans
1 teaspoon vanilla

Boil sugar, syrup, cream and butter to hard ball stage. (In summer 250°, in winter 246°.) Grease a 12x8-inch pan and cover the bottom with pecans. When candy is done, mix in the vanilla. Pour candy over pecans. When cool, cut in squares and wrap in waxed paper. (Hint: Use a foil pan for candy.) This is Walter's grandmother's recipe. I have made it many times. The recipe makes a lot of candy. Good for Christmas gifts.

Madeline Russell

MEGAPHONE PECAN TARTS

SHELLS
½ cup margarine, softened
1 (3-ounce) package cream cheese, softened

1 cup flour, sifted

Blend margarine and cream cheese. Mix in the flour. Chill for 1 hour. Form into small balls and shape into small muffin cups.

FILLING
1 cup ground pecans
1 egg, lightly beaten
½ teaspoon salt

1 teaspoon vanilla
¾ cup light brown sugar
1 tablespoon butter, melted

While dough chills, prepare the filling. Stir ingredients together. Pour about 1 full teaspoon into each tart shell. Bake at 325° for 30 minutes. Remove and cool well before removing from muffin pan. Makes 2 dozen.

Mrs. E.B. Moyers (Kay)

CLASSIC MILESTONE

1982 - Paul "Bear" Bryant made his last Cotton Bowl appearance with the Alabama Crimson Tide and came to Dallas as college football's winningest coach. But, it was an unhappy visit, as Texas quarterback Robert Brewer rallied the Longhorns to a 14-12 victory.

BANANA NUT ICE CREAM

3 eggs	1 tablespoon vanilla
2¾ cups sugar	¼ cup banana liqueur
3 cups milk	¼ teaspoon salt
3 cups whipping cream	Chopped pecans, toasted
7 bananas, crushed	

In a large mixing bowl, beat eggs until foamy. Gradually add sugar and beat until thickened. Add milk, cream, crushed bananas, vanilla, banana liqueur and salt; mix thoroughly. Chill. Churn freeze. Remove dasher and stir in toasted chopped pecans. Yields 1 gallon.

TOASTING PECANS
To toast pecans, spread pecans on a cookie sheet or in a shallow baking dish and bake at 300° for about 10 to 12 minutes, stirring occasionally to ensure even toasting.

Miriam Curry, R.D./L.D.
Nutrition Consultant
Associated Milk Producers, Inc.

PEACHES 'N CREAM ICE CREAM

Peaches	1 quart whipping cream
3 eggs	1 pint half and half
3 cups sugar	

Mash enough well-ripened peaches to make 1 quart of pulp; set aside. Blend eggs with sugar. Add peaches and whipping cream. Pour into freezer container and add half and half to fill line. Freeze until firm.

Kendall and Beth Clayton
Baylor '60 and '61

CLASSIC MILESTONE

1983 - Unbeaten SMU returned to the Cotton Bowl for the first time since 1967. Lance McIlhenny, the winningest quarterback in Southwest Conference history, accompanied by the Pony Express—Eric Dickerson and stablemate Craig James—handed Dan Marino and his Pitt Panthers a 7-3 defeat.

RASPBERRY FREEZER DESSERT

1 cup flour
½ cup margarine, softened

¼ cup brown sugar
½ cup chopped nuts

Mix with pastry blender. Put into large Pyrex pan and bake at 275° for 1 hour, stirring with a fork every 10 to 15 minutes to separate. Separating is very important.

TOPPING
2 unbeaten egg whites
1 cup sugar
1 tablespoon fresh lemon juice

2 (10-ounce) packages frozen
raspberries, partially thawed
1 large carton Cool Whip

Mix egg whites, sugar and lemon juice. Stir in raspberries and beat for about 10 minutes. Fold in the Cool Whip. Pour over cooled crumbs. (I always reserve a few of the crumbs to sprinkle on top.) Place in freezer. Note: Strawberries may be used instead of raspberries.

Mrs. Jim Dickey (Nancy)
Wife, Past President
Fort Worth Metroplex Chapter
Southwest Football Officials Association

LEMON-LIME CHIFFON MOLD

4 eggs
1 cup water
2 envelopes unflavored gelatin
½ cup sugar
2 tablespoons lemon juice

1 (6-ounce) can frozen limeade
concentrate
1 cup whipping cream
Few drops green food coloring

Separate eggs, placing whites in medium size bowl, and yolks in top of double boiler. Add water to yolks and beat slightly with a fork. Mix gelatin with ¼ cup sugar in a 1 cup measuring cup. Stir into egg yolk mixture. Cook over simmering water, stirring constantly, for 5 minutes or until mixture coats a metal spoon. Strain into a large bowl. Stir in lemon juice and defrosted limeade until well blended. Chill mix until it begins to thicken. Beat egg whites until foamy; beat in remaining ¼ cup sugar, 1 tablespoon at a time, until meringue forms in peaks. Beat cream until stiff in another bowl. Beat gelatin mixture until fluffy. Gently fold in meringue, then whipped cream until no streaks of white remain. Fold in a few drops of green food coloring until mixture is a pale green or whatever shade of green you desire. Pour into gelatin mold and chill overnight. Serves 8 to 12.

Mrs. Gordon R. Miller (Rita)

MARSHMALLOW DELIGHT

½ pound marshmallows
1½ cup diced or crushed pineapple
1 pint whipping cream

2 tablespoons sugar
2 teaspoons vanilla

Cut marshmallows into fourths. Add pineapple. cover and refrigerate overnight. Next day, whip cream; mix in sugar and vanilla. Fold sweetened whipped cream into fruit and marshmallow mixture. Pour into freezing tray and chill thoroughly or partially freeze before serving. Serves 8 to 10.

Harlan Streater
Mama's Pizza

STATUE OF LIBERTY STRUDEL

DOUGH
1½ cups flour
¼ teaspoon salt
2 tablespoons flour
1 egg
⅓ cup oil
¼ Mogen David concord grape wine,
   warmed

Graham cracker crumbs
Additional oil
Sugar
Cinnamon

Sift together flour, salt and sugar. Add egg, oil and wine, mixing thoroughly. Cover with towel and allow to rest while preparing filling. Sprinkle graham cracker crumbs onto rolled pastry and brush with oil after rolling. Knead dough about 5 minutes on lightly floured pastry board. Divide dough in 2 parts. Work with 1 part and keep remainder covered. Roll to paper thinness. Spread dough with oil and sprinkle with mixture of sugar and cinnamon. Divide circle of dough in half. Make a roll of filling and put at beginning of dough. Roll tightly and fold ends under. Arrange on a well-oiled jelly roll pan. Continue with remainder of dough and filling. (This will make 4 strips about 18 inches long.) Brush strips well with oil and sprinkle with cinnamon and sugar. Make several slices in each section, cutting only halfway through. Bake at 350° for approximately 1 hour. Check after about 30 minutes and brush with oil again, if needed.

FILLING
2 apples, grated
1 cup fruit preserves (any flavor)
1 tablespoon sugar
½ cup coconut

½ cup chopped pecans
A little lemon juice
Graham cracker crumbs

Mix ingredients well. Note: If using blackberry preserves, be sure to use seedless. There are many other things to use for the filling: strawberry preserves, orange marmalade, coconut, lots of pecans, orange peel and lemon peel. Cornflakes or graham crackers are used to keep it from being too loose.

Sheldon Labovitz
King's Liquors

BANANA FRITTERS—ACAPULCO STYLE

4 large bananas (ripe but firm)	4 eggs, separated
Milk	Oil for frying
3 tablespoons vanilla	Cinnamon
Flour	Sugar

Cut bananas in half and soak in milk to cover with the vanilla added. Refrigerate for 1 hour. Turn bananas and soak for 30 more minutes. Remove bananas from milk and roll them in flour. Beat the egg whites until foamy. Add yolks and beat well. Dip bananas in eggs and deep fry in hot oil for 1 or 2 minutes or until brown. (A fry-daddy is perfect.) Drain on paper towels. Mix cinnamon and sugar. Roll bananas in the mixture and place in an oblong baking dish. Cover with sauce and refrigerate. At serving time, warm in a low oven for 20 minutes. Serves 8.

SAUCE

1 cup sugar	1 cinnamon stick
1 cup brown sugar	½ stick butter
1 cup water	½ cup rum
½ lime, squeezed (rind added)	

In a saucepan, mix sugar, brown sugar, water, lime, cinnamon and butter. Cook until syrupy. Remove from heat and stir in the rum. Cool and pour over bananas.

Mrs. John P. Thompson
Wife, Cotton Bowl President 1978-1980

BLUEBERRY DELIGHT

1 stick margarine or butter	1 cup sugar
2 cups graham cracker crumbs	2 eggs
½ cup confectioners' sugar	2 tablespoons lemon juice
½ cup chopped pecans	1 can blueberry pie filling
1 (8-ounce) package cream cheese	1 large carton Cool Whip

Melt margarine and mix with graham cracker crumbs, confectioners' sugar and chopped pecans. Press in bottom of 13x9-inch baking pan to form crust. Beat cream cheese, sugar, eggs and lemon juice until smooth. Spread over crust and bake at 350° for 20 minutes. Remove from oven and cool. Spread on the pie filling. Top with Cool Whip. Refrigerate until ready to serve. Cut in squares. Serves 24.

Kenneth Stone

CRUNCHY PEACH PARADE DAY DESSERT

5 cups peeled pitted peaches, cut up
1 cup sugar
¾ cup flour
¾ cup baking powder
⅛ teaspoon salt
1 egg

⅓ cup butter, melted
Cinnamon, to taste
Nutmeg, to taste
Whipped cream or ice cream, for topping
  (optional)

Preheat oven to 350°. Put peaches in a buttered 10-inch pie plate. Combine sugar, flour, baking powder and salt; mix in egg. Sprinkle mixture evenly over the peaches. Pour the melted butter over mixture. Sprinkle with cinnamon and nutmeg. Bake for 50 to 60 minutes or until golden brown. Serve warm or at room temperature. Garnish with whipped cream or ice cream, if desired. Serves 8.

Mrs. J. Herman Musick (Celeste)

COTTON PICKIN' PEACH COBBLER

¾ cup flour
⅛ teaspoon salt
2 teaspoons baking powder
1 cup sugar
¾ cup milk

½ cup butter
1 (29-ounce) can sliced peaches
¼ teaspoon almond extract
½ cup sugar
Cinnamon, to taste

Sift flour, salt and baking powder. Mix in sugar. Stir in milk, beating to mix well. Melt butter in baking pan. Pour batter over melted butter. DON'T STIR. Pour peaches and almond extract over batter. Mix sugar and cinnamon and sprinkle the mixture over the batter. Bake at 350° for 1 hour.

Vance Godbey

HOMEMADE YOGURT

1 quart fresh milk or 1 pint fresh and 1
  pint canned
1 (¼-ounce) package unflavored gelatin

⅓ cup water
½ cup yogurt starter

Heat milk to warm, not hot. Dissolve gelatin in water and add to milk. Cool to room temperature (70°). Add yogurt starter and mix in a blender. Let stand in warm place until thickened. Refrigerate. Serve with fruit or cereal as desired.

Mrs. Kenneth P. Dowell (Jo)
Wife, Cotton Bowl President 1970-1972

Tex-Mex

TEXAS A&M UNIVERSITY

TEXAS A&M UNIVERSITY

Texas A&M University, Texas' first public institution of higher learning, has been the nation's leader in enrollment gains during the past decade. Since opening in 1876, the university has ballooned in enrollment to its current record level of 36,840.

In the 1983-84 academic year, Texas A&M enrolled more National Merit Scholars than any other public university in the nation. Strictly a military school for many years, A&M continues to commission more reserve officers than any other institution and has the largest cadet corps outside the military academies.

The university has 10 academic colleges and offers 88 degree programs at the undergraduate level and 225 at the graduate and professional level.

Dr. Frank Vandiver presides over the administration of the university. Key athletic department personnel include Tom Adair, SWC faculty representative, and Jackie Sherrill, athletic director and head football coach.

A favorite of Willie's

"One More Jalapeno" Cornbread

1 cup yellow corn meal
2 eggs, beaten at room temperature
1 cup buttermilk, room temperature
1 T. bacon drippings, room temperature
½ t. soda
½ t. sugar
1 ¼ t. baking powder
3/4 t. salt
1 can (17oz) cream style corn
1 lb. hot pork sausage, browned, drained and crumbled
1 medium onion, chopped
½ lb. chedder cheese, grated
3 jalapeno peppers, seeded and chopped
1 T. pomentos, chopped

Mix first 8 ingredients well; add the next 6 and stir well.

Pre-heat oven 375 degrees, grease # 10 iron skillet with bacon drippings and heat in oven. Pour mixture into hot iron skillet and bake about 1 hour. Serves 8 to 10.

Connie Nelson

WARM LOBSTER TACO WITH YELLOW TOMATO SALSA AND JICAMA SALAD

yield: 6 people

Ingredients:

3 tablespoons	corn oil
4	1 pound, chick lobsters, ** (this step can be prepared up to one day ahead) all meat removed from shell; meat cut into small medallions or medium dice
6 each	flour tortillas – heated and kept covered
1 cup	grated jalapeño jack cheese
1 cup	shredded spinach leaves

Method:

1. Bring a large sauté pan to medium high heat.

2. Add oil, then add lobster medallions and sauté until heated thoroughly. (about 4 minutes)

3. Lay all heated tortillas flat on a table, with a spoon portion all lobster meat to the middle of the tortillas. Portion all cheese and spinach on top of the lobster. Roll up into a cylinder shape.

4. Place each taco on a warm plate, surround with yellow tomato salsa and garnish with jicama salad.

YELLOW TOMATO SALSA

yield: 6 people

Ingredients:

2 pints	yellow cherry tomatoes
1 large bulb	shallot, finely minced
1 large clove	garlic, finely minced
2 tablespoons	finely minced cilantro
3 tablespoons	white wine vinegar
2 each	serrano chilies, finely minced (seeds and stem removed)
2	limes, juice only
	salt to taste
** 1 tablespoon	maple syrup ** if tomatoes are not sweet enough

Method:

1. Grind yellow tomatoes through a small dye into a small bowl.

2. Add all other ingredients to tomatoes and incorporate by stirring.

YELLOW TOMATO SALSA, continued

3. Adjust seasoning, cover, and refrigerate until very cold.   (about 2 hours)

JICAMA SALAD

Ingredients:

1 small	jicama, peeled and finely julienne
1 small	red bell pepper, finely julienne
1 small	yellow bell pepper, finely julienne
1 small	zucchini, the green skin only, finely julienne
1 small	carrot, finely julienne
6 tablespoons	peanut oil
3 tablespoons	lime juice
	salt and cayenne to taste

Method:

1. Combine all ingredients in a mixing bowl and toss.

Executive Chef
Dean Fearing

PHIL GRAMM
TEXAS

CHILI-CON CARNE
(Serves 4)

1 lb. meat cut in small cubes
1 medium size can tomato juice
1 small can tomato sauce
1 small onion chopped
3 tablespoons chili powder

Brown meat and onions
Add tomato juice and tomato sauce
Add chopped onion and chili powder

Simmer 2 hours

Wendy Lee Gramm

BAYLOR UNIVERSITY
SCHOOL OF LAW
WACO, TEXAS 76798

Edwin P. Horner • Mills Cox Professor of Law

CHICKEN ENCHILADA CASSEROLE

1 pkg. (12) corn tortillas, cut in ¼'s
3 cups, cooked and chopped chicken
    (season lightly with garlic & onion)
1 can cream of chicken soup <u>OR</u> 1 can cream of mushroom soup
1 can beef bouillon <u>OR</u> 1 can chicken broth + 1 beef bouillon
    cube
½ lb. grated Monterrey Jack Cheese

Cover bottom of 2 qt. greased Casserole with one layer of
tortillas and add some of the chicken, soups and cheese. Repeat
in layers, ending with cheese on top.

Heat thoroughly. Serve with taco sauce.

OFFICE OF THE GOVERNOR

MARK WHITE
GOVERNOR

STATE CAPITOL
AUSTIN, TEXAS 78711

May 6, 1986

Dear Russell:

I am delighted that you are producing another "Texas" cookbook.
Below is a recipe that is truly Texan and was passed on to me by my
aunt, Sue Pearce.

COMIDA MEXICANA

1 Pound of bulk Sausage (Hot and Spicy if you like it that way)
1 Cup Diced Onion
1 Cup Diced Green Pepper
1 Can Stewed Tomatoes
1 Can Rotel Tomatoes with Green Chilies
2 Cups Buttermilk
2 Cups Thin Spaghetti
1 Tablespoon Chili Powder
½ Teaspoon Comino Seed
1 Teaspoon Salt

Brown and thoroughly cook sausage with diced onion and green pepper in
large skillet. Add tomatoes, buttermilk, thin spaghetti, chili powder,
comino seed and salt. Cover and simmer for 20 minutes. Serves 8.
Warning: If you prepare a day in advance, the seasonings become HOTTER!

Yours truly,

Sheila Simmons
Administrative Assistant
to Governor Mark White

T.J. Tuckers' Famous TACO SALAD......

2lbs. ground beef
12-14 plump tomatoes
3 tablespoons Cayene pepper
½ cup chili powder
small pinch tomato puree
dash of salt
white pepper
THE ABOVE INGREDIENTS COMPRISE THE <u>FILLING</u>

romaine or bibb lettuce (coarsely chopped)
monterey jack cheese (long strips)
cheddar cheese (long strips)
hot or mild salsa (whichever you prefer)

PREPARE THE DISH AS FOLLOWS:

1. cook only the FILLING, the remainder is used <u>cold</u>.
2. place lettuce down first
3. serve the cooked filling on top
4. crush plain corn chips on top of the filling (light sprinkle)
5. coarsely chopped fresh tomatoes
6. cheese
7. salsa
8. jalopeno (if desired)

ABOVE DISH SERVES 6-8... it's yummy.

Since I don't know how to turn on a stove, or boil an egg,
this is not, obviously, a favorite family recipe. It is,
however, a favorite dish served at T.J. TUCKERS 59th Street
and First Avenue in New York. Recipe compliments of Chef
David Vasquez.

Thank you

Dick Stockton

CHILI CON CARNE FOR A CROWD

10 lbs.	lean cubed beef
5 lbs.	ground beef
1/2 cup	vegetable oil

Sear beef in vegetable oil until meats loose pink color.

| 2 qts. | water |

Add water and bring to a simmer.

2 1/4 cups	chili powder
1/3 cup	salt
1 tbls.	chopped garlic
1 cup	paprika
1/4 cup	cumin
1/3 cup	crushed red pepper

Mix spices together.

| 2 qts. | water |

Add water to spices slowly mixing with a whisk. Add to meat and cook approximately 45 minutes until cubed beef is tender. Skim any fat from top.

| 5 cups | browned flour |

Brown in oven, stirring occasionally.

| 2 qts. | water |

Beat water into flour slowly, beating with a whisk. Pour thru a china cap or large strainer to remove any lumps. Add to chili and cook on low heat 15 more minutes, making sure chili does not scorch on bottom of pot.

Serve over Mexican rice or white rice, topped with grated Colby cheese and chopped scallions or onions.

TAMALE PIE
(Serves 8-10)

3 Tbls. butter
3 Tbls. olive oil
1 small onion, minced
1 clove garlic, minced
1 lb. ground beef
½ lb. pork sausage meat
1 can (No. 2½) tomatoes
1 can (No. 2) whole kernel corn

2 tsps. salt
2 tsps. chili powder
20-24 pitted ripe olives
1 C. cornmeal
1 C. milk
2 eggs, well beaten
1½ C. grated cheese

Heat the butter and oil in a frying pan and saute' the onion and garlic until golden. Add the ground beef and sausage meat and brown slightly. Put the tomatoes, corn, salt, and chili powder in a saucepan and simmer for 20 minutes. Let cool, then combine with the meat and pour into a shallow pan about 10x14 in size. Press olives into mixture. Combine the cornmeal, milk, and well-beaten eggs and spread with a spoon over the filling. Sprinkle the grated cheese over the top. Bake in a moderate oven (350) for 1 hour. (The filling can be prepared well ahead of time, and the cornmeal topping added before baking.)

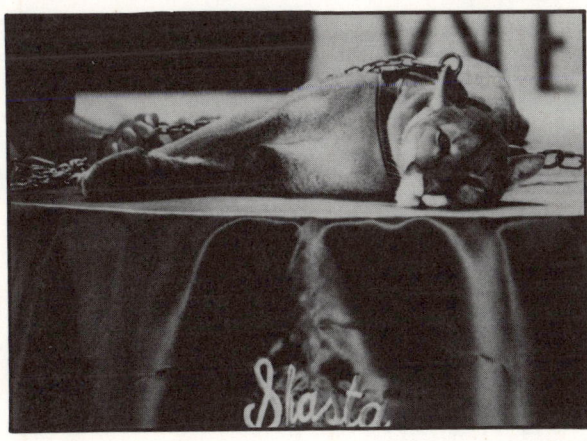

Bill Clements ★▬

FIRST LADY OF TEXAS CHICKEN ENCHILADAS

3 large-sized chicken breasts
Salt
1 cup chopped onion
1 clove garlic, minced
2 tablespoons butter or margarine
1 can (16 oz.) tomatoes, coarsely chopped
1 can (8 oz.) tomato sauce
1/4 cup chopped green chile peppers
1 teaspoon sugar
1 teaspoon ground cumin
1/2 teaspoon salt
1/2 teaspoon dried oregano, crushed
1/2 teaspoon dried basil, crushed
12 corn tortillas
2-1/2 cups shredded Monterrey Jack cheese
3/4 cup sour cream

Simmer chicken breasts in water to cover until tender. Skin and debone.
Sprinkle with salt, cut into 12 strips and set aside. Saute onion and garlic
in butter until tender. Add tomatoes, tomato sauce, chile peppers, sugar,
cumin, salt, oregano and basil. Bring to boil, reduce heat. Simmer, covered,
20 minutes. Remove from heat. Dip each tortilla in tomato mixture to soften.
Place 1 piece of chicken and 2 tablespoons cheese on each tortilla, roll,
place seam down in 2-quart baking dish. Mix sour cream into remaining sauce
mixture, pour over tortillas, sprinkle with remaining cheese. Cover, bake at
350° until heated thoroughly. Serves 6.

SPANKY McFARLAND

FRIJOLES BORRACHOS
(Drunk Beans)

1 lb. dried pinto beans
1 cup cubed ham
½ cup salad oil
1 medium onion, chopped
1 medium green pepper, chopped
1 can (16 oz.) tomatoes
½ bunch fresh cilantro (fresh coriander plant), washed and chopped
1 12-oz. can of regular beer

Prepare beans as directed, add ham. Set aside.

In smaller pan, combine remaining ingredients (mash tomatoes before adding)
including juice from tomatoes. Bring to boil and simmer for about 5 minutes.

Add this mixture to beans and ham, and return to boil on low heat for 30 minutes.

Spanky suggests serving Frijoles Borrachos with hot flour tortillas. He also
suggests bottled red pepper sauce for those who like their beans spicier!!

Spanky got this recipe from a Laredo restauranteur after having eaten
them on one of his trips. It has long been a favorite of the McFarland
family, and Spanky hopes you enjoy it as much as he has over the years.

Your "Little Rascal"
Spanky McFarland

MARCHING BAND BREAKFAST BURRITOS

Owens Country pork sausage
2 eggs
Milk
2 butter pats
1 package flour tortillas

½ teaspoon chopped onion
1 teaspoon chopped green pepper
¼ cup grated Longhorn Cheddar cheese
¼ cup grated Monterey Jack cheese
Mexican hot sauce

First get your 3 pans out: 1 to scramble eggs, 1 to fry sausage, and 1 for flour tortillas. Then chop and grate ingredients. Turn on oven to warm. Fry 1 sausage patty, then drain grease. Mix 2 eggs with a little milk and scramble in a pat of butter. Melt remaining pat of butter in a separate pan on low heat. Take 1 flour tortilla and place in pan with melted butter. Turn tortilla until butter has spread over one side of tortilla and it is warm. Mix scrambled eggs with onion, green peppers and cheese. (Reserve a little cheese to melt on top of burrito.) Break sausage patty into small pieces and add to egg mixture. Spoon egg mixture onto buttered side of tortilla and roll up. Sprinkle extra cheese on top; heat to melt cheese. Serve with Mexican hot sauce and favorite fruits.

Pam Seal
Former Dallas Cowboy Cheerleader

BREAKFAST TWO MINUTE WARNING TACOS

1 medium potato, chopped into ½-inch
  cubes
4 ounces oil or shortening

8 ounces chorizo (Mexican sausage)
6 eggs
12 flour tortillas

Fry potatoes in hot oil until golden brown; drain grease. Add chorizo to potatoes and cook over medium heat for about 6 minutes. Add eggs to mixture and cook until done. Set aside. Heat flour tortillas until soft and warm. Spoon egg mixture onto tortillas and roll up. Wrap in foil until ready to serve.

Gilbert Gamez Jr. and Tommy Gamez
Dos Hermanos Restaurant

CLASSIC MILESTONE

1984 - Again, a possible national championship lay in the balance for Texas in the Classic. The Longhorns were ranked No. 2 behind top-ranked Nebraska which would fall later that evening in Miami. Texas seemed to have the game well in hand in the closing minutes, leading 9-3, but a fumbled punt paved the way to Georgia's comeback for a 10-9 upset.

CON QUESO DIP

1 onion, chopped
1 green pepper, chopped
6 celery stalks, chopped
½ cup butter
3 pounds Velveeta cheese

1 to 2 cans green chilies, chopped
1 cup grated Monterey Jack cheese
1 cup grated Colby cheese
Worcestershire sauce, to taste
Garlic salt, to taste

Sauté onion, pepper and celery in butter. Transfer into double boiler and melt with Velveeta. Stir in chopped green chilies, Monterey Jack and Colby cheeses. Season with Worcestershire and garlic.

Mrs. Rodger Meier (Joyce)
Wife, Cotton Bowl Director

GUACAMOLE

4 large California avocados
1½ to 2 tablespoons finely chopped
    onion
1 small tomato, finely chopped

½ teaspoon salt, or to taste
¼ teaspoon garlic powder
1 teaspoon lemon juice

Peel and mash avocados. Add onion and chopped tomato; mash with avocados to blend. Add salt, garlic powder and lemon juice, mixing well. May be served as a dip, salad or appetizer. Serve with tortilla chips.

Rosemary S. Garbett
President
Los Tios Mexican Restaurants

B & B'S FOOTBALL SPECIAL

1 (14½-ounce) can whole tomatoes
1 can Ro-Tel tomatoes
1 (4-ounce) can Old El Paso Taco Sauce
1 pinch sugar

1 pinch salt
½ teaspoon Wesson oil
Green chili relish, to taste

Combine ingredients in a blender and blend for 2 seconds; stop and repeat. Pour contents into a jar, cover and refrigerate overnight. It can be prepared on the spur of the moment, but it's better if it's refrigerated overnight. Serve with corn chips. This recipe was created by Bill Ferguson and me in 1967.

Billy A. Lloyd
PaineWebber

HOT CHILI DIP

2 pounds ground chuck
2 large onions, chopped
4 garlic cloves, pressed
1 tablespoon sugar
1 small bottle Mexene chili powder
2 tablespoons cumin powder
6 or 8 chili pequins

1 tablespoon salt or to taste
1 tablespoon black pepper
2 large cans tomato sauce
4 cups hot water
2 cans Austex hot tamales, sliced
2 pounds grated sharp cheese
2 bunches green onions, chopped

Sauté meat and next 8 ingredients in a large heavy iron or aluminum pot until the meat is no longer pink. Stir in tomato sauce and hot water. Cover the pot and simmer for about 3 hours. Cool and refrigerate overnight. The next day, skim and discard the grease from the top; reheat the mixture, add hot tamale slices, and cook until they disintegrate. Add cheese, reserving 2 cups, and stir until the cheese has melted. Transfer the chili into 2 greased oblong flat baking dishes. Sprinkle the remaining cheese on the top and bake until cheese melts. Remove from the oven and sprinkle the chopped green onions on top. Serve with king-size Fritos. This freezes very well, but do so before adding cheese and onion topping. Great for after-game parties. Serves 40 to 50 people.

Sam S. Stollenwerck (Carol)
Cotton Bowl Committee

TORTILLA SOUP

1 large onion, chopped
1 garlic clove, minced
1 (12-ounce) can tomatoes, chopped, reserving liquid
1 ounce vegetable oil
8 ounces chicken breast, cut in small cubes
1 teaspoon cumin

1 teaspoon chili powder
1 can beef broth
1 can chicken broth
1 can tomato soup (or tomato paste)
2 cans water plus tomato liquid
Tortillas

Sauté onion, garlic and tomatoes in pot with oil. Add chicken, cumin, chili powder, beef broth, chicken broth, tomato soup and water; simmer for about 1 hour. Cut thin tortillas into small 1-inch strips or pieces; fry lightly until crisp. Serve soup with tortilla strips, diced avocado and grated cheese on the side.

Mrs. Finley Ewing (Gail)
Wife, Cotton Bowl Director

FAVORITE CHILI

4 dried chiles anchos
4 dried chiles arbols
2 dried chiles japones
3 teaspoons cumin seed
7 garlic cloves
1 teaspoon crushed chiles pequins
5 fresh jalapeño peppers, stemmed and
    seeded
1 pound (450 g) tomatoes, canned or
    fresh, undrained

2 teaspoons salt
Fat trimmed from beef or ¼ pound
    (115 g) chopped beef suet
4 pounds (1¾ k) lean beef, such as
    trimmed chuck roast or chuck tender,
    cut in ¼-inch (¾-cm) cubes
1 teaspoon sugar
1 cup (240 ml.) red wine
2 to 3 cups (425 to 700 ml.) water
¼ cup (35 g) masa trigo

This chili is a project; it takes nearly all day by the time you've shopped for and found the fresh and dried chiles, softened them, and proceeded with the rest of the recipe. But it's worth it. If you can't find these exact chiles, don't be afraid to experiment with what's available or your own combinations. Mexican markets usually have a wide variety of dried and fresh chiles.

Remove stems, membranes, and seeds from dried chiles (anchos, arbols, japones). Place in small saucepan and barely cover with water. Bring to a boil over medium heat and simmer 15 minutes. Remove peppers from liquid and set aside. Reserve liquid and add to chili sparingly as desired for a hotter stew. Place softened peppers in food processor along with cumin, garlic, chiles pequins, jalapeños, tomatoes and salt. Process until smooth.

Meanwhile, in a cast-iron pot or Dutch oven, render enough fat from trimmings or suet to make ¼ cup (60 mL). Cook meat in rendered fat over high heat until meat loses color and turns gray. Cook meat in 2 batches if pot is crowded. Cook away most of the water the meat gives up, but do not brown.

To meat, add pepper and tomato mixture, sugar, and wine. Add just enough water to raise level of liquid to that of meat. Do not cover completely with liquid. Bring to a boil, reduce heat, and simmer, uncovered, about 1½ hours, stirring occasionally. Add water as needed to maintain desired level.

Combine masa trigo and just enough water to make a smooth paste. Press out all lumps with the back of a spoon. Gradually stir into chili to thicken. Taste for seasoning and adjust. If a hotter chili is desired, add a bit of reserved chili liquid. Cook about 30 minutes longer over very low heat, stirring frequently.

Dotty Griffith
Food Editor
The Dallas Morning News
Reprinted with permission, Wild About Chili, published by Barron's Educational Series, Inc., 113 Crossways Park Drive, Woodbury, N.Y. 11797.

JALAPEÑO QUICHE SQUARES

½ cup butter
10 eggs, beaten
1 pound grated Monterey Jack cheese
8 ounces jalapeños, diced (2 small cans Old El Paso)

1 pint small curd cottage cheese
½ cup flour
1 teaspoon baking powder
Salt

Preheat oven to 400°. Melt butter, add to beaten eggs. Add remaining ingredients, mixing well. Pour into a 14x9x2-inch (3-quart) casserole dish. Bake at 400° for 10 minutes. Reduce heat to 350° and bake for 45 more minutes. Let cool and cut into squares. Or, may be prepared ahead and reheated in microwave before serving.

Rosemary S. Garbett
President
Los Tios Mexican Restaurants

MINERVA GORDITAS

1 pound ground beef
1 small onion
2 teaspoons salt
1 teaspoon garlic salt
¼ teaspoon chili powder
2 cups masa harina
1 teaspoon baking powder

2 teaspoons salt
1 cup water
2 tablespoons grated Longhorn cheese
2 bacon strips, fried and crumbled
Lettuce, shredded
Tomatoes, diced
Grated cheese

Fry beef with onion. Season with salt, garlic salt and chili powder. While meat is cooking, mix with hands the masa harina, baking powder, salt, water and Longhorn cheese. Pinch off a small portion of dough and roll into a 2-inch ball. With quick patting motion, flatten out to ½-inch thickness, about 3 inches in diameter. Fry in hot grease until golden brown, turning once; drain. Make a slit through the middle, open slightly (like a taco shell) and stuff with meat mixture, bacon, lettuce, tomatoes and cheese. Serve with taco sauce. Serves 6.

Richard A. Laswell

COTTON BOWL MILESTONE

1985 - The "magic" Doug Flutie became the fourth Heisman winner to play in the Cotton Bowl. And it was the fourth appearance in nine years for Houston. The Cougars' Earl Allen raced 98 yards for the longest kickoff return in Cotton Bowl history, but Flutie passed for a record-tying three touchdowns to lead his Boston College Eagles to a 45-28 victory. The Eagles' 45 points were the most scored by a Classic team.

ENCHILADAS

MEAT

2 to 3 pounds ground meat
½ pound ground pork (pan sausage)
½ can Ro-Tel tomatoes
1 small can tomato sauce
3 buds garlic minced very fine
1 cup minced onion

1 cup minced celery
1 bell pepper chopped fine
⅛ teaspoon each of oregano, cumin
2 teaspoons chili powder
Salt to taste

To prepare meat, brown meat first. Add vegetables and let them sauté a few minutes. Add tomatoes and tomato sauce, and enough water to keep from being dry. Add other ingredients (oregano, cumin, salt, chili powder). Bring to boil and simmer until vegetables are cooked (about 25 minutes).

1 pound (approximately) mild Cheddar
    cheese (grated)

1 large onion (minced fine)

SAUCE (To soften tortillas)

1 large can tomato sauce
Chili powder
Bacon drippings (cooking oil or
    shortening)

Salt to taste
3 packages tortillas

To prepare tortillas, in a skillet bring to a boil ½ tablespoon bacon drippings (or substitute), tomato sauce, chili powder, salt. Turn heat down to simmer while you do each tortilla. In sauce, soften one tortilla at a time before laying it flat in pan where you are going to make enchiladas. Soften four or five tortillas before putting in filling of meat, grated cheese, and minced onion. Roll these and arrange in pan. (About 1 tablespoon of meat, cheese, onion per enchilada is enough for each tortilla to make rolling easier.) After doing all tortillas into enchiladas sprinkle remaining meat (as much as you want) the left-over cheese and onions on the prepared enchiladas. Also pour enough sauce over them so that they won't be dry. Do not pour too much sauce or they will become soggy. Put pan of enchiladas in oven (250-275°) until cheese melts. If you prepare ahead of time, cover with foil and heat with foil on them about 30 minutes at 250-275°.

Dr. and Mrs. William H. Nelms (Ailsa)

COTTON BOWL MILESTONE

1985 - Boston College became the first team to take home a two-million dollar paycheck for its appearance in the Cotton Bowl.

HOOK 'EM JALAPEÑO CORN BREAD

2 eggs
1 can yellow cream corn
1 tablespoon baking powder
1 (8-ounce) carton sour cream or
  buttermilk
⅔ cup corn oil

1 cup yellow cornmeal
½ teaspoon salt
2 cups grated Cheddar cheese
1 can jalapeños (remove seeds and chop)

Mix together eggs, corn, baking powder, sour cream, oil, cornmeal and salt. Pour half into a greased baking dish. Cover with cheese and jalapeños. Cover with remaining mixture. Bake at 350° for 1 hour. Note: This recipe came from East Texas via Dorothy Doss.

Mrs. Darrell Royal (Edith)

MEXICAN CORN BREAD

1 cup cornmeal
1 cup flour
½ teaspoon soda
1 teaspoon salt
½ teaspoon sugar
¼ pound sharp cheese, shredded

1 cup creamed corn
1 medium onion, chopped
2 or more seeded peppers
1 cup buttermilk
½ cup oil

Combine cornmeal, flour, soda, salt and sugar. Stir in cheese, corn, onion and peppers. Add buttermilk, oil and eggs, mixing well. Pour into greased iron skillet. Bake at 450° for 25 to 30 minutes.

Jerry Moore

EL SOMBRERO DE LA RED RAIDER CORN BREAD

1½ cups cornmeal
1 teaspoon salt
3 teaspoons baking powder
2 eggs, lightly beaten
⅔ cup oil

1 cup sour cream
1 (16-ounce) can cream style corn
3 canned jalapeño peppers, seeded and
  chopped
1 cup grated Cheddar cheese

In a mixing bowl, combine cornmeal, salt and baking powder. Add eggs, oil and sour cream, stirring until just blended. Stir in corn and chopped peppers. Pour half the batter into a greased 8x8x2-inch pan. cover with half the cheese. Repeat with remaining batter and cheese. Bake at 350° for 35 to 40 minutes. Cut into squares and serve hot.

Miriam Curry, R.D./L.D.
Nutrition Consultant
Associated Milk Producers, Inc.

HALL OF FAME FLOUR TORTILLAS

4 cups flour
3½ teaspoons baking powder
2 teaspoons salt

⅔ cup shortening
1⅓ cups water, warmed

Sift flour with baking powder and salt. Cut shortening into dry ingredients until mixture resembles rice granules. Mix in warm water and work in with well-greased hands. Divide the dough into shares slightly smaller than a racquetball and roll out each on a floured board. Cook on a hot griddle until both sides are lightly browned.

Mrs. Frank Chairez (Helen)

BUÑUELOS NICKLE DEFENSE

1 cup sugar
1½ teaspoons cinnamon
½ teaspoon nutmeg

12 (8-inch) flour tortillas
Hot vegetable oil

In a large plastic bag, mix sugar, cinnamon and nutmeg. Shake to mix well; set aside. Cut tortillas into 3x2-inch strips; fry until crisp and golden brown, turning once. Drain on paper towels. While still warm, place a few at a time in sugar mixture in bag; shake gently to coat. Store in an airtight container. Yields about 5 dozen.

Mrs. John W. Carpenter (Cele)
Wife, Cotton Bowl Director

MOON PIE ESPANOL A LA ZAPATA

Take two Moon Pies from wrappers. Sprinkle Moon Pies liberally with Four Alarm chili sauce, chopped fresh onion, Tabasco, diced jalapeño peppers, and drollops of boiling chili concaso. Take deep breath, shout "Viva Zapata!" and eat quickly with eyes closed. Do not throw away Moon Pie wrappers, as they will be found handy for fanning your tongue.

Larry L. King
Author
"Best Little Whorehouse in Texas"

FAJITAS AND PICA DE GALLO

8 pounds beef skirts (fajita meat)
Pepper
Garlic powder
5 (10-ounce) bottles Worcestershire sauce
1 bottle red or white wine
1 stick butter, melted
1 small squeeze-bottle lemon juice
1 medium can pickled jalapeño peppers
6 large ripe tomatoes

3 celery stalks
1 bunch fresh cilantro
1 bunch scallions
5 fresh serrano peppers
2 large onions
2 limes
2 large bell peppers
2 dozen flour tortillas

Have your butcher run the fajitas through the tenderizer at least once and also trim excess fat. To prepare marinade, use a large deep pan or bowl, add meat that has been peppered liberally and dusted with garlic powder. Cover with all the Worcestershire, half the wine, melted butter, lemon juice and 2 chopped jalapeños. Add more wine and water if meat is not covered. Let stand at room temperature for at least 3 hours. To prepare the Pica de Gallo, scald the tomatoes to remove skin by briefly submerging them in boiling water. After removing the skin, chop into cubes about ½-inch square or smaller. Place the chopped tomatoes in a 1-quart pitcher or bowl. Add finely chopped celery, 1 cup cilantro, 3 cups sliced scallions, serrano peppers, to taste. Stir and add more onions, peppers or cilantro, if necessary. Squeeze fresh lime juice over pica and refrigerate. Grill meat with sliced onions and bell peppers. Sear meat on both sides, then cook on reduced flame for 10 to 15 minutes. Baste with marinade if you like. Test meat periodically to keep from overcooking. Slice meat into strips about 1x3-inches. Place several strips of meat in a flour tortilla, add a spoonful of pica and guacamole and enjoy. Serve with refried beans and guacamole. Serves 6 to 8.

George M. Young, Jr.
Young Oil Company

MEXICAN PRALINE ICE CREAM

4 eggs separated
2 cans sweetened, condensed milk
1 quart half and half
⅔ cup maple flavored syrup
1 teaspoon salt

2 to 3 cups milk
5 Mexican pralines (the kind purchased
   in Mexican food restaurants)
2 chocolate covered toffee (Heath) candy
   bars

Beat egg whites stiff. Mix yolks with next 6 ingredients, fold in egg whites. Put in freezer can and freeze 10 minutes according to directions with freezer. Meanwhile, coarsely grate or crumble candies in blender or food processor. Add candies to ice cream and complete freezing process.

Mrs. John W. Carpenter III (Cele)
Wife, Cotton Bowl Director

Wine & Food

TEXAS CHRISTIAN UNIVERSITY

TEXAS CHRISTIAN UNIVERSITY

Texas Christian University, founded in 1873, is a private, coeducational university, located on 245 acres in southwest Fort Worth. The student body of about 6,900 includes representatives from every state and many foreign countries.

TCU is composed of six schools and colleges: Arts and Sciences, Business, Fine Arts, Nursing, Educational, and Brite Divinity School. Bachelor degrees are offered in over 65 major fields. A comprehensive program of continuing education is offered to area adults.

The university employs 314 full-time faculty members; almost 80 percent hold the highest degrees in their fields. Classes are small and the student-faculty ratio is about 15-1.

Prominent figures in the TCU athletic program include Chancellor Dr. William E. Tucker, Tom Badgett, SWC faculty representative; Frank Windeger, athletic director; and head football coach Jim Wacker.

WINE LIST

Barbecue Beef

Rose of Cabernet – Texas
Pinot Noir – California
Côtes du Rhone – France
Chianti – Italy
Rioja Red – Spain
Beer

Beef Bourguignon

Light Zinfandel – California
Chianti – Italy
Red Burgundy – France

Beef Curry

Zinfandel – California
Petit Sirah – California
Hermitage Red – France

Beef Wellington

Red Burgundy – France
Bordeaux – France
Barolo – Italy
Cabernet Sauvignon – California

Caviar, Paté

White Burgundy France
Pinot Grigio – Italy
Champagne – France
Chardonnay – California

Casserole, Meat

Beaujolais – France
Gamay Beaujolais – California
Chianti – Italy
Zinfandel – California

Chef's Salad
(no vinegar dressing)

White Zinfandel – California
Rhines – Germany
Chiaretto – Italy
Beaujolais – France

Chicken a la King

Chenin Blanc – Texas/California
Vouvray – France
Orvieto – Italy
Soave – Italy
Chardonnay – California
White Burgundy – France

Chicken, Baked

Johannisberg Riesling – California
Bordeaux – France
Barbera – Italy
Pinot Noir – California
Rhine – Germany

Chicken, Barbecued

White Zinfandel – California
Lugana – Italy
Gavi – Italy
Riesling – Germany/California

Chicken Breast Sandwiches

Table white, chablis – California
Sauvignon Blanc – California
French Colombard – Texas
Frascati – Italy
Riesling – Germany
White Sparkling – California/New York
Dry Rosé – France

Chicken, Broiled or Roasted

Chardonnay – Italy/California
Gavi – Texas
Bardolino – Italy
Riesling – Germany
Sauvignon Blanc – California

Chicken, Coq au Vin

Red Burgundy – France
Chianti Riserva – Italy
Petit Sirah – California

Chicken, Curry

Beer as first choice
Gewürztraminer – France (Alsace)/
 California
White Bordeaux – France
Sauvignon Blanc – California
Pouilly Fumé – France
Macon Blanc – France
Pinot Grigio – Italy

Chicken, Fried

White Zinfandel – California
Rose of Cabernet – Texas
Beaujolais – France
Bardolino – Italy
Valpolicella – Italy
Riesling – Germany
Pinot Noir – California

Chicken Hash

Table Red – California
Chianti – Italy

Chicken Kiev

White Burgundy – France
Chardonnay – Italy/California/Texas
Rhine – Germany

Chicken Paprika

Very Dry Red – California
Chianti – Italy

Chicken Salads with Mayonnaise

Champagne – France
Rose d'Anjou – France
White Zinfandel – California
Chenin Blanc – Texas

Chicken with Spicy Sauce

Gewürztraminer – Germany
Macon Blanc – France
Chardonnay – Texas
Pinot Grigio – Italy
Beer

Chili

Beaujolais – France
Burgundy – California
Strong Red – New York/California
Chianti – Italy
Torgiano Rosso (Rubesco) – Italy
Red Rhone – France
Beer

Chinese Food

White Zinfandel – California
Dry White – Italy/California/New York/
France
Soave – Italy
Vernaccia di San Gimignano – Italy
Beer – China

Cantonese Dishes

Rhine – Germany
Gewürztraminer – California

Chicken Chow Mein

Chenin Blanc – California
Rhine – Germany
Tsingtao – China

Chinese Roast Duck

Macon Blanc – France
Beaujolais – France
Champagne, Extra Dry –

Hunan-Szechuan Dishes

Rhine – Germany
Rosé of Pinot Noir – California
Petit Sirah – California
Hermitage Red – France

Peking Dishes

Beaujolais – France
Zinfandel – California

Clams, Fried

White Burgundy – France
Chablis – France
Verdicchio – Italy

Shrimp Tempura

White Graves – France
Alsatian Riesling – France
Chardonnay – California
Champagne – Brut
Sauvignon Blanc – California
Chefoo White Wine – China

Clams, Steamed

White Burgundy – France
Chardonnay – California
White Bordeaux – France
Soave – Italy

Cold Cuts

White Zinfandel – California
Riesling – Germany
Pinot Grigio – Italy
Gamay Beaujolais – California
Beaujolais – France
Rose of Cabernet – Texas

Crab

White Burgundy – France
Chardonnay – Italy/California
White Bordeaux – France
Fumé Blanc – California

Dover Sole, Halibut, Turbot

White Burgundy – France
Chardonnay – California
Lugana – Italy
Gavi – Italy
Sauvignon Blanc – California

Duck a L'Orange

Rine – Germany
White Zinfandel – California
Vouvray – France

Duck, Wild

Reserve Zinfandel – California
Barolo – Italy
Barbaresco – Italy

Duck with Wine Sauces

Red Burgundy – France
Chianti Riserva – Italy
Barolo – Italy
Petit Sirah – California
Pinot Noir – California
Cabernet Sauvignon – California
Zinfandel – California

Eggplant Parmesan

Chianti – Italy
Bardolino – Italy
Valpolicella – Italy

Eggs Benedict
(cheese or mushroom sauce)

Chablis – France
Chenin Blanc – California/Texas
Sylvaner – Germany/California
Gewürztraminer – Germany/California
Mimosa (champagne mixed with orange juice)

Eggs, Scrambled

White Zinfandel – California/Texas
Grenache Rosé – California
Bardolino – Italy
Verdicchio – Italy
Beaujolais – France
Gamay Beaujolais – California
Mimosa (champagne mixed with orange juice

Fish, Bass

Chardonnay – California/Texas
Rhine – Germany/Texas
Liebfraumilch – Germany
Chardonnay – California
Pinot Blanc – California
Chablis – France

Fish, Broiled

Chardonnay – California/Texas
White Burgundy – France
Verdicchio – Italy

Fish and Chips

Chablis – California
Dry Rosé – California
Portugese White – Portugal

Fish Filet, Sautéed

Riesling – Germany
Chardonnay – California
Verdicchio – Italy
Vouvray – France
Mâcon Blanc – France
French Colombard – California
White Graves – France

Fish, Trout

Chardonnay – California
Gamay Beaujolais – California
Gavi – Italy
Bardolino – Italy

Foie Gras (Liver)

Pommard – France
Médoc – France
Champagne – France
White Sparkling – Spain/Ger./Italy/Calif./ N.Y.
Gewürztraminer – Germany/California

Game

Red Rhone (Bordeaux) – France
Médoc – France
Brunello – Italy
Barbaresco – Italy
Barolo – Italy
Cabernet Sauvignon – California/Texas
Pinot Noir – California
Zinfandel – California

Goose

White Burgundy – France
Alsatian Riesling – France
Vino Nobile de Montepulciano – Italy
Cabernet Sauvignon – California

Ham

White Zinfandel – California/Texas
Rhine – Germany
Rosé – France/California
Beaujolais – France
Gamay Beaujolais – California
Chianti – Italy
Orvieto (Secco) – Italy
Chablis – France
Gewürztraminer – Germany

Hamburgers

White Zinfandel – California/Texas
Valpolicella – Italy
Beer
Beaujolais – France
Rose of Cabernet – Texas

Hors d'oeuvres

Beaujolais – France
Bordeaux – France
Chardonnay – Italy
Soave – Italy
Valpolicella – Italy
Tavel Rosé – France
Beaujolais – France
White Zinfandel – California

Kabobs

White Zinfandel – California
Beaujolais – France
Bardolino – Italy
Cabernet Sauvignon – Texas
Valpolicella – Italy
Chianti – Italy

Lamb Chops, Broiled

Barbera – Italy
Beaujolais – France
Gamay Beaujolais – California

Lamb, Leg

St. Emilion – France
Margaux – France
Cabernet Sauvignon – California

Lamb, Curry

Cabernet Sauvignon – California/
    South America
Chianti – Italy
Gewürztraminer – California/France
White Rhone – France

Lamb, Roasted

Bordeaux – France
Brouilly – France
Brunello di Montalcino – Italy
Tignanello – Italy
Pinot Noir – California
Petit Sirah – California
Zinfandel – California

Lamb Stew

Pinot Noir – California
Zinfandel – California
Petit Sirah – California
Barbaresco – Italy
Merlot – California
Beaujolais – France

Liver and Onions

Valpolicella – Italy
Zinfandel – California
Beaujolais – Villages France

Lobster, Baked

White Burgundy – France
Chardonnay – California
Montrachet – France
Pinot Grigio – Italy

Lobster, Boiled

Johannesberg Riesling – Germany/
    California
Sauvignon Blanc – California
Soave – Italy

Mexican Food

Mateus – Portugal
Lancers – Portugal

Omelet

Rosé – France
Beaujolais – France
Bardolino – Italy
Gamay Beaujolais – California

Oysters and Cream Sauce

Champagne, Extra Dry – France
Pinot Noir Blanc – California

Oysters, Fried or Rockefeller

White Burgundy – France
Chardonnay – California
Lugana – Italy
Chablis – France

Oysters, Raw

Soave – Italy
Chardonnay – California

Pasta, Red Sauce

Zinfandel – California
Chianti – Italy
Bardolino – Italy
Barbera – California

Pasta, White Sauce

Dry Chenin Blanc – California
Soave Italy
Frascati – Italy
Sauvignon Blanc – California
Riesling – Germany
Gewürztraminer – California/France

Paté, Coarse

Light Red Bordeaux – France
White Zinfandel – California

Paté, Fine

Alsatian Riesling – France
Côtes de Beregerac – France

Peppers, Stuffed

Dry Rosé – California/France
Bardolino – Italy

Pheasant

Cabernet – California
Chianti Riserva – Italy
St. Emilion – France
Burgundy – France

Pizza

Bardolino – Italy
Chianti – Italy
Rosé – Portugal
White Zinfandel – California/Texas
Beer

Pork Chops

White Zinfandel – California/Texas
Gamay Beaujolais – California
Rhine – Germany
Beaujolais – France
Bardolino – Italy

Pork Roast

White Zinfandel – California/Texas
Rhine – Germany
White Graves – France
Chardonnay – Italy/California
Gavi – Italy
Rosé – California/France/Portugal

Pork Sausage

Sauvignon Blanc – California
Alsatian Riesling – France
Spanish White – Spain

Poultry
(general)

Chardonnay – California/Texas
Pomerol – France
Rubesco – Italy
Bardolino – Italy
White Bordeaux – France

Pot Roast

Cabernet Sauvignon – Texas
Petit Sirah – California
Gamay Beaujolais – California

Quail, Roasted

Cabernet – California/Texas
Côte de Beaune – France
Barbaresco – Italy

Quiche, Lorraine or Seafood

Champagne, Brut – France
White Sparkling – California
Frascati – Italy
Sauvignon Blanc – California
Mersault – France
Muscadet – France
Chardonnay – California

Rabbit

Petit Sirah – California
Cabernet – California/Texas
Barolo – Italy
Pomerol – France

Ravioli, Meat Filled

Beaujolais – France
Bardolino – Italy
Burgundy – California

Ravioli, Cheese Filled

White Rhone – France
Chablis – Caifornia
Frascati – Italy

Roast Beef

St. Emilion – France
Graves, Red – France
Barbaresco – Italy
Chianti – Italy
Rubesco – Italy
Cabernet Sauvignon – California/Texas
Red Burgundy – California
Zinfandel – California
Pauillac – France
Côtes de Nuits – France
Beaujolais Grand Crus – France
Côte Rotie – France

Salmon or Trout, Baked

White Burgundy – France
Johannesberg Riesling – Germany
Bardolino – Italy

Salmon, Poached

Dry White Bordeaux – France
Chardonnay – California
Dry Rosé – California

Seafood

Sauvignon Blanc – California
Pouilly Fumé – France
Lugana – Italy
Verdicchio – Italy
Graves – France
Muscadet – France

Seafood Casserole

Chenin Blanc – California/Texas
Soave – Italy
Riesling – Germany

Shellfish

Chablis – France
Muscadet – France
Chardonnay – California
Pinot Grigio – Italy

Shellfish with Rich Sauce

Beaujolais – France
Lacryma Christi – Italy
Dry Rosé – France/Portugal

Shrimp, Boiled

White Burgundy – France
Riesling – California/Texas
Chardonnay – California/Texas
White Bordeaux – France
Lugana – Italy
Beer

Shrimp Creole

Dry Rosé – California

Chenin Blanc – California
Bardolino – Italy
Anjou Rosé – France
Beer

Shrimp, Fried

Sauvignon Blanc – California/Texas
Muscadet – France
Verdicchio – Italy
Lugana – Italy
Chardonnay – California/Texas

Spaghetti

White Zinfandel – California/Texas
Chianti – California/Italy
Valpolicella – Italy
Red Rhone – France

Spicy Snacks

Dry Sherry – Spain/California

Steak

St. Emilion – France
Barbaresco – Italy
Graves, Red – France
Cabernet Sauvignon – California
Chianti – Italy
Burgundy – American
Zinfandel – California
Châteauneuf-du-Pape – France
Pinot Noir – California

Stew

Médoc – France
St. Emilion – France
White Zinfandel – California/Texas
Barbaresco – Italy
Cabernet – California

Stroganoff

Beaujolais – France
Pommard – France
Petit Sirah – California
Zinfandel – California
Rioja, Red – Spain

Teriyaki

Châteauneuf-du-Pape – France
Zinfandel Reserves – California
Côtes du Rhone – France
Barolo – Italy

Turkey, Roasted

White Zinfandel – Texas
Chardonnay – California
St. Emilion – France
Bardolino – Italy
Champagne, Extra Dry – California
Riesling – Germany

Veal Chops

Beaujolais – France
Riesling – California
Riesling – Germany
Pinot Grigio – Italy

Veal Orloff

Bordeaux – France
White Burgundy – France
Barbaresco – Italy

Veal, Roast

Beaujolais – France
Pouilly-Fuissé – France
Chardonnay – California
Bardolino – Italy
Johannesberg Riesling – Germany

Veal Scaloppine

White Burgundy – France
Soave – Italy
Vinho Verde – Portugal

Venison

Côtes du Rhône – France
St. Emilion – France
Barolo – Italy
Brunello di Montalcino – Italy
Côtes de Beaune – France
Côtes de Nuits – France
Chàteauneuf-du-Pape – France

Weiner Schnitzel

Valpolicella – Italy
Beaujolais – France
Rhine – Germany
Riesling – Germany/California
Dry Rosé – France/Portugal

Desserts and Cheeses

General

Champagne – France
Sparkling – American
Auslese – Germany
Spätlese – Germany
Beerenauslese – Germany
Asti Spumante – Italy

Melons and Pineapple

Orvieto Abbocoto – Italy

Nuts and Fruit Cake

Port – Portugal/Texas
Vin Santo – Italy
Madeira – Portugal
Marsala – Italy
Malvasia Bianco – California

Pastry Cream Fillings

Sauternes – France
Asti Spumante – Italy
Vouvray – France
Champagne (Demi-Sec) – France
Vin Santo – Italy

Imported Beers

Carta Blanca – Mexico
Corona – Mexico
Dos Equis – Mexico
Löwenbräu – Germany
St Pauli Girl - Germany
Heineken – Holland
Amstel – Holland

Diners' Dictionary

TEXAS TECH UNIVERSITY

TEXAS TECH UNIVERSITY

"The most beautiful campus in the West—till you get to Stanford." That's author James Michener's description of the Texas Tech 1,800-acre spread.

The university lists more than 160 acres of study. In addition to six colleges—Agricultural Sciences, a 26-department Arts and Sciences, Business Administration, Education, Engineering and Home Economics—there are the Graduate and Law Schools.

Founded in 1923, the Lubbock campus has a student body of about 24,000. The university also operates the 980-acre agricultural Lubbock County Field Laboratory, the 15,000-acre Texas Tech University Center at Amarillo (emphasizing agriculture), the 400-acre Texas Tech University Center at Junction in Texas hill country, and a 90-acre natural sciences and archeological field laboratory in Val Verde County.

Serving as the school's president is Dr. Lauro Cavazos. Dr. Robert Sweazy is the SWC athletic representative, T. Jones is the athletic director and David McWilliams is head football coach.

© *1986, Jim Bradford, Pres., Dining Publications*

A

à blanc *(ah-BLAHN)*—French. To cook raw meat in boiling water.

à point *(ah-POINT)*—French. Literally means, "just in time." To serve food at the exact moment it is ready.

abalone *(aba-LONE-e)*—An edible mollusk which is similar to a large scallop. Usually expensive due to its rarity.

agneau *(AN'yoh)*—French. Lamb.

ail *(aye)*—French. Garlic.

à la carte *(ah-lah-KART)*—Common menu term meaning that each selection is priced and ordered separately.

à la king—Any dish served in a creamy white sauce which contains pimientos, green peppers and mushrooms.

à la mode—French. Originally a style of preparation where beef is braised with vegetables, although the Americanization of the term has come to mean pie topped with ice cream.

albacore *(AL-ba-core)*—A large edible fish that is a primary source for canned tuna.

al dente *(ahl-DEN-tey)*—Italian. Term meaning to cook food until it is tender, but not soft or mushy.

allemande *(ah-lee-MAHND)*—German. Although the name is German, it is a classic French white sauce.

amandine *(AH-mahn-deen)*—French. Refers to blanched almonds thinly sliced and served as a garnish, typically with fish.

ambrosia *(am-BROZH-ah)*—American. Usually denotes Southern desserts in which marshmellows and fruits such as apples, oranges and bananas are blended with shredded coconut.

anchovy *(AN-chovie)*—A very small fish used mainly as a garnish for salads and pizza topping. Because it is preserved in brine, the taste is typically salty.

angels on horseback—American. An hors d'oeuvre of oysters wrapped in bacon and baked, then served on toast.

antipasto *(ahn-te-PAHS-toh)*—Italian. An hors d'oeuvre or appetizer, meaning "before the pasta."

apéritif *(ah-PAIR-eh-TEEF)*—French. An alcoholic beverage taken to stimulate the appetite before a meal.

arrowroot—A tropical root used to thicken soup and gravy. Usually in the form of a dry powder.

arroz con pollo *(ah-ROSE-cone-POYO)*—Spanish. "Rice with chicken." Combines seasonings such as garlic and peppers with tomatoes.

asado *(ah-SAH-doh)*—Spanish. Roasted meat.

aspic *(AS-pik)*—French. A clear gelatin made from various meat or vegetable stocks.

au buerre *(oh-BUHR)*—French. Cooked in or with butter.

au blanc *(oh-BLAHN)*—French. To keep white by cooking in a stock of acidulated water and flour.

au gras *(oh-GRAH)*—French. To cook in a fat-based sauce. Any meat cooked and dressed with a rich sauce or gravy.

au gratin *(oh-GRAH-tihn)*—French. A dish garnished with bread crumbs or cheese and baked in an oven until lightly browned on top.

au jus *(oh-ZHU)*—French. Any meat dish served in its natural juices.

B

bagel—Jewish. A doughnut-shaped bread roll.

baklava *(BAH-klah-VAH)*—Greek. Classic pastry made from layers of filo dough and filled with various nuts, spices and syrup.

basil *(bazel)*—A common herb used primarily as a spicy flavoring in tomato sauces.

béarnaise sauce *(behr-NAZE-sohs)*—French. Hollandaise sauce flavored with wine, shallots and herbs.

béchamel sauce *(BAY-she-mel)*—French. A white sauce made with flour, butter and milk.

bel paese *(bell-pa-ACE-ah)*—Italian. A well known cheese with a mild, delicate flavor.

beluga sturgeon *(beh-LOO-ga-STIR-jun)*—A large, slender fish which is prized for its high quality roe (eggs), from which comes the finest of caviar.

bercy *(behr-SEE)*—French. A sauce with fish stock, white wine, shallots and lots of butter.

beurre *(buhr)*—French. Butter.

beurre manié *(buhr-mahn'YEA)*—French. A mixture of butter and flour used as a thickening agent.

bisque *(beesk)*—French. Shellfish soup.

blanch—To cook rapidly in boiling water.

blue *(blue)*—French. Method of cooking whereby live or extremely fresh fish, usually freshwater trout, are cooked in boiling water which has been seasoned with vinegar and salt.

blintz—Jewish. Thin egg pancake.

boeuf *(bef)*—French. Beef.

bok choy—Chinese. Oriental cabbage.

bonne femme *(bon-FAHM)*—French. Prepared in a very simple way. French home cooking.

bordelaise *(bohr-duh-LAZE)*—French. A sauce demi-glace with red or white wine, shallots, tomato sauce and beef marrow.

bouillabaisse *(bou-ya-BESS)*—French. A classic dish that is a creative jumble of many variations. Lobster, eel and leeks are imperative, as well as saffron. After that, most any variation is permissible and possible.

bourguignon *(boor-gi-N'YON)*—French. A method of preparation originating in Burgundy. The main item is usually prepared in a red wine sauce and garnished with chopped onions and mushrooms.

braise *(braze)*—To cook meat or vegetables by browning in fat, then simmering in a small quantity of liquid in a covered container.

brasserie *(brahz-eh-REE)*—French. A casual restaurant.

bratwurst—German. Sausage of lean pork heavily seasoned with herbs and spices.

brie *(bree)*—French. A mold-ripened, whole-milk cheese, the center of which is soft.

brill—English. An edible flatfish of European waters.

brine—A very salty solution used to preserve foods.

broiled—English. Cooked with heat over or under a broiler, frequently brushed with oil.

C

canapé *(kan-ah-PEH)*—French. An appetizer of biscuits, crackers, bread, etc., topped with savory mixtures.

canard *(kah-NAR)*—French. Duck.

cannelloni *(kan-nel-LO-nee)*—Italian. Cooked pasta which is stuffed and browned in an oven.

capers—A flower bud preserved in vinegar and used as a garnish.

capon *(KA-pon)*—A rooster castrated to improve the quality of its flesh for food.

carafe *(ka-RAHF)*—A glass bottle used for serving water or wine at the table; a decanter.

cassis *(kah-SEES)*—French. Made from the famous black currants of Burgundy, it is a pungently flavored syrup for use in beverages or desserts.

cayenne *(kai-YEN)*—A condiment made from a very pungent pepper plant. Also known as "red pepper."

cèpes *(sehp)*—French. Large, wild, edible, strongly-flavored mushrooms ranging in color from yellow-brown to reddish-brown. To be sauteed in butter with garlic and parsley. Especially good with veal chops.

ceviche *(seh-VEECH-e)*—Mexican. Raw fish marinated in lime juice.

champignon *(sham-pee-N'YOHN)*—French. An edible mushroom. Also called a button mushroom.

chanterelles *(shahn-t'REHL)*—French. Yellow, trumpet-shaped mushrooms.

chateaubriand *(sha-toe-bree-AHN)*—French. A porterhouse steak.

chaud *(sho)*—French. Hot.

chaud-froid *(sho-FRWA)*—French. Poultry or game cooked, covered in a cream sauce and glazed with aspic. Served cold.

chile *(CHILL-e)*—Mexican. Pepper.

chili *(CHILL-e)*—English. A dish attributed to Texas made of meat stew and variously seasoned with chili peppers.

chinese parsley—Coriander.

chorizo *(ko-REEZ-O)*—Mexican. A spicy pork sausage frequently used in egg dishes or burritos.

choron sauce *(sho-RONE)*—French. Béarnaise sauce with a diced tomato puree.

comino *(ko-MEEN-O)*—Mexican. Cumin.

chutney *(CHUT-nee)*—East Indian. A spicy, sweet relish used as a condiment.

cilantro *(se-LAHN-tro)*—Mexican. The parsley-like leaves of fresh coriander. Called Chinese parsley in Oriental cookery.

clarify—To make soups, jellies, butter, etc., absolutely clear by filtering.

coddle *(kod'l)*—To cook in water just below the boiling point.

compote *(English, KOM-pote; French, kon-POHT)*—Fruit, fresh or dried, cooked in a syrup and served cold.

condiments—Any food seasonings.

consommé *(kohn-so-MAY)*—French. A clear soup made of meat or vegetable stock, or both.

coquille st. jacques *(ko-KEE)*—French. Method of preparation whereby scallops are prepared in butter and served with parsley butter or cream sauce in their shells.

cordon bleu *(kor-dohn-BLUE)*—A famous French cooking school. Denotes dishes prepared according to such methods.

coriander *(KOR-e-an-der)*—English. An aromatic herbal plant whose leaves and seeds are frequently used in condiments. Referred to as cilantro in Mexican cookery and Chinese parsley in Oriental cookery.

court bouillon *(kur-bu-YOHN)*—French. A liquid in which vegetables and herbs have been cooked. Used mostly for poaching fish.

crêpe *(krape)*—French. A very light, delicate pancake.

crêpe suzette—French. A thin dessert pancake usually rolled with hot orange or tangerine sauce and often served with a flaming brandy or curacao sauce.

croissant *(kwa-SAHN)*—French. A rich, crescent-shaped roll of leavened dough or puff pastry.

croquette *(kro-KET)*—French. A small cake of minced food often coated with bread crumbs and deep fried.

croutons *(kru-TOHN)*—French. Tiny bread shape, fried or toasted. Used as a garnish, or when larger, as a base.

cru *(kru)*—French. Uncooked, raw.

cuisine minceur *(kwi-ZEEN-mha-SIHR)*—French. a way of cooking for dieters.

curry—A condiment of dried spices ground into a powder. Frequently used in East Indian and Asian cookery.

D

decant *(dee-KANT)*—To pour off any liquid from one container to another without disturbing the sediment.

deglaze—To dilute pan juices with wine, stock, etc., to make gravy.

demi-glace *(demi-GLAS)*—French. A basic brown sauce, reduced and strengthened with meat jelly or a strong veal stock.

dolci *(DOLE-see)*—Italian. Sweet.

dom pérignon *(pere-N'YON)*—A noted French champagne whose name is derived from a 17th century Benedictine monk who developed the process of making sparkling champagne.

drambuie—A Scottish liqueur made from Scotch whiskey, heather honey and various herbs and spices.

drawn butter—The clarified butter that separates from the salt and curds after melting. Often used with herbs as a sauce.

dumpling—Small chunks of slices of dough cooked in soups or stews with various meats.

E

éclair *(a-KLARE)*—French. A light, tubular pastry made of chou pastry with cream or custard filling and usually iced with chocolate frosting.

edam *(E-dahm)*—A mild yellow cheese from the Netherlands, pressed into balls and usually covered with red paraffin.

en brochette *(ahn-bro-SHET)*—French. Broiled on a skewer.

enchilada *(in-chee-LA-da)*—Spanish. A tortilla filled with meat and / or cheese.

en coquille *(ahn-ko-KEE)*—French. Served in the shell; in shell-shaped ramekins.

endive *(in-dive)*—A green plant cultivated for its crown of crisp, succulent leaves and used in salads; a variety of common chickory.

en papillote *(ahn-pah-pee-YOHT)*—French. Baked in an oiled paper bag.

entrecôte *(AHN-tre-kote)*—French. A cut of steak taken from between the ribs.

entrée *(ahn-TREY)*—French. Meaning the main course.

entrements *(ahn-tre-MAY)*—French. A side dish or dishes. Especially those served between principal courses or as a desseret.

escalope *(es-SKALLOP)*—French. Thin slices of boneless meat or fish.

escargots *(es-kar-GO)*—French. Snails.

espagnole *(es-pah-N'YOL)*—A classic brown sauce.

espresso—Italian. A strong coffee brewed by forcing steam under pressure through long-roasted, powdered coffee beans.

F

faisan *(feh-ZAHN)*—French. Pheasant.

farci *(FAHR-see)*—French. Stuffed.

feta—Greek. White, salty cheese made from goat's milk.

fettuccine *(fet-tu-CHEEN-e)*—Italian. Pasta cut in ribbon-like strips.

fillet *(fee-LAY)*—Also filet. A strip of boneless meat, fish or poultry. Also, to fillet, or cut from the bone in thin strips.

filo *(FEEL-o)*—Greek. Very thin sheets of pastry used to make Greek sweets.

financiere *(fee-nan-see'AIR)*—French. A rich sauce made with Madeira wine, mushroom broth and slivers of truffles.

fines herbes *(feenz-AIRB)*—French. A mixture of finely chopped parsley, tarragon, chervil and chives.

flambé *(flahm-BAY)*—French. Denotes foods which are served flaming in ignited liquor.

flan *(flahn)*—French. A tart with a filling of custard, fruit or cheese.

florentine *(FLO-rhen-teen)*—French. Served with spinach.

foie *(fwah)*—French. Liver.

foie gras *(fwah-GRAH)*—French. A famous pâté made from the ground liver of a goose, seasoned with spices and Cognac.

fondue *(fohn-DU)*—French. A Swiss dish made of melted cheese and wine in a heated pot at the table. Bread is dipped in the mixture. American version more typically refers to steak cubes dipped in hot oil to cook, then dipped in a selection of sauces.

foo yung—Chinese. Omelet.

fresco—Italian. Fresh, raw or uncooked.

fricassée *(fri-ka-SAY)*—Poultry or meat cut into pieces, stewed, and served with a thick gravy.

frijoles *(free-HOLEY)*—Spanish. Beans.

froid *(frwah)*—French. Cold.

fromage *(froh-MAHJ)*—French. Cheese.

fumet *(fu-MAY)*—French. Any concentrated meat, fish or vegetable stock.

fusilli *(fu-SEEL-lee)*—Italian. Pasta made in the shape of a corkscrew.

G

galantine *(GAL-en-teen)*—English / French. A dish of boned, stuffed meat, fish or poultry cooked and served hot or cold, coated with aspic or its own jelly.

garbanzos *(gahr-BAHN-zos)*—Spanish. Chick peas.

garni *(gar-NEE)*—French. Garnished.

gazpacho *(gahz-POTCH-o)*—Spanish. A cold soup made with raw tomatoes, onions, sweet peppers and cucumbers. All are chopped, soaked in vinegar and mixed with oil and minced garlic.

glacé *(gla-SAY)*—French. Coated with a sugar glaze or icing; candied.

goahn *(GO-hahn)*—Japanese. Rice.

gouda *(GOO-da)*—A mild, close-textured, pale yellow cheese made from whole or partially skimmed milk. Originally made in Gouda in The Netherlands.

grand marnier *(mar-N'YEA)*—French. A sponge cake filled with custard or butter cream and flavored with grand marnier liqueur.

gras *(grah)*—French. Meaning fat.

gratin *(graht'n)*—French. A crust of bread crumbs with butter, and often cheese, browned in an oven.

grenouilles *(gre-NU-ya)*—French. Frog legs.

grill—English. Cooked on top of a flat metal surface. Grilled foods are frequently dipped in an egg wash and dusted with flour to prevent sticking.

grillades *(gree-YAHD)*—French. Any meat or fish grilled over a high heat.

grits—Ground corn served boiled, having the consistency of a very thick soup. A popular breakfast dish in the South, served with eggs.

guacamole *(gua-ka-MOLE-e)*—Mexican. An avocado mashed with onions, tomatoes, lemon juice, herbs and other spices.

gumbo—Creole. A thick soup or stew combining fish, meat, poultry and vegetables thickened with okra or file powder.

H

hai-tai *(HI-tie)*—Japanese. An edible seaweed.

hake—A fish related to and resembling the cod.

halibut—Large, edible flatfish found in the northern Atlantic or Pacific waters.

headcheese—A savory jellied loaf or sausage containing chopped and boiled parts of the feet, head, and sometimes the tongue and heart of an animal, usually a hog.

hoisin sauce *(hoy-SIN)*—Chinese. A reddish-brown sauce whose primary ingredient is soybeans.

hollandaise *(HOLLEN-daze)*—A basic rich sauce made wtih drawn butter, lemon juice and egg yolks.

homard *(o-MAR)*—French. Lobster.

hors d'oeuvre *(or-DURV)*—French. Appetizer.

huevos *(WAY-bohs)*—Mexican. Eggs.

hush puppy—A deep-fried cornmeal fritter usually rolled into a ball.

I, J & K

ichiban dashi *(itchy-bahn-DA-she)*—Japanese. A simple soup stock made from kelp and dried fish.

imperial crab—Crab meat which has been baked in its shell and mixed with various seasonings.

imperiale *(em-peri-AHL)*—French. Refers to a garnish of mushrooms, foie gras, truffles, etc.

insalata *(in-sah-LAH-tah)*—Italian. Salad.

irish coffee—American. A beverage of sweetened hot coffee and Irish whiskey, topped with whipped cream. Usually served as an after dinner drink.

irish stew—A stew of meat, usually mutton or lamb, and vegetables, typically potatoes and onions.

jambalaya *(jum-ba-LIE-ya)*—Louisiana Acadian. Highly seasoned dish whose basic ingredients are shrimp and rice. Several variations, most including tomatoes, garlic, herbs, red pepper and other spices.

jarlsberg—A nut-flavored cheese of Norwegian origin.

jerusalem artichoke—A North American sunflower producing a white, tuberous root eaten as a vegetable and used in salads.

jicama *(HE-ka-ma)*—Mexican. A root vegetable frequently used in sauces.

jubilee, cherries—A flaming dessert made with vanilla ice cream topped with black cherries and Cognac.

julienne *(ju-l'YEN)*—French. Anything thinly sliced.

kabob—Middle Eastern. A dish consisting of pieces of seasoned meat roasted and served with condiments on skewers.

kir *(keer)*—French. An aperitif of white wine and Creme de Cassis.

knockwurst—German. Garlic flavored sausage.

L

langosta *(lahn-GOS-ta)*—Spanish/Mexican. Spiny lobster.

lapin *(lah-PEHN)*—French. Rabbit.

lasagna *(LA-ZAHN-ya)*—Italian. Flat, wide pasta. Also a dish made with such pasta with layers of ground meat, tomato sauce and cheese, then baked.

leek—An edible root akin to onion, having a white, tubular bulb and dark green leaves.

liaison *(lee-a-ZOHN)*—French. Any thickening or binding agent.

linguini *(leen-GWEEN-e)*—Italian. long, narrow noodles.

lobster newburg—Sauteed lobster with brandy and Madeira wine in a cream and egg sauce.

lobster thermidor—Halved lobster, grilled slowly and then replaced in the shell which is lined with sauce bechamel, to which English mustard has been added.

lox—Jewish. Smoked salmon.

M

MSG—Monosodium glutamate. Also known under the brand name Accent.

maitre d' *(may-tre-DEE)*—French. Originally maitre d'hotel, meaning "master of the hotel." The head steward responsible for greeting and seating of guests.

manicotti *(mah-nee-KOT-tee)*—Italian. A dish where hollow tubes of pasta are stuffed with a filling of chopped ham and ricotta cheese.

marinate—To tenderize and flavor meat, poultry, game or venison by steeping in a marinade, usually wine or alcohol with oil, vinegar and spices.

matzo balls *(MAH-tsoh)*—Jewish. dumplings.

medallion *(may-DY-yohn)*—French. Refers to any food cut in rounds.

menudo *(men-U-doh)*—Mexican. A pungent soup with a reputation for curing hangovers.

meuniere *(men-Y'ERE)*—French. A style of preparing fish whereby it is lightly dusted with flour and sauteed in butter.

mole *(moh-LAY)*—Mexican. A pungent hot sauce of chile and other spices.

moo goo gai pan—Chinese. A Cantonese dish of chicken, mushrooms, vegetables and spices steamed together.

mornay *(mor-NAY)*—French. A creamy white sauce flavored with grated Swiss or Parmesan cheese.

moussaka *(moo-sah-KAH)*—Middle Eastern/Greek. A baked dish of ground meat and egg plant.

mousse *(moos)*—French. A light, fluffy dish usually made with ham, chicken livers or fish. However, most popular as a dessert when sweet ingredients are used. The main ingredient is finely minced and mixed with cream and egg whites. Cooked in a mold and served cold.

mousseline *(moo-s'LEEN)*—French. To enrich with whipped cream.

N & O

noix *(nwah)*—French. Walnuts.

normande *(nor-MAHND)*—French. A cream sauce for fowl and poultry. Several variations.

oeufs *(oeh)*—French. Eggs.

omelette—French. An egg scrambled and fried mixed with meats and/or vegetables. Folded like a crêpe.

oysters bienville—Oysters on the halfshell topped with a thick egg sauce containing wine and onions, then mixed with pieces of shrimp and mushrooms and sometimes truffles. Baked in an oven before serving.

oysters casino—Oysters on the halfshell topped with chili sauce, bacon and horseradish, then broiled.

oysters delmonico—Oysters on the halfshell topped wtih bacon and sweet red and green peppers. Flavored with lemon juice and cooked au gratin with breadcrumbs.

oysters rockefeller—Oysters topped wtih chopped spinach, shallots, garlic, Pernod and anchovies, then baked on a bed of rock salt.

P

paella *(pah-EH-yah)*—Spanish. The world famous dish with numerous variations. Combines rice with such things as chicken, vegetables, sausage, meat and seafood; flavored with saffron and garlic.

panaché *(pah-nay-SHAY)*—French. Mixed.

parfait *(pahr-FAY)*—French. A light, frozen dessert made of several layers of different flavors of ice cream or ices, variously garnished and served in a tall glass.

parmigiano *(parh-mee-JAH-noh)*—Italian. Parmesan cheese.

pâté *(pah-TAY)*—French. A finely ground mixture of meat or poultry, with the addition of salt and spices, with or without truffles. Pâté is always served well chilled, without any garnish or dressing, usually at the beginning of the meal.

peking duck—Chinese. Crisp-roasted duck, cut into squares and served in a light crepe with sweet sauce and scallions.

periwinkles—English. A small, marine snail.

picante *(pee-KAN-tey)*—Mexican. A tomato-based sauce which is highly seasoned with chilies.

piccata di vitello *(pee-KAH-tah-dee-veeTAY-loh)*—Italian. Slices of veal flavored with a light lemon butter sauce.

pilaf—Near Eastern. A steamed rice dish cooked in butter and mixed with various vegetables in a seasoned broth. Usually served as a side dish.

piquante sauce *(pee-KAHNT)*—French. A demi-glace with vinegar, shallots and gherkins, flavored with tarragon.

pita *(PEET-ah)*—Middle Eastern/Greek. Flat bread.

poach—To cook in simmering liquid.

poireaux *(pwah-ROH)*—French. Leek.

poivrade, sauce *(sohs-pwah-VRAHD)*—French. Carrots, onions and celery mixed with game trimmings, vinegar and sauce demi-glace. Seasoned with freshly ground pepper.

polonaise *(poh-loh-NEZZ)*—French. To garnish with breadcrumbs.

potage *(po-TAHJ)*—French. Soup.

potée *(po-TEE)*—French. A thick soup made with pork, green cabbage base and vegetables.

prosciutto *(proh-SHOO-toh)*—Italian. A spicy, dried ham.

provencale *(pro-vahn-SAHL)*—French. A style of cooking in Southern France using various combinations of tomatoes, onions, garlic, breadcrumbs, olives and anchovies, sometimes accompanied with mushrooms and parsley.

Q & R

quenelles *(kuh-NEHL)*—French. Light dumplings made of forcemeat and bound with eggs, poached in stock or water.

quesadillas *(kah-sah-DEE-yahs)*—Mexican. Tubular or crescent-shaped tortillas made with chilies, filled with cheese and deep fried.

queso *(KAH-soh)*—Mex./Spanish. Cheese.

quiche *(keesh)*—French. A creamy egg custard tart or pie made with various fillings.

radicchio *(ra-DEEK-e-o)*—Italian. Red lettuce.

ravioli *(rav-e-O-lee)*—Italian. Small pasta envelopes stuffed with meat or spinach, ricotta cheese and herbs.

remoulade *(ruh-moo-LAHD)*—French. Sauce mayonnaise with mustard, gherkins, capers, herbs and a little anchovy essence.

render—To obtain fat by cooking meat trimmings, etc.

ricotta *(ree-CAWT-tah)*—Italian. A fresh, moist cottage cheese made from ewe's milk.

risotto *(ree-ZOH-toh)*—Italian. Rice cooked in butter or oil with a small chopped onion, then in stock or wine with additional meat, vegetables, etc., until the liquid is absorbed.

roux *(ru)*—French. A mixture of fat and flour used as a sauce base.

royale *(ro-Y'AL)*—French. Unsweetened custard cut into strips or decorative patterns. Used in soups.

rumaki—Hawaiian. Boiled chicken livers served on a skewer.

S

saffron—A strong yellow spice. Very expensive and typically used in minute amounts.

sake *(SAH-kee)*—Japanese. Fermented rice wine.

salmis *(sal-ME)*—French. A stew of game first roasted then cooked in wine.

salpicon *(sal-pe-KONE)*—French. A mixture of diced ingredients bound with a sauce.

sauerbraten *(ZAHWR-brah-tuhn)*—German. A top round pot roast marinated in various ingredients.

sauté *(so-TAY)*—French. To stir fry in a shallow pan, making ingredients "jump," until uniformly brown.

scaloppine *(skah-loh-PEE-neh)*—Italian. Thin slices of veal sauteed in butter and served in various ways.

scampi *(SKAHM-pee)*—Italian. Large shrimp used in Italian cooking.

schnitzel *(SHNIHT-suhl)*—German/Austrian. A veal cutlet lightly dusted with flour and fried in butter.

sear—To brown meat rapidly to seal in the juices.

sec *(sek)*—French. Dry.

shallot—An edible bulb similar to an onion.

smorgasbord *(SMEUHR-gohs-board)*—Swedish. A large sandwich table, but Americanized to mean an array of all types of food.

soba *(SO-bah)*—Japanese noodles.

sole *(sohl)*—French/English/American. One of the finest and most delicate of flatfish.

souffle *(su-FLAY)*—French. An airy affair in which the main taste is merely suggested in a froth of egg yolks, baked so that it rises.

sorbet *(sowr-BAY)*—French. Sherbet. A frozen dessert with a semi-mushy consistency. Commonly used to cleanse the palate between appetizers and the entree.

spaetzle *(SHPEHTZ-luh)*—German. Dumplings made with eggs and flour.

spanakopita *(spah-nah-KOH-pee-tah)*—Greek. Triangular flaky pastry pies filled with spinach and feta cheese.

subgum—Chinese. Various dishes served with an assortment of meats and vegetables.

sukiyaki *(su-kee-YAH-kee)*—Japanese. World-famous dish of beef cooked with scallions, bamboo shoots, mushrooms, onions, noodles and bean curd.

supreme, sauce *(sohs-sew-PREHM)*—French. Chicken veloute with cream and a little meat jelly.

sushi *(SOO-shee)*—Japanese. A molded bed of rice topped with a variety of raw fish.

T

tagliolini *(tahl-leo-LEENY)*—Italian. Flat strips of pasta, made with egg.

tempura—Japanese. Fish and vegetables deep fried in a crispy batter.

terrine *(teh-REEN)*—French. Earthenware crock, typically used for foie gras.

tofu *(TOH-fu)*—Japanese. A bland, soybean dish served as a vegetable. Also known as bean curd.

torte *(TAWR-tuh)*—German. A light cake which has been filed with various sweets.

tortellini *(tawr-teh-LEE-nee)*—Italian. Stuffed, twisted pasta.

tournedos *(toor-nuh-DOH)*—French. Small, thick, round slices of beef fillet.

truffes *(troof)*—French. Truffles. An aromatic, flavorsome member of the fungus family. The finest, coming from France, are often called "black diamonds," and are found growing wild under oak trees. Unsurpassed as a flavoring agent for numerous dishes.

truss—To bind a bird or cut of beef with string.

turbot *(tewr-BOH)*—A large, flatfish.

U & V

udon—Japanese. Noodle soup.

uni—Japanese. A marine animal of the urchin family which produces desirable roe.

veau *(vo)*—French. Veal.

velouté *(vuh-loo-TAY)*—French. Basic white sauce made with bouillon and white roux.

vermicelli *(vehr-mee-TCHEH-lee)*—Italian. Spaghetti-shaped pasta, but thinner.

vichyssoise *(vee-shee-SWAHZ)*—French. The classic cream of soup of pureed potatoes, chicken stock and leeks. Best served chilled and garnished with chives.

vitello *(vee-TEH-loh)*—Italian. Veal.

W, X, Y & Z

weiner schnitzel *(VIGHN-ner-shniht-suhl)*—Austrian/German. Escalopes of veal coated in flour, egg and breadcrumbs and fried in a mixture of lard and butter.

won ton *(WAHN-tahn)*—Chinese. Rolls of dough stuffed with meat and vegetables.

xato *(KHAH-toh)*—Spanish. Salad dish made with endives which have been marinated in various seasonings.

yakitori *(yahk-tory)*—Japanese. Pieces of chicken and vegetables skewered, dipped in a marinade of soy sauce, sake, sugar and cayenne pepper, grilled and dipped repeatedly.

yorkshire pudding—British. World famous dish which combines a batter of flour, milk and eggs, then baked. Traditionally served with roast sirloin.

ziti *(TSEE-tee)*—Italian. Largest of the tube pasta.

☆ INDEX ☆

☆ INDEX ☆

✯ INDEX ✯

RUSSELL M. GARDNER is a lifelong resident of Fort Worth, Texas and is son of a prominent Fort Worth physician. Russell attended the Summer Academy in Architecture at the University of Texas at Austin in 1981. He graduated from Arlington Heights High School in 1982. Upon graduation, Russell studied petroleum engineering at the University of Oklahoma, and has attended classes at Texas Christian University in Fort Worth. He is majoring in communications with a minor in journalism. He is a member of Sigma Alpha Epsilon Fraternity. Russell plans to graduate from Texas Christian University, then attend graduate school. He is the Co-Editor and Co-Publisher of the **TEXAS CELEBRITY COOKBOOK**, a regional bestseller. He is the Co-Owner and Executive Vice-President of Gardner-Farkas Press, Inc. which plans to publish several books in 1987. Russell enjoys snow skiing, hunting, racing cars, water sports, and is an avid weekend golfer.

F. CHRIS FARKAS is a lifelong resident of Fort Worth, Texas where his maternal great grandfather settled in the early 1870's. He graduated in 1971 from Texas Christian University with a B.A. degree in journalism. Chris also served as president of Sigma Alpha Epsilon fraternity. After graduation, he became a professional restauranteur as owner of Mama's Pizza restaurants in 1973. The chain has since expanded to 25 locations across Texas. Chris has served on the board of directors of the Fort Worth Chapter of Texas Restaurant Assn. and became president of the Tarrant County Chapter in 1981-2. He was elected to the state board of directors in 1985 and 1986. Restauranteur of the year honors were won in 1985. Other service includes 1986 board of directors Tarrant County National Safety Council. He is also a member of Confrérie de la Chaine des Rôtisseurs, TCU Alumni Association, Century II Club, and the Fort Worth Club. Chris is an amateur archeologist, and an avid hunter, fisherman, and outdoorsman.

GARDNER-FARKAS PRESS, INC.
P.O. BOX 33229
FORT WORTH, TEXAS 76162

Please send me _____ copies
of TEXAS CELEBRITY COOKBOOK .... @ $15.95 each _____
Texas residents add 5⅝% sales tax .... @ .86 each _____
Postage and handling .... @ $ 2.00 each _____
Enclosed is my Check or Money Order in the amount of _____
Make checks payable to Gardner-Farkas Press, Inc.

Drivers license # _____ State _____

Please charge to my MasterCard or Visa No. _____

Expiration date _____ Signature _____

NAME _____

ADDRESS _____

CITY _____ STATE _____ ZIP _____

(PLEASE PRINT)

GARDNER-FARKAS PRESS, INC.
P.O. BOX 33229
FORT WORTH, TEXAS 76162

Please send me _____ copies
of COTTON BOWL CLASSIC COOKBOOK:
50th ANNIVERSARY .... @ $17.95 each _____
Texas residents add 5⅝% sales tax .... @ .95 each _____
Postage and handling .... @ $ 2.00 each _____
Enclosed is my Check or Money Order in the amount of _____
Make checks payable to Gardner-Farkas Press, Inc.

Drivers license # _____ State _____

Please charge to my MasterCard or Visa No. _____

Expiration date _____ Signature _____

NAME _____

ADDRESS _____

CITY _____ STATE _____ ZIP _____

(PLEASE PRINT)

Reorder Additional Copies

The Cotton Bowl
The First Fifty Years

J. Curtis Sanford had a dream for Dallas. A bowl game to rival the Rose Bowl in Texas, the football hotbed of the United States.

Now 50 years later, the Cotton Bowl Classic is the showcase event for college football in the Southwest.

Carlton Stowers has captured all the pageantry of this great classic in a new book, *The Cotton Bowl Classic: The First Fifty Years*. It's available to you for only $29.95 per limited commemorative edition. The same book in soft cover is yours for just $17.95

☐ Soft Bound
☐ Hardbound Limited Commemorative Edition

FORM OF PAYMENT ☐ Check enclosed
☐ VISA   ☐ MasterCard   ☐ American Express

_____   _____
Card Number (please print)   Card Exp. Date

_____
                        Signature

_____
Name

_____
Address

_____
City

_____   _____   _____
State   Zip   Phone

Mail Your Check To: P.O. Box 47420 Dallas, Texas 75247

The Cotton Bowl
The First Fifty Years

J. Curtis Sanford had a dream for Dallas. A bowl game to rival the Rose Bowl in Texas, the football hotbed of the United States.

Now 50 years later, the Cotton Bowl Classic is the showcase event for college football in the Southwest.

Carlton Stowers has captured all the pageantry of this great classic in a new book, *The Cotton Bowl Classic: The First Fifty Years*. It's available to you for only $29.95 per limited commemorative edition. The same book in soft cover is yours for just $17.95

☐ Soft Bound
☐ Hardbound Limited Commemorative Edition

FORM OF PAYMENT ☐ Check enclosed
☐ VISA   ☐ MasterCard   ☐ American Express

_____   _____
Card Number (please print)   Card Exp. Date

_____
                        Signature

_____
Name

_____
Address

_____
City

_____   _____   _____
State   Zip   Phone

Mail Your Check To: P.O. Box 47420 Dallas, Texas 75247